MIDLOTHIAN
PUBLIC LIBRARY

Ruth, Maris, McGwire and Sosa

Also by William F. McNeil

The King of Swat:
An Analysis of Baseball's Home
Run Hitters from the Major, Minor,
Negro and Japanese Leagues
(McFarland, 1997)

The Dodgers Encyclopedia
(1997)

Ruth, Maris, McGwire and Sosa

Baseball's Single Season Home Run Champions

by
William F. McNeil

McFarland & Company, Inc., Publishers
Jefferson, North Carolina, and London

Cover: (clockwise from top left): Babe Ruth, Roger Maris, (BRACE PHOTO), Mark McGwire (W. McNEIL), and Sammy Sosa (BRACE PHOTO)

Library of Congress Cataloguing-in-Publication Data

McNeil, William F.
    Ruth, Maris, McGwire and Sosa: baseball's single season home
run champions / William F. McNeil.
      p. cm.
    Includes bibliographical references and index. ∞
    ISBN 0-7864-0747-6 (sewn softcover : 50# alkaline paper)
    1. Home runs (Baseball)—United States—History. 2. Home
runs (Baseball)—United States Statistics. 3. Ruth, Babe, 1895–
1948. 4. Maris, Roger, 1934–1985. 5. McGwire, Mark, 1963–
6. Sosa,Sammy, 1968– . I. Title.
GV868.4.M38   1999
796.357'26—dc21   99-29681
                                                 CIP

British Library Cataloguing-in-Publication data are available

Manufactured in the United States of America

McFarland & Company, Inc., Publishers
  Box 611, Jefferson, North Carolina 28640
    www.mcfarlandpub.com

This book is gratefully dedicated to
my wife Janet.
She is the best thing that ever happened to me.

Contents

Contents

Preface

Big brawny sluggers who hit baseballs prodigious distances have fascinated baseball fans since the first game was played on the Elysian Fields in Hoboken, New Jersey, in 1846. With the introduction of the lively ball 75 years later, the home run became the single most electrifying feat in the game.

Babe Ruth, a left-handed hitting outfielder for the New York Yankees who had first set a home run record in 1919, established a stunning new single season home run record in 1920 by putting 54 balls in orbit. He again broke his own record with 60 home runs in 1927.

That achievement was one of the major league's "untouchable" records until a handsome blonde bomber from North Dakota displaced the Babe as the record holder for the first time in 42 years. Smooth swinging Roger Maris set the mark at 61 in 1961.

Another 37 years passed before the mark fell again, and then it was broken twice the same year. Mark McGwire, the monstrous slugger of the St. Louis Cardinals, hit an astounding 70 home runs in 1998. Sammy Sosa of the Chicago Cubs was the first to hit 66, but was passed by McGwire on the last weekend of the season.

As usual, fans continue to ask whose record breaking achievement was the most important? Whose accomplishments were the most heroic? Who is the greatest home run king of all? Those questions and more are addressed within these pages, and each player's accomplishments are put in perspective.

The careers of the four legendary home run champions are covered, with a special emphasis placed on their record breaking seasons. The conditions under which each of them performed his historic feat is analyzed. the advantages each of them enjoyed during their grueling quests as well as disadvantages they had to overcome, are reviewed in detail.

Ruth, Maris, McGwire, and Sosa. Who is the mightiest slugger of them all? This book answers that question.

PART ONE : THE TEXT

1. The Evolution
of the Home Run

Professional baseball began in 1869 when the city of Cincinnati organized and paid a team to play baseball full time. The club, known as the Cincinnati Red Stockings, toured the United States from coast to coast in 1869 and 1870, taking on all comers. They played some of the top amateur clubs in the country, including Forest City of Cleveland, the Athletic of Philadelphia, and the Mutual of Brooklyn, but for the most part their opposition consisted of local town teams of questionable talent.

In their opening game, they crushed Great Western at Cincinnati, 45–9. Several Reds players hit home runs in the game, including shortstop George Wright. It was a portent of things to come.

The Reds were practically unbeatable, running up an 80-game undefeated streak over two seasons, and outscoring the opposition by an average score of 53–6. The only blemish on their record a 17–17 tie with the Haymakers of Troy, New York. Cincinnnati's first Big Red Machine was finally beaten by The Atlantics of Brooklyn 8–7 on June 14, 1870. The game, played at the Capitoline Grounds in Brooklyn, has been called the greatest game of the nineteenth century. The Atlantics pushed across the winning runs in the bottom of the eleventh inning after the Reds had tallied twice in their half. The Red Stockings disbanded after the 1870 season.

In 1871, a full fledged professional league took the field, when the National Association of Professional Base Ball Players was formed. The first home run hit in a professional baseball league was credited to Ezra Sutton, the 153-pound third basemen of the Forest Citys of Cleveland.

Sutton stepped to the plate in the fourth inning against George "The Charmer" Zettlein of the Chicago White Stockings, and sent a drive over the head of center fielder Tom Foley for a home run. Sutton hit another homer three innings later, thus becoming the first player to hit two homers in one game. In spite of Sutton's big day however, home runs were nothing more than a curiosity in the early days of baseball. The first games were played on open fields, with a ball that was soft and misshapen. Games were high-scoring affairs, but singles, doubles, and triples were the big offensive weapons of the day. In fact, there were only 47 home runs hit in 127 league games in 1871, compared to 434 doubles and 239 triples. The few home runs that were hit were usually inside-the-park jobs, with the batter hitting the ball over the fielder's head or between the fielders, and racing around the bases to score before the relay throw could reach home plate. Both of Sutton's homers were fashioned in that manner.

The first enclosed baseball parks were built for other endeavors, such as horse races or bicycle races. The oval tracks, which were ideal for races, were not well suited for the game of baseball, which was played inside the oval. The fields necessarily had extremely short foul lines of approximately 200 to 250 feet, and obscene center field distances, occasionally exceeding 500 feet.

Charlie Gould, a first baseman for the Boston Red Stockings and a former member of the original Cincinnati Red Stockings, hit one of the league's most exciting home runs on September 5, 1871. The blow, a grand slam home run off former Brooklyn Atlantic ace George Zettlein, whom Gould had faced as a member of Cincinnati's first professional team, actually sailed over the 250-foot left field fence at Boston's South End Grounds, an unusual feat in those days. Newspaper headlines around the league celebrated the historic event.

The National Association however, was beset by numerous financial, administrative, and disciplinary problems during its turbulent existence. Gambling scandals, thrown games, players jumping from one team to another, and other unsavory practices, caused chaos within the league's administrative offices. Unable to control the situation, the owners disbanded the league after five seasons. It was immediately replaced by the National League, which began operations in 1876.

The first National League game was played on April 22, 1876, at

Jefferson Street Grounds in Philadelphia, with the Boston Red Caps defeating the Athletics 6–5. Ross Barnes, an outstanding second baseman for the Chicago White Stockings smashed the first National League home run on May 2, 1876. Barnes' drive off "Cherokee" Fisher at Cincinnati's Avenue Grounds carried down the left field line to the spectators' horse-drawn carriages that encircled the playing field. It was Barnes' only home run of the season. George Hall of Philadelphia captured the home run championship with five circuit blows. Charlie Jones of Cincinnati, with four home runs, was the only other National League player to hit more than two.

The first National League baseball parks were nightmares for batters. In most parks, it was impossible to hit a ball over the distant fences. This was especially true for right-handed batters. For instance, the left field fence at the Philadelphia Base Ball Grounds was 500 feet distant while the right field fence was a more comfortable 310 feet away, still a good poke in the old dead ball days. Robison Field in the American Association measured 470 feet down the left field line, 500 feet to dead center, and 290 feet to right field. Exposition Park III in Pittsburgh and National League Park II in Cleveland both had over 400-foot carries to the right and left field foul poles. The average distance to the outfield fences in major league parks in the 1880s and 90s was 358 feet to left field, 473 feet to center, and 322 feet to right. This advantage for left-handed hitters continued for more than 100 years, benefiting such future home run kings as Babe Ruth and Roger Maris, and penalizing right-handed hitting challengers like Jimmie Foxx, Hank Greenberg, and Harmon Killebrew.

Major league baseball was on a learning curve for most of the nineteenth century. Pitching evolved from underhand to sidearm, and finally to overhand. The number of balls and strikes were changed periodically during the first 13 years, finally settling on three strikes and four balls in 1889. Catcher's chest protectors were introduced in 1885, and fielder's gloves became normal attire by the late 1880s. Balls, bats, and other equipment were standardized in order to create uniformity in the game. The modern game actually began in 1893 when the distance from the mound to home plate was fixed at 60'6".

The first bonafide home run hitters emerged during the 1880s to wreak havoc on National League pitchers. For the most part, they were big, strapping left-handed hitters like Dan Brouthers, Roger Connor, and Sam Thompson. In an age when the average player weighed in the neighborhood of 150 pounds, these big sluggers all stood over six feet tall and topped the scales at more than 200 pounds. They averaged between eight and 12 home runs a season each, a hefty total in those days. Sam Thompson once led the league with a monstrous 20 home runs, which by today's standards, could have been in the 50–60 range.

"Big Dan" Brouthers was the most fearsome of the nineteenth century sluggers. Standing 6'2" tall and weighing a muscular 207 pounds, the big first baseman terrorized opposing pitchers. In addition to his nine home runs, he averaged 38 doubles and 17 triples a year, to go along with a .342 batting average. His .519 slugging percentage was the highest of any nineteenth century batter, and is higher than such modern sluggers as Harmon Killebrew, Ernie Banks, and Eddie Mathews.

Another notable slugger of the nineteenth century was Harry Stovey. Unlike the other big boomers of the 1880s, Stovey was a fleet-footed outfielder for the Philadelphia Athletics who had all the qualifications of a superstar. He could hit, hit with power, run, field, and throw. The trim 180-pound gazelle racked up 122 homers during his career, leading the league in that category five times. He averaged 11 homers a year, in addition to 32 doubles, 15 triples, and 90 stolen bases.

Bobby Lowe, the brilliant second baseman of the Boston Beaneaters, set a home run record that may never be broken, on May 31, 1894. Playing against the Cincinnati Reds at the Congress Street Grounds in Boston, Lowe deposited four consecutive balls over the left field fence off the slants of Cincinnati righthander "Icebox" Chamberlain, sparking the Beaneaters to a 20–11 victory. The 150-pound infielder must have been proficient at dropping balls over the short left field fence because, of his 17 home runs in 1894, 16 of them were hit at home, either at the Congress Street Grounds or at the South End Grounds III, a similarly designed park.

Big Ed Delahanty of the Philadelphia Phillies duplicated Lowe's feat of four home runs in one game on July 13, 1896, in Chicago's West Side Grounds. The National League was in a state of flux during the middle of the 1890s, having expanded from eight teams to 12 teams in 1892, then increasing the pitching distance from 55 feet to 60 feet 6 inches the following year. Home runs and batting averages jumped up significantly for three or four years as pitchers tried to adjust to the new conditions and the league tried to absorb the diluted pitching staffs. Lowe and Delahanty took advantage of the confusion to etch their names in the record books. In spite of the heroics by Lowe and Delahanty, the home run remained an elusive force throughout the late nineteenth and early twentieth century, due to the outrageous geometry of the ball fields and the poor construction of the baseballs.

As exciting as baseball was to watch, and as difficult as it was to play, the game was not considered to be an honorable profession by most of nineteenth century society. The Victorian Age had become deeply imbedded in the United States by the 1890s, and the moral and social climate in the country decried improprieties of any sort. Women in particular were protected from the evil environment by being kept in the home as much as possible, and by draping their bodies with layers and layers of cloth whenever they entered the outside world. Women's dresses extended from the neck to the floor, with sleeves covering their arms down to their hands. Only the head was exposed, and that was usually shaded by a large floppy hat. Bustles were added to the attire to prevent men from being distracted by a woman's form. Women did not travel about unescorted, but were always in the company of a responsible adult, usually a male relative. They were not allowed to frequent taverns or saloons, and never attended sporting events, which were considered to be barbarous contests unfit for the delicate female psyche.

Baseball players of the time were looked down upon as ruffians, drunkards, and carousers. The brawling, tobacco chewing, gambling low-lifes that gravitated to the game detracted from the overall clean competition and sportsmanship that actually defined the game. Baseball had such a poor image that law-abiding citizens were embarrassed when a member of their family chose professional baseball as a career. Harry Stovey, whose real name was Stowe, changed it to Stovey when he began playing baseball to protect his mother from public humiliation. When he retired from the game, he returned to his home town of Fall River, Massachusetts, where he joined the police force. At the time of his death in 1937, very few townspeople realized their friend and co-worker was one of the greatest baseball players of the nineteenth century.

National League owners returned to an eight-team format in 1900, and revamped the style of play to provide a more exciting game for the fans to enjoy. As the twentieth century got underway, the image of the game gradually improved. College athletic programs produced outstanding baseball players like Christy Mathewson, Eddie Collins, and Harry Hooper, who subsequently chose professional baseball as a worthy profession. Over three dozen college men were playing major league baseball by 1916. Eddie Grant from Harvard, Chief Meyers from Dartmouth, Bob Bescher from Notre Dame, Dick Rudolph from Fordham, and Bill Carrigan from Holy Cross, brought a measure of respect and dignity to the game. Gentlemen players like Walter Johnson, Cy Young, and Honus Wagner, whose on- and off-field demeanor was exemplary, further made the game more palatable to the general public. Soon, women and children began attending games in greater numbers, and the sport rapidly grew to become America's national pastime.

The strategy of the game changed during the first decade of the new century. Big, powerful sluggers were no longer in demand in the professional ranks. Baseball owners shunned the burly muscle men, considering them to be brutish oafs, who were defensive liabilities and who clogged up the base paths. Major league players of the 1900s were smaller, faster, and more adept at handling a bat than their predecessors had been. The game evolved into a low-scoring affair, with bunts, stolen bases, and hit and run plays the keys to victory. Home runs declined from an average of 38 per team during the last two decades of the nineteenth century to 22 per team during the first decade of the twentieth century.

Pitchers dominated the game. The maximum height of the pitcher's mound was set at 15 inches in 1903, giving the pitcher a distinct advantage. Earned run averages dropped from about 3.80 during the 1890s to under 2.99 from 1904 to 1910. The improved pitching statistics were due to the higher mound, deeper pitching staffs, tighter defense resulting from bigger and better gloves and other equipment, and more professionally groomed playing fields. Fielding averages jumped up from .931 in 1893 to .961 in 1908. Slugging averages, on the other hand, plummeted by 50 to 100 points. The number one offensive tool of the 1900s was the stolen base, which was popularized by such speedsters as Ty Cobb, Bob Bescher, and Max Carey. Cobb's single-season record of 96 stolen bases stood for 48 years until broken by Maury Wills in 1962. His career total of 892 thefts lasted until 1990 when it was buried under an avalanche of stolen bases by Ricky Henderson, who is now closing in on the 1300 mark.

Home run champions had modest totals to show for their efforts as the new century got underway. Sam Crawford of Cincinnati led the National League with 16 homers in 1901, the highest total of the decade. Socks Seybold of the Philadelphia Athletics hit 16 homers in 1902 to lead the American League. No other slugger hit as many. In fact, the National League leader had less than ten home runs five times during the decade, and the junior circuit leader had less than ten home runs four times. Tommy Leach of Pittsburgh led the N.L. with six home runs in 1902.

Things began to change for the sluggers in 1910 when a new cork-centered baseball was introduced. The ball was livelier than the old ball and seemed to jump off the bat when it was hit. It wasn't long before the big boys with the big lumber zeroed in on the friendlier ball. Frank Schulte of the Chicago Cubs, who had hit just 17 home runs in 5½ previous seasons, was the first slugger to exploit it. The solidly built 170-pound left fielder pounded out 69 homers over the next six years, including a league-leading 21 homers in 1911.

The most prolific home run hitter to play major league baseball before the emergence of Babe Ruth was Clifford "Gavvy" Cravath. The 5'10", 180-pound bruiser kicked around the minor leagues for the better part of ten years, with two unsuccessful major league trials along the way. In his early years, from 1902 through 1907, he was a hard-hitting outfielder with the Los Angeles Angels in the Pacific Coast League. His .303 batting average, powerful bat, and 50 stolen bases, brought him to the attention of the Boston Red Sox, who acquired his contract in 1908. After unsuccessful trials with Boston, Chicago, and Washington of the American League, Cravath found himself back in the minor leagues, holding down an outfield spot for the Minneapolis Millers of the American Association. There, at the age of 27, he suddenly blossomed into a dangerous offensive threat. In 1910, the big basher from Escondido, California, led the league in batting (.326), hits (200), and home runs (14). The next year he did even better, showing the way in batting (.363), hits (221), doubles (53), and home runs (29).

That performance brought him to the attention of the Philadelphia Phillies who purchased his contract and inserted him in right field in

Baker Bowl, where he remained for eight years. He went on to lead the National League in home runs during six of those years. His league-leading totals included two years with 19 homers and one year with 24 homers. Although Cravath was a right-handed hitter, he learned to hit the ball to all fields to take advantage of the dimensions of his home park. Baker Field had a 335-foot left field foul line, but the right field fence was only 272 feet from home plate and the right center field power alley was just a 300-foot chip shot away. Cravath quickly became proficient at hitting the ball to right field. In spite of the fact that the playing dimensions at Baker Bowl made right field an inviting target, only teammate Fred Luderus was able to take advantage of it. Luderus, a left-handed hitting first baseman hit 56 home runs over a four-year period, with 43 of them coming at home. No visiting player was able to capitalize on the short right field porch, as evidenced by the fact that the Phillies outhomered the opposition by a count of 224 to 86 between 1912 and 1919.

Over the six-year period from 1912 to 1917, Gavvy Cravath accounted for 7.2 percent of all home runs hit in the National League. By comparison, Harry Stovey, the top nineteenth century slugger hit 5.7 percent of all home runs in the American Association between 1883 and 1889. Babe Ruth, whose career will be reviewed in the following chapters, accounted for 10.8 percent of all American League homers between 1919 and 1924, and 9.5 percent of all homers hit between 1926 and 1931. No other players in major league history have dominated the home run statistics like Babe Ruth and Gavvy Cravath.

Gavvy Cravath's career average of 17 home runs for every 550 at bats was by far the highest average during the dead ball era, and would equate to an average of about 43 home runs in the lively ball era, second only to the great Bambino. In truth, Gavvy Cravath was the Babe Ruth of the dead ball era.

Other changes that were taking place in major league baseball during the first two decades of the twentieth century favored the home run hitters. New steel and concrete stadiums being built in such cities as Philadelphia, Pittsburgh, Brooklyn, Boston, Chicago, Detroit, and St. Louis were more homer friendly. Prior to 1900 most parks had large playing fields surrounded by wooden fences. Center field was usually in the neighborhood of 500 feet distant from home plate, and the left field fence stood a good 350 feet away. Right field was a cozier 322 feet from home plate, but the field opened up quickly to expose cavernous 400-foot power alleys. The new steel stadiums provided more uniform dimensions, but they were still far from perfect. The left field foul line was shortened by 14 feet, but remained a distant 339 feet from home plate. Center field was shortened to 446 feet, a decrease of more than 60 feet. Right field was 329 feet from home plate on average, but six of the 16 major league parks still had right field fences less than 300 feet away. It is not surprising, therefore, that the most prodigious power hitters of the first 100 years of major league baseball were left-handed hitters. Most of the stadiums in use during that period favored southpaw swingers. It is only in the 1990s that right handed hitters have achieved parity.

The more unusual early twentieth century major league parks included Ebbets Field in Brooklyn, the Polo Grounds in New York, and Fenway Park in Boston. The right field wall in Ebbets Field was only 297 feet from home plate but it rose to a height of 38 feet, with the top half being a 19-foot screen and the bottom half a 19-foot concave concrete wall. It was always an adventure for the right fielder when a batted ball caromed off the concave section of the wall. The Polo Grounds had the typical nineteenth century oblong shape measuring 250 feet, 485 feet, and 249 feet, in left, center, and right. Pull hitters like Mel Ott had a field day in the Polo Grounds (Ott hit 323, or 63 percent, of his 511 career home runs there), but straight away hitters were frequently victimized by the distant 440-foot power alleys (Walker Cooper hit only 21 home runs at home and 42 away, a home field percentage of just 33 percent). Fenway Park's distinctive feature is "The Green Monster," an inviting 37 foot high green plastic wall hovering over the left fielder, just 320 feet from home plate. The right field power alleys of 380 to 400 feet and the 420-foot center field area give the park respectability.

Off the field, in the everyday world, the economy was strong again thanks to increased industrialization, but several events lurking on the horizon would have a significant effect on the future prospects of major league baseball. World War I, which began in the Balkans in 1914, would soon engulf the United States, drawing hundreds of major league baseball players into the fray. The 1919 World Series between the Cincinnati Reds and the Chicago White Sox would turn out to be a dirty affair endangering the very future of the game. The major league owners would hire a new tough baseball commissioner, former judge Kenesaw Mountain Landis, and endow him with absolute authority over the conduct of the game and its players.

Finally, a hero would emerge to save the game from extinction. A young man by the name of George Herman Ruth would take the popularity of the game to a new level.

2. Babe Ruth— The Early Years

George Ruth was born in Baltimore, Maryland, on February 6, 1895, near the historic inner harbor area of the city. The harbor and the fort that defended it became celebrated events in American history for an incident that had taken place 80 years before Ruth's arrival. During the War of 1812, as British forces bombarded Fort McHenry, Francis Scott Key, a prisoner on board one of the British war ships, on seeing the American flag still flying over the fort at sunrise, penciled a song that would eventually become our national anthem. Ruth's parents, George Herman Ruth and Katherine (Schamberger) Ruth, owned the Union Bar on Frederick Avenue when Babe was born, but moved closer to the harbor several years later, buying another saloon at 426 West Camden Street. They lived over the saloon with their eight children.

The area where Ruth grew up, down by the docks, was a poor, slum-like neighborhood. Visiting sailors wandered the streets, frequenting the dozens of saloons that dotted the waterfront. Derelicts harassed passersby for money. Ladies of the evening decorated the street corners and parks. Fights were an everyday occurrence, with knifings and beatings commonplace.

Although George Ruth, Sr., was Lutheran and his wife Katherine was Catholic, they didn't attend church regularly, and Babe received his moral training on the streets of Baltimore. The dirty, scruffy-faced urchin was on his own, even as a young boy. His father, known as Big George (Babe was known as Little George), worked 14-hour days at the bar. And his sickly mother was kept busy full time trying to care for the family's needs, so young Ruth hung out around the docks with his pals.

Babe's mother gave birth to eight children in 11 years, with Babe being the oldest, but only he and his sister Mamie lived to adulthood. Most of his brothers and sisters died before they reached the age of five.

According to Mamie, in Dorothy Ruth Pirone's book, *My Dad, the Babe*, "George wasn't a bad boy. He was a mischievous boy." He spent all his time with his buddies, on the streets, looking for excitement. He avoided school like the plague, even defying his parents when they tried to make him attend school.

Babe was only seven years old but, by his own admission, he was a little bum. He didn't know right from wrong. He went where he wanted to go. And whenever he got the urge to do something, he just did it. If he wanted something his parents had, he took it. He wasn't a criminal. He didn't belong to an organized street gang. He and his friends didn't steal (except for occasional vegetables from a wagon on its way to market). They didn't destroy property, and they didn't accost people. They just hung out on the streets, looking for something to do. They were never in serious trouble with the law, but the police harassed them anyway, just to keep them on their toes. Ruth said later, that he always "hated the coppers."

Babe was chewing tobacco and smoking by the time he was seven. But even at that early age, he loved the game of baseball. He spent much of his free time in the vacant lots around the neighborhood, playing the game that would make him famous. Even then, he was big for his age and could hit the ball farther than most of the other boys.

Many of the characteristics that would one day define the adult Babe Ruth were already ingrained in his personality. He was completely honest, outspoken, uninhibited, undisciplined, irresponsible, happy-go-lucky, friendly, uncouth, and stubborn. He never cared much for authority figures. He had a short temper but also a charm that encouraged people to overlook his faults. With his size and his short temper, he had all the qualifications for being a bully, but he was just the opposite. He was a caring person who liked people and who wanted people to like him.

On February 7, 1904, a horrible conflagration consumed Baltimore's business district, causing over $125,000,000 in damages. The city was rebuilt within three years, but Babe Ruth wasn't around to witness the rebirth. The waterfront waif who, at eight years old, could neither read nor write, and who resisted his father's frequent beatings for missing school, had been removed from society.

According to Grantland Rice in *The Tumult and the Shouting*, "When

Babe was about seven, it seems he tapped the family till. 'I took one dollar,' said Babe, 'and bought ice cream cones for all the kids on the block. When my old man asked me what I'd done I told him. He dragged me down cellar and beat me with a horsewhip. I tapped that till again—just to show him he couldn't break me. Then I landed in the Home, thank God.'"

Babe's parents had him committed to St. Mary's Industrial School, known as "The Home," at Wilkens and Caton Avenue, about four miles south of the city center. The school was not a reform school per se, but more a boarding school, where runaways and incorrigibles were sent to receive the discipline and guidance they failed to get at home. Parents, reportedly, had to pay monthly board to send their child there.

St. Mary's was run like a prison although it was not officially a penal institution. It was run by the Xaverian Brothers, a Jesuit order that avows strict discipline. Whippings for infractions were daily occurrences, and young Ruth received more than his share of such rewards for insubordinate behavior. Strangely enough, Babe Ruth came to love the Home. He was once quoted as saying, "I'm as proud of it [St. Mary's] as any Harvard man is proud of his school." He claimed it was the most important time of his life. Brother Matthias, a 6'6", 240-pound human tower, was the Prefect of Discipline at St. Mary's, so he crossed swords with Babe many times over the first few months. Eventually, they became very close, with Babe looking upon Brother Matthias as a father figure.

Babe spent most of the next ten years at St. Mary's, with a few visits home along the way. The youngster learned a semblance of discipline although he never became what could be called a model citizen. He also accepted religion, assuming his mother's Roman Catholic faith at St. Mary's. He even served as an altar boy at the school.

What was most important for Babe's future was that he was forced to attend school, where he finally learned to read and write. He also studied arithmetic, history, geography, and spelling.

While Babe was at the Home on April 18, 1906, one of the worst natural disasters in American history struck the West Coast. A devastating earthquake and fire destroyed the city of San Francisco, California. Over 1,000 people were killed in the quake and ensuing three-day conflagration, with property losses estimated at $350,000,000. Babe knew nothing of the disaster, his world being limited to the area inside the walls of the Home.

Four years later, a more personal tragedy struck young Ruth. On August 23, 1910, his mother Katherine died of tuberculosis. She was just 35.

Babe's life at the Home was well regimented. His daily routine consisted of 6 A.M. wake-up, breakfast, Mass, about five hours of classwork, another four hours learning a trade, and several hours of free time. The boys at the school had a number of trades they could choose from, including printing, carpentry, farming, and shoe repair. Babe chose to be a tailor. After several years as a student and an apprentice, Babe bragged that he could sew a shirt in 15 minutes.

The priests at St. Mary's tried to provide a well-rounded regimen for the 850 boys at the school, so, in addition to education and trades, they also placed heavy emphasis on athletics. The most popular game at school was baseball, and the school was blessed with several baseball diamonds, which were spacious and well kept. As Babe grew older, the happiest moments in his life were those spent on a baseball field. It became obvious from the first time he held a bat that the former juvenile delinquent had a natural affinity for baseball. Brother Matthias noticed this and took Babe under his wing. He spent countless hours working with him, perfecting his pitching and fielding. The big, gentle priest caught Babe's pitches day after day, so Babe could improve his control and his movement on the ball. Brother Matthias also hit Babe hundreds of fungoes, and watched as the youngster happily ran them down. According to Marshall Smelser, Babe noted, "I could hit the first time I picked up a bat, but Brother Matthias made me a fielder." Ruth called the Xaverian brother the greatest man he ever knew.

There were so many boys playing baseball at St. Mary's that the school organized six intramural leagues with a total of 44 teams. Babe Ruth developed into a star player at St. Mary's. He was an outstanding pitcher, and he also played first base, shortstop, and the outfield. He may have done some catching as well because one of the team photos shows Ruth holding a catcher's mitt and a mask.

On April 14, 1912, while the baseball season was heating up at St. Mary's, a tragedy was taking place in the north Atlantic Ocean. The world's largest passenger ship, the *Titanic*, the 853-foot leviathan thought to be unsinkable, struck an iceberg off the coast of Newfoundland while on its maiden voyage from England to New York, and sank. Fifteen hundred of the 2,223 passengers were lost at sea. Another passenger ship, the *Carpathia*, heard the *Titanic*'s distress signal, and raced to the scene in time to rescue over 700 passengers. The sinking of the *Titanic* remains the largest sea disaster in the history of the world.

In 1913, the Red Sox won the school championship, led by Babe Ruth who went undefeated as a pitcher, striking out 22 batters in one game, and who hit a lusty .537 to boot. Babe was big for his age, and by this time, at the age of 18, he stood 6'2" tall and weighed in at a trim 150 pounds. He was a southpaw pitcher with a blazing fast ball, a sharpbreaking curve, and a decent change of pace. At bat he was already noted for his long distance clouting.

The St. Mary's baseball teams played other schools around the Baltimore area, in addition to playing intramural games. Jack Dunn, a former major league pitcher who once won 20 games for the Brooklyn Bridegrooms and was now the owner and manager of the Baltimore Orioles of the International League, heard about Ruth from friends in the city, including Brother Gilbert, the Athletic Director at Mt. St. Joseph's College, and Bill Byers, a former player for Dunn at Baltimore. Byers coached an all-star team that was defeated by Ruth's St. Mary's team in 1913, with Ruth fanning 20 batters along the way. Byers, who was not only impressed by the Babe's pitching savvy, but also by his big bat, told Dunn he thought Ruth should be an every day player.

The following February, Dunn visited St. Mary's Industrial School to watch the young southpaw pitch. At a subsequent meeting with Brother Matthias, Dunn expressed an interest in signing Ruth to a professional baseball contract. A deal was consummated; Babe signed with the Baltimore Orioles for $600 for the 1914 season, and Jack Dunn became his legal guardian until Ruth reached the age of 21.

The world that Babe Ruth entered in 1914 was a far different world from the one he left when he entered St. Mary's in 1904. The world was changing at breakneck speed, with technological advances bringing automation into American manufacturing and farming. Spectacular new inventions were increasing the quality of life.

The gasoline-driven automobile, introduced in 1893, was an important means of transportation by 1911. Over 100,000 Ford Model T's, selling for $600, were already on the road.

Motion pictures, invented in 1893 by Thomas Alva Edison, were being shown for five cents in 10,000 nickelodeons by 1908.

The first subway train sped beneath the streets of New York in 1904, traveling eight miles from the Brooklyn Bridge to 145th Street at Broadway.

The Wright brothers flew an airplane 120 feet in 1903. The first cross-country flight took place only eight years later.

Cities were being lighted by electric lights. Telephones were becoming consumer items. Railroads criss-crossed the country, making long distance travel practical.

And the *San Francisco Chronicle* began publishing comic strips in 1907.

Babe Ruth began his professional career on March 7, 1914, when he took the field for his first intra-squad game for the Orioles in Fayetteville, North Carolina. Playing for the Buzzards against the Sparrows, the powerful southpaw swinger wasted no time in impressing his teammates, as well as the coaches and the fans. In the seventh inning, he sent a monstrous 400-foot drive over the right fielder's head and raced around the bases for a two-run home run. The Buzzards won the game 15–9, and Babe sparkled both at shortstop and on the mound.

Two weeks later, the Babe received his first real baptism of fire when the Orioles entertained the major league Philadelphia Phillies, who had held down second place in the National League in 1913. Ruth pitched three innings in his first outing, yielding two unearned runs, but not being involved in the decision, as the Phils won a squeaker, 4–3.

It was about this time, that young Ruth received his nickname. Many of the Baltimore players started calling Ruth, "one of Dunn's babies." The newspapers quickly picked up the statement and began referring to the 19 year old southpaw as "Dunn's Baby," in the spring training reports. Over a period of weeks, it was modified to Babe. The name stuck.

Babe Ruth gained a lot of valuable experience during spring training. The Orioles played a number of games against major league teams, and Babe quickly got his baptism of fire against the big boys. He knocked off the Phillies and Dodgers, split with the A's, and lost to the Yanks and Giants, finishing with a 3–3 record, a respectable performance for a 19-year-old kid playing with his first professional team.

The International League season opened on April 21, with the Orioles hosting the Buffalo Bisons. Ruth pitched the second game of the season, and whitewashed the Bisons by a score of 6–0. He also began his professional baseball career by scorching a single to right field in his first at bat.

After dropping his second start, a 2–1 pitchers duel to Rochester, the southpaw sensation tossed a 1–0, ten-inning shutout at the Montreal Royals, doubling home the winning run himself. For two months, the young rookie pitched regularly, winning some, losing a few, and gaining valuable experience. His 14–6 record through the end of June helped keep the Orioles in first place, but the hand writing was on the wall. Unfortunately, the Orioles were not drawing many people to their games, being outdone by the outlaw Federal League's Terrapins. Jack Dunn did everything he could to keep the team solvent, but to no avail. By the first of July, he was forced to conduct a full-scale fire sale.

On July 9, 1914, Babe Ruth, along with pitcher Ernie Shore and catcher Ben Egan, was sold to the Boston Red Sox for $20,000. The teenager made his major league debut in Boston's Fenway Park on July 11, against the cellar-dwelling Cleveland Indians. The rookie pitched a creditable game, going seven innings and yielding three runs on eight hits. Tris Speaker's RBI single in the bottom of the seventh brought in the run that made Ruth the winning pitcher.

Three days later, an incident 7000 miles to the east of Boston, threw the entire world into chaos. Archduke Franz Ferdinand of Austria-Hungary was assassinated by a Serbian, in Sarajevo, Bosnia. Within days, Austria-Hungary declared war on Serbia. Russia entered the conflict on the side of Austria, Germany declared war on Russia and soon more than 32 nations were embroiled in the hostilities.

In spite of all the technological advances that had been made in the United States during the early years of the new century and in spite of the automation that improved manufacturing and farming efficiency and provided more leisure time for the working people, there was still a feeling of anxiety in the air. Immigrants, to the tune of half a million in 1900, were taking jobs from native-born Americans, and were driving down wages in the process. And urbanization, which saw people moving from the country to the city to work in factories, had its downside. The big cities, with their crowds of people, street traffic, noise, and confusion, were depressing to thousands of new city dwellers.

The mood in the country had actually been on a downward spiral for almost a quarter of a century, going back to the depression of 1893. The Spanish-American war that sent U.S. troops halfway around the world just five years later, placed a huge drain on the economy. In 1899, an insurrection in the Philippines kept American forces engaged in a guerrilla war halfway around the world for two years. Then, in 1900, the Boxer Rebellion in China, where members of a secret society waged war on all foreigners in an attempt to drive them from the country, brought troops from England, France, Germany, Japan, Russia, and the United States to the rescue.

One of the most demoralizing tragedies to strike the American people was played out in Buffalo, New York, on September 6, 1900, when Leon Czolgosz, an anarchist, shot President William McKinley twice at close range. McKinley died eight days later and was succeeded by Vice President Theodore Roosevelt.

Four months previous, on May 1, a coal mine explosion in Schofield, Utah, killed more than 200 miners. Then, in September, a violent hurricane slammed into Galveston, Texas, killing an estimated 7000 people, a fifth of the population, leaving the Gulf Coast devastated. Mini-depressions in 1904 and 1907 further dampened the spirits of the people. And the San Francisco earthquake mentioned earlier, caused unimaginable destruction to the West Coast.

A feeling of impending doom permeated the United States of America. The clouds of war were coming closer and closer to the homeland. The feeling of desperation would reach its lowest point in 1918 when more than 4,000,000 men would march off to war.

The mood in the country was even affecting major league baseball. Attendance, which had reached an all-time high of 7,200,000 in 1909, declined the following year, and by 1914 it had fallen off almost 40 percent, to 4,400,000.

World events, even those affecting his own country, didn't interest the Babe however. He was only interested in playing the game of baseball. His major league career lasted five weeks, during which he pitched in four games, winning two and losing one. Manager Bill Carrigan, whose Red Sox were not quite ready to make a run at the powerful Philadelphia Athletics, decided that further seasoning with the Providence Grays would benefit Ruth more than sitting on a bench in Boston.

Carrigan was right. Babe Ruth's eight wins helped the Grays capture the International League pennant by four games over his old team, the Baltimore Orioles. His hitting improved also. After a tepid .200 batting average in Baltimore, the Babe hit a more respectable .247 for Providence, with ten triples (in just 121 at bats) and one home run. The homer on September 5 in Toronto came in support of his own one-hitter. It was a three run shot in the sixth inning of a 9–0 whitewashing.

Nineteen fourteen was a significant year in the life of Babe Ruth in another respect. He got married. The young, virile major leaguer, who was now earning $2500 a season after another raise, was always on the prowl for good-looking women. While in Boston, Ruth regularly had breakfast at Landers Coffee Shop on Huntington Avenue. He became infatuated with a waitress named Helen Woodford, a 17-year-old immigrant from Nova Scotia. Supposedly, after visiting the shop a couple of dozen times over a period of three months, Ruth proposed to her during one of his morning visits. She accepted, and on October 17 of that year, they were married in St. Pauls Church in Ellicott City, Maryland.

The marriage was doomed from the start. Ruth was too young and immature to be a responsible husband. The frequent road trips he took with his team, the different cities he visited, and the countless temptations he encountered and surrendered to, soon alienated him from his wife. Helen was just the opposite of the boisterous, carousing Babe. She was petite, pretty, and shy. She enjoyed being a housewife.

The next year, 1915, Babe Ruth came of age as a major league pitcher. When the season got underway, the St. Mary's graduate was not being counted on to be a major contributor to the Red Sox drive to the top of the American League. Bill Carrigan had rightys Ernie Shore, Rube Foster, "Smokey Joe" Wood, and Carl Mays, and southpaws Dutch Leonard and Ray Collins in the rotation. Ruth was odd man out.

On May 6, when Ruth got one of his infrequent starts, against the New York Yankees, his record stood at 1–1. In the third inning of a scoreless game, Yankee pitcher Jack Warhop tried to throw a fastball past the youngster, and Ruth promptly hit a mighty wallop into the upper right field stands at the Polo Grounds. It was his first major league homer, and a tape-measure shot at that. Although Ruth lost the game 4–3 in 13 innings, he impressed manager Carrigan with his pitching skills.

The next day, the war was brought closer to America's shores when a German U-boat torpedoed the British passenger ship Lusitania off the coast of Ireland, sending 1200 people to their deaths. At least 128 of the fatalities were American citizens, causing considerable outrage among U.S. citizenry.

Babe Ruth, the new Boston slugger, had a return match with Jack Warhop less than one month after their first encounter. This time Babe hit another towering home run to practically the same spot as the first one, only longer.

The 20-year-old rookie hit another tape-measure job on July 21. He slammed a towering drive over the right field pavilion in Sportsmans Park in St. Louis. As reported by William J. Jenkinson in the SABR Home Run Encyclopedia, the ball "cleared the wide breadth of Grand Boulevard and landed on the sidewalk approximately 470 feet from home plate."

In spite of the fact that the 6'2", 198-pound phenom could pound the ball with authority, his teammates resented the fact that he insisted on taking batting practice with the team. In those days, pitchers were not allowed to take batting practice. Some players decided to teach the young upstart a lesson. They sawed his bats in half when he was not in the club house.

Ruth also drew criticism from the players because he was so relaxed with everyone. He never held anyone in awe, which some people took as a sign of disrespect, particularly with regard to the veteran players on the club. But Babe was just being Babe. He treated presidents the same way he treated kids—as equals. One time, several years later, on meeting President Coolidge, he remarked, "Hot as hell, ain't it Prez."

Some players resented him because he was generally uncouth. He had horrible table manners, his language was disgusting, and his hygiene was deplorable. All these things were true. Over time, he improved in some areas like hygiene, but he was never able to clean up his language. One player claimed Ruth wasn't recruited. He was trapped. Other players called him "The Big Baboon."

The talented southpaw eventually moved up in the pitching rotation and pitched some outstanding games down the stretch. One

Opposite: **Babe Ruth began his career as a left-handed pitcher for the Boston Red Sox in 1914. He won 65 games for the Sox between 1915 and 1917.**

memorable game took place in Fenway Park on August 14, when he faced the great Walter Johnson. Ruth prevailed 4–3. The pitching duels between Ruth and Johnson became legendary over the years. The two fireballers met on the field of battle ten times Between 1915 and 1918. The Red Sox southpaw came away the winner on six occasions, while Johnson was the victor twice. Three times, the two hooked up in brilliant 1–0 pitching duels, with Babe Ruth winning all three. One of the games went 13 innings.

In another key game against the second-place Detroit Tigers, Ruth outpitched 24-game winner, Hooks Dauss, 3–2.

By season's end Babe Ruth was tied with Ernie Shore for the second best record (18–8), just one game behind Foster's 19–8, and was third in innings pitched. In addition to his fine pitching, Babe's batting statistics were an omen of things to come. He batted a healthy .315, and accumulated 15 extra base hits in only 92 at bats—ten doubles, one triple, and four home runs. Braggo Roth of Cleveland led the American League in home runs with seven in 384 at bats.

Babe Ruth's total of four home runs in 92 at bats is even more impressive when you realize that the entire Red Sox team hit a total of only 14 home runs. No one on the team hit more than two homers, and only seven position players in the league hit more than four.

Bill Carrigan's Red Sox won the 1915 American League pennant by 2½ games over the Detroit Tigers. In the World Series, the Sox faced the National League champion Philadelphia Phillies. It was strictly no contest. Carrigan, going with his veteran pitchers Shore, Foster, and Leonard, took the title in five games. Ruth watched from the bench, except for one pinch hitting chore in game one.

As 1916 dawned, Babe Ruth stepped to the front of the line, becoming Bill Carrigan's ace. He began the season in grand style, knocking off Walter Johnson by a score of 5–1 on April 17. "The Big Train" lasted only six innings, being raked for 11 hits by the Sox batters. On June 1, Ruth took the measure of Johnson again, this time by a slim 1–0 score. The Senators managed to hit just one ball out of the infield against the Boston southpaw. On August 15, the two great pitchers met a third time. This one was a sizzling pitching duel, with both pitchers at the top of their game. After 12 innings, the score stood at 0–0. Then in the bottom of the 13th, the Red Sox bunched three hits together to win the game 1–0.

Ruth won a fourth encounter, 2–1, with Johnson finally taking a 4–3 decision on September 12.

The pennant race was a nail biter, with Boston, Detroit, and Chicago bunched together on September 14, as the Red Sox began a grueling ten-game road trip. They immediately dropped the opener of a three-game set to the White Sox, then righted themselves to take the next two. They went on to sweep the Tigers in three, and win two more at Cleveland, opening up a three-game lead over Chicago. They clinched the pennant six days later.

Ruth and Johnson dominated the league's pitching statistics for the season. In spite of going 1–4 against the Bambino, "The Big Train" led the league with 25 victories, 228 strikeouts, 371 innings pitched, and 36 complete games. The 21-year-old Ruth, with a 23–12 record, showed the way with a sparkling 1.75 earned run average and nine shutouts, still an American League record.

Boston's opponent in the World Series was the Brooklyn Dodgers, who had captured the National League pennant by 2½ games over the Philadelphia Phillies. The Dodgers, who had a better all-around team on paper, and were favored in the Series, were beaten by Boston, four games to one.

Babe Ruth pitched the best game of the Series, defeating hard luck pitcher, Sherry Smith of Brooklyn, 2–1 in 14 innings. Ruth's 13⅓ consecutive scoreless innings plus Larry Gardner's game-winning single in the bottom of the 14th were the highlights of the Series. Ruth's 14-inning complete game is still the longest complete game in World Series history.

Babe Ruth was on the verge of becoming the best left-handed pitcher in major league baseball. On the heels of his sensational year in 1916, the Boston ace won 24 games against 13 losses in 1917 and led the league in complete games with 35. He split two decisions with Walter Johnson, winning 1–0 and losing 6–0.

The year 1917 was a momentous one in American history. On April 6, the U.S. Congress declared war on Germany after repeated acts of aggression by the European nation against American citizens. Hundreds of thousands of able-bodied men were drafted into the armed forces, but Ruth received a deferment as a married man. He later enlisted in the Massachusetts Home Guard. A total of 227 major league players marched off to war in 1918, seriously depleting the quality of play in the big leagues.

Even though Babe Ruth was a world class pitcher, 1917 was his last full year on the mound. The following year, he split his time between the mound and left field. He still pitched enough to be the number four man on manager Ed Barrow's staff, winning 13 games against seven losses, with an ERA of 2.22 in 166 innings, but his main value was as a world class hitter.

In a war-shortened season of 126 games, the Boston Red Sox took the American League pennant by 3½ games over the Cleveland Indians. In Boston's pennant clincher, Babe Ruth tossed a 6–1 three-hitter over Philadelphia, and contributed a single and a double to the cause. For the season, the Bambino, playing 110 games in left field, stroked the ball at an even .300 clip, and tied for the league lead in home runs with Tilly Walker, with 11. Many of his home runs were tape-measure jobs that excited the fans and brought flowering comments from the sports writers.

In the World Series against the Chicago Cubs, the big southpaw went 2–0 on the mound, establishing a Series record of 29⅔ consecutive scoreless innings, including 13⅓ from 1916. The record stood until 1961 when it was broken by Yankee ace Whitey Ford.

Ruth took the opener of the World Series, 1–0, over Hippo Vaughn. The only run of the game came across the plate in the fourth inning on a walk and consecutive singles by Whiteman and McInnis. Ruth also took game four, 3–2, with ninth-inning help from Joe Bush. Boston took the sixth game and the Series, 2–1 behind Carl Mays.

The season was not all fun and games for the young slugger however. On August 27, his father was killed in a brawl. Apparently George Ruth, Sr. had gotten into an argument with his partner, Benjamin Sipes, over an incident in their Baltimore bar. The argument moved outside the bar where it turned into an out-and-out fight. George, Sr., struck the first blow, Benjamin Sipes, the second. The elder Ruth fell to the sidewalk, striking his head on the curbstone and fracturing his skull. He died hours later, at the age of 46.

Nine weeks after the World Series ended, the global conflict also came to an end when Germany capitulated on November 11. The war had lasted over four years and took more than 8,000,000 lives. Russia alone had 1,700,000 deaths, while France buried over 1,350,000 of its people. The American war dead in less than two years totaled 126,000, including three major league players.

The big baseball news of the winter concerned the prodigious slugging feats of George Herman Ruth. The Babe was already being called the greatest home run hitter in baseball history, at the tender age of 23. His legendary exploits with the bat had the entire country mesmerized. It soon became obvious to Boston Red Sox management that his future was as an outfielder, not as a pitcher.

Babe Ruth appeared in 130 of the team's 140 games in 1919, but only 17 of them were as a pitcher. His win-loss record for the year was 9–5, bringing his major league record to 89–46. Five additional victories over the next 14 years would bring his major league career totals to 94–46, a winning percentage of .671. The debate has continued over the years as to just how good a pitcher Babe Ruth was.

His statistics indicate that Boston's ace was the best left-handed pitcher of his time, and just a shade behind Walter Johnson and Grover Cleveland Alexander. His winning percentage is better than Eddie Plank's or Rube Waddell's, the two greatest southpaws of the first two decades of the twentieth century, and two members of Baseball's Hall-of-Fame. His earned run average is better than Plank's and slightly higher than Waddell's. His nine shutouts in 1916 is still the American League record for a left hander. And his 29⅔ consecutive scoreless innings in the World Series was the record for 44 years.

Babe Ruth's winning percentage is #5 on the all-time major league list, and his earned run average of 2.28 is #10 all-time. Detractors claim that Babe's pitching career of about five years wasn't long enough to be able to evaluate his pitching skills. However, as one former player said, "If you can't tell how great a player is, in five years, you shouldn't be in the game." It should be remembered that Sandy Koufax, who was elected to the Baseball Hall-of-Fame in his first year of eligibility, had only six successful seasons. His first six years in the National League, when he compiled a record of 36–40, were completely forgettable.

Make no mistake, Babe Ruth was a great pitcher.

Babe Ruth was also a great hitter, which he would soon prove. Over the winter, the Boston strongman worked out diligently at his Sudbury, Massachusetts, country home. His regimen included clearing the trees behind his home, chopping wood, and running. Helen saw to it that he maintained a healthy diet.

As a result, he arrived at spring training camp in Tampa, Florida, in top physical condition. And he arrived with the mentality of a hitter. In his book *The Tumult and the Shouting*, when Grantland Rice called Ruth a good hitting pitcher, Babe replied, "I may be a pitcher, but first off I'm a hitter. I copied my swing after Joe Jackson's. His is the perfectest."

Joe Jackson was considered by many experts, including Ruth and Ted Williams, to be the greatest natural hitter of all time. Both sluggers copied their swings after "Shoeless Joe." At the time he was barred from baseball for life, Jackson had a career batting average of .356, #3 all-time.

Now that he was to be a full-time outfielder, Babe Ruth also began to take a serious interest in the kind of bat he used. He did considerable experimentation with bats, purchasing bats with many different lengths, weights, and shapes. At one time, he ordered several bats that weighed an enormous 52 to 54 ounces but found them to be unwieldy and seldom used them. His favorite bats were Hillerich-Bradsby Louisville Sluggers, 40–44 ounces and about 35" long. He was the first player to order bats with a knob at the end to keep his hand from slipping off the bat when he swung.

Until Babe Ruth appeared on the scene, players used thick, heavy bats and choked up several inches on the handle to allow them to make contact with the trick pitches that were then part of the game. Over the years, Babe Ruth revolutionized, not only the game of baseball, but also the bat design. Babe went to a lighter, thinner-handled bat that allowed him to whip the bat through the strike zone more quickly, increasing the bat speed at time of contact and giving him greater distance on his drives.

Baseball owners shortened the baseball season to 140 games in 1919 but went back to the 154-game schedule the following year. From a team standpoint, 1919 was a disaster. Shortly before the season began, Red Sox owner Harry Frazee sold three of his star players to the New York Yankees, outfielder Duffy Lewis and pitchers Carl Mays and Ernie Shore. Mays had won 21 games for the Sox in 1918 while Lewis and Shore were both in the army.

The Red Sox started slowly in 1919, hovering around the .500 mark for two months, then collapsing completely, finishing in sixth place, 20½ games behind the pennant-winning Chicago White Sox. Babe Ruth, catcher Wally Schang, and pitchers Allan Russell and Herb Pennock were the only bright spots in an otherwise dismal year.

Ruth got off the mark quickly when the season began, smacking a home run against the Yankees, in support of Carl Mays' 10–0 shutout of the New York team. For the first couple of months, Babe Ruth alternated between the mound and left field, but the wear and tear of the dual role finally brought the experiment to an end. Babe became a full-time outfielder.

As summer wore on, Babe's spectacular hitting exploits had the baseball writers rushing to their record books to verify the existing home run record. At first it was thought that Buck Freeman's 25 home runs in 1899 were the record. Then someone discovered that Ned Williamson had dropped 27 balls over the short fence in Chicago's Lake Front Park in 1884.

No matter, Babe would not be stopped. His first challenge, Sock Seybold's American League record of 16 home runs, set in 1902, fell before a fussilade of home runs, on August 14. Within weeks Ruth passed Gavvy Cravath's modern major league record of 24 set in 1915, then beat Freeman's mark of 25. On September 20, the mighty Bambino tied Williamson's mark with an unusual Fenway Park home run. Ruth, a notorious pull hitter, hit an outside pitch from Lefty Williams of the White Sox over the left field wall in the bottom of the ninth, to win the game. Finally, on September 24, Ruth hit #28, to pass Williamson. The record-breaking home run came in the ninth inning of the second game of a doubleheader against the New York Yankees, in the Polo Grounds. It was hit against New York's 20-game winner, Bob Shawkey, and was called the longest home run in Polo Grounds history, clearing the right field stands and landing in Manhattan Field which adjoins the stadium. He hit one more home run before the season ended, finishing with 29, an unbelievable total in those days of the dead ball and trick pitches. And—he outhomered four American League teams.

Babe Ruth's slugging accomplishments in the years between 1915 and 1919 are truly amazing. Gavvy Cravath had the highest home run frequency in baseball history, prior to the arrival of Ruth, 17 homers for every 550 at bats. In his tenure in Boston, Babe averaged 24 home runs per year, an extraordinary number. But it was even more extraordinary

when examined in detail. Babe Ruth played half his games in spacious Fenway Park, at that time one of the most difficult parks in which to hit a home run. Fenway Park had a 405-foot power alley in right center field and an unconscionable 550-foot center field wall.

The Boston strong boy hit a total of 49 home runs during his stay in Boston. Only 11 of them were hit in Fenway Park, with the remaining 38 being hit on the road. Babe's home run frequency was a modest 11 home runs a year at home, but an astronomical 38 home runs a year on the road. And this with a dead ball!

The 1919 World Series pitted the powerful Chicago White Sox against the National League champion, Cincinnati Reds. Although the White Sox were heavy favorites, betting was light because there were already rumors that the Series was fixed. Ed Cicotte, the White Sox ace, who went 29–7 during the season, was clobbered in the opening game of the Series, then lost game four, 2–0, when his two errors in the fifth inning led to both Cincinnati runs. Lefty Williams, a 23-game winner during the season, went down to defeat three times, compiling a suspicious 6.61 earned run average. The only bright spot in the Chicago lineup was the pitching of little Dickie Kerr, who did everything in his power to win the Series. He shutout the Reds 3–0 in game three, then won game six 5–4 with a gutty ten inning performance. But it wasn't enough. Cincinnati took the best five of nine Series in eight games.

On October 28, 1919, the United States Congress passed the 18th amendment to the Constitution, making the manufacture and sale of alcoholic beverages illegal in the country. It was the culmination of a 200-year effort on the part of various organizations and governments, to control the excessive use of alcohol. Women like Carrie Nation were in the forefront of the movement. The 6' tall, 175-pound leader of the Women's Christian Temperance Union gained notoriety by marching into saloons, carrying a hatchet and laying waste to the furniture, the bar, the whiskey kegs, and the bottles.

The Anti Saloon League, which was organized in Ohio in 1873, united the different organizations under one banner. By 1916, 23 of the 48 states had anti-saloon laws. On December 22, 1917, Congress

Opposite: **Babe Ruth, in his first full season as an outfielder in 1919, set a new home run record when he socked 29 round trippers.**

submitted the 18th amendment to the states for ratification. It became law on January 16, 1920.

Prohibition would have a profound effect on American society during the decade of the 20s, but not in the way its adherents expected.

On the baseball front, the big news of the off season was the sale of Babe Ruth to the New York Yankees. Harry Frazee, the owner of the Boston Red Sox, experienced serious financial difficulties in 1919. He had lost a considerable sum of money producing Broadway plays he had loans due to Joseph Lannin, the former Red Sox owner, and Ruth was squeezing him for more money. In desperation, Frazee sold his "franchise" player to New York for $120,000 and a $350,000 loan. The deal was finalized on January 5, 1920.

Ruth's sale was followed in subsequent years, by the sale of Waite Hoyt, Herb Pennock, Joe Bush, Sam Jones, Everett Scott, and Wally Schang, to those same Yankees. Frazee's disgraceful acts destroyed the greatest team of the decade, a team that had captured four World Championships between 1912 and 1918.

The wholesale shipment of Boston's star players to New York led to the creation of the great Yankee dynasties that dominated the major leagues from 1921 until 1964.

Boston has never recovered from the Babe Ruth fiasco. They have won only four American League pennants in the ensuing 80 years. They have never won another World Championship.

3. Babe Ruth—
A Hero Emerges

Nineteen hundred and twenty was a historic year in major league baseball. Prohibition went into effect. "The Roaring Twenties" got underway. The major leagues began using a new juiced-up baseball, establishing the lively ball era in professional baseball. Babe Ruth joined the New York Yankees, and broke all single season home run records. Trick pitches like the spit ball were banned forever. And the Black Sox scandal captured the public's attention.

The beginning of the lively ball era was not a figment of someone's imagination. The ball shot off players' bats like it was shot from a cannon. Major league home runs increased by 41 percent from 1919 to 1920. They continued to increase over the next decade as more and more batters began to swing for the fences instead of just trying to make contact with the ball.

Major league hitters pounded out a total of 447 home runs in 1919. They hit 631 homers in 1920, and a mind-boggling 1565 homers in 1930. There were two major culprits, the new ball and Babe Ruth. The A.G. Spalding Company, manufacturer of major league baseballs, reportedly began using Australian yarn in 1920. The new yarn, which was stronger and tougher than American yarn, could be wound tighter, giving harder, livelier balls than those manufactured prior to 1920.

Babe Ruth himself contributed significantly to the home run craze. His mighty blasts created such excitement around the country that other players soon began to copy his swing. Until Ruth revolutionized the game, players were more concerned with making contact with the ball than they were with hitting it out of the park. The baseball mentality was such that it was a disgrace to strike out, so most players just protected the plate when they had two strikes on them, making sure they put the ball in play.

The tremendous increase in home runs however, is not the reason that so many modern-day hitters strike out 100 to 150 times a year. In 1930, when major league hitters pounded out 1,565 home runs, which was an increase of 250 percent over 1920, strikeouts only increased by 9 percent, from 7,282 to 7,936.

Today's hitters are guess hitters, who commit to swinging at a pitch before they know what kind of a pitch it is. Yesterday's hitters were controlled hitters, who waited on a pitch until the last moment before swinging at it. As a result, they knew what kind of pitch they were swinging at and were able to put it in play more often.

The other factor that impacted significantly on the home run production in the major leagues was the banishment of trick pitches from the game. Pitchers were no longer permitted to throw the spitball, emery ball, shine ball, and other trick pitches, but major league pitchers who threw the spitball were grandfathered. They were allowed to continue throwing it until they retired. Burleigh Grimes was the last of the spitball pitchers, finally retiring in 1934.

As the 1920 season got underway, Miller Huggin's New York Yankees were poised to make a run for the top. The previous year, they won 80 games against only 59 losses, finishing in third place, 7½ games behind the Chicago White Sox. Now, with Ruth in tow, Huggins was confident he could take it all.

Babe Ruth was already referred to as the Sultan of Swat by the baseball community after his long distance bludgeoning of opposing pitchers during the preceding two years. His record-breaking clouts brought the fans out by the thousands. Even opposing players held Ruth in awe. Players and fans alike stopped whatever they were doing to watch the Bambino take batting practice before a game.

The big slugger was an imposing sight at the plate. He was one of the bigger players in the league at 6'2", and 210 pounds, and his chiseled body seemed to be designed for destruction. His broad shoulders and huge chest, tapering down to a svelte waist and powerful legs, exuded power. His swing was vicious but graceful. It was copied from "Shoeless Joe" Jackson's swing, except that Babe Ruth kept his feet closer together than Jackson did, so he could stride into the ball, utilizing all his power at the moment of contact. As Ruth said, his swing was an all-or-nothing swing. He either hit the ball with tremendous power or he looked good striking out.

Ruth was the most glamorous and exciting player in baseball history. Unlike his contemporaries who swung the bat level to the ground in order to hit line drives back through the infield, the Yankee slugger used his powerful wrists to uppercut the ball, sending the little white pellets into orbit whenever he connected.

Ruth got off the mark slowly when the 1920 season opened however, going homerless in New York's first 11 games. Then, on May 1, Babe Ruth hit his first Yankee home run, a towering drive over the right field roof at the Polo Grounds, also known as Brush Stadium, sparking the team to a 6–0 whitewashing of the Red Sox. The Yankees were tenants in the New York Giants home park for ten years, until they moved into their own stadium, in 1923. Ruth played in the Polo Grounds for three years and enjoyed tremendous home run success in the homer-friendly park. He averaged an astounding 63 home runs for every 550 at bats in the Polo Grounds.

The Yankee slugger hit 11 home runs in May and 13 in June as he took baseball to a level it could never imagine. On July 15, in just his 93rd game of the season, Babe Ruth tied his own major league mark with home run number 29. Five days later, he broke the record, smashing #30 against the Chicago White Sox in the Polo Grounds.

The excitement of Babe Ruth's home run rampage was brought back to earth on August 16, when tragedy visited the Yankees' home park. In a game against the Cleveland Indians, New York submarine pitcher Carl Mays hit Cleveland shortstop Ray Chapman in the temple with a fastball after Chapman inadvertantly ducked into the pitch. The 29-year-old infielder died within 24 hours, becoming the only fatality in major league baseball history.

Cleveland, under manager Tris Speaker, wore black arm bands the rest of the season, in tribute to their fallen comrade. The Indians went on to capture the American League pennant after eight Chicago White Sox players were suspended for complicity in fixing the 1919 World Series. They also won the World Championship, beating the Brooklyn Dodgers five games to two.

Ruth continued his cannonading through the months of August and

September. He hit a milestone on September 24 when he launched #50 off the right field facade at the Polo Grounds in the first game of a doubleheader. He hit number 51 in game two. The Sultan of Swat climaxed his explosive season by hitting home run #54 on September 29, breaking his own record by 25 home runs.

Babe Ruth's inaugural season in New York was a smashing success. He not only set a new major league home run record, but he also showed the baseball world he was not a one-dimensional player. The big outfielder ripped the ball at a sizzling .376 clip, with 36 doubles and nine triples to go along with his 54 home runs. His .847 season slugging average has never been approached. His nearest competitor was Lou Gehrig, who had .765 in 1927. In fact, Ruth holds the second and third spots with averages of .846 in 1921 and .772 in 1927.

And New York Yankee owner, Col. Jacob Ruppert, was generously rewarded for his investment in the big slugger. The Bronx Bombers' home attendance shot up from 619,000 fans in 1919 to almost 1,300,000 fans in '20. They broke the major league attendance record by almost 400,000 people, on their way to becoming the first major league team to break the magical 1,000,000 attendance barrier.

Babe Ruth totally dominated the major leagues in 1920. He led the majors in runs scored (158), home runs (54), runs batted in (137), bases on balls (148), on base percentage (.530), and slugging average (.847). The immensity of his home run accomplishments can be better understood when they are put in proper perspective. Babe Ruth outhomered every team in the American League! The entire St. Louis Browns ballclub hit only 50 home runs all year. The Philadelphia Athletics hit 44. No other team hit more than 37. The Babe's closest individual rivals in the home run race were George Sisler who hit 19, and Tilly Walker who hit 14. Only 11 players in the entire American League hit as many as ten home runs.

Although Ruth was the major league leader in strikeouts during his career, he would be considered a contact hitter by today's standards. His average of 87 strikeouts per 550 at bats pales by comparison to modern day sluggers who average anywhere from 100 to 175 strikeout a year. Reggie Jackson, for instance, fanned an unbelievable 145 times for every 550 at bats during his career, while Philadelphia Phillies slugger Mike Schmidt went down swinging 124 times.

Ruth was also an intelligent base runner who stole 14 bases in 1920. In the outfield he combined good range with a strong, accurate throwing arm, as evidenced by his 21 assists.

As the 1920 season wound down, the rumors of a fix in the 1919 World Series reached a point where a Cook County Grand Jury began investigating the allegations. Finally, on September 28, with just five days remaining in the season, Chicago White Sox owner Charles Comiskey suspended eight White Sox players pending an investigation of the incident. The players involved included Eddie Cicotte, Lefty Williams, Happy Felsch, Swede Risberg, Fred McMullin, Buck Weaver, Chick Gandil, and "Shoeless Joe" Jackson. Chicago lost the pennant to the Cleveland Indians by two games.

Eventually, the eight players, now known as the "Black Sox," were indicted and tried in Chicago. They were eventually cleared of all charges against them due to a lack of evidence, but the verdict didn't help their professional baseball careers. In November of 1920, major league owners, disturbed by the rumors of thrown games that had persisted for years, hired a new baseball commissioner. Judge Kenesaw Mountain Landis was given absolute power to take any necessary action to restore the integrity of the game. Landis' first act was to ban the Chicago eight from playing organized baseball for life.

Gandil, Felsch, Williams, Cicotte, McMullin, and Risberg were certainly guilty of the crime. But many people still feel that Joe Jackson (who hit .375 with a record 12 hits in the Series, and who fielded flawlessly) and Buck Weaver (who hit .324 and also fielded flawlessly) received bum raps. Many people have tried, over the years, to have Jackson exonerated so he could be inducted into baseball's Hall-of-Fame. As recently as 1998, Ted Williams pleaded Jackson's case. He may yet be awarded the honors that have eluded him for the past 79 years.

Nineteen twenty was the beginning of the decade that has been called the Golden Age of Sports. It has also been called the most hedonistic decade of the twentieth century—the Jazz Age, the Roaring Twenties. The two—sports and the Roaring Twenties—went hand in hand. Everything seemed surrealistic during the 20s. The athletes were larger than life. The nightlife was one wild, never-ending roller coaster ride. On the athletic front, until the 20s, baseball and boxing were essentially the only sports that most Americans were familiar with. Then beginning in 1919, when increased leisure time made spectator sports more popular, the entire field of athletics exploded with legendary figures. Babe Ruth stood baseball on its ear with his electrifying home run feats, personally carrying the game to a new level of popularity. In the ring, a young fighting machine out of Colorado, named Jack Dempsey, captivated the sporting public. The Manassa Mauler, a veritable tiger at only 182 pounds, manhandled heavyweight champion, Jess Willard, to win the title on July 4, 1919. Dempsey, in as ferocious an attack as had ever been seen in the squared circle, knocked the 6'6" 250-pound "Pottawatomie Giant" to the canvas six times in the first two minutes of the fight, en route to a third round TKO. He would rule the division for seven years until dethroned by Gene Tunney in 1926.

Other sporting figures who captivated the American public over the next decade included football legend Red Grange of Illinois University, Notre Dame's famed Four Horsemen, golfer Bobby Jones, Tennis champions Helen Wills and Bill Tilden, swimmer Gertrude Ederle, and aviator Charles Lindbergh.

American society changed dramatically in the years following World War I. Call it a fatalistic attitude brought on by the horrors of war, just another step in evolution, or the result of a booming economy. Whatever it was, it turned the country upside down.

The automobile had made long-distance traveling practical. By 1929, there were 23 million autos on the country's highways. Stock market investments made thousands of millionaires overnight. Even the small investor was living comfortably as a result of the huge profits being generated by American business. And movies were influencing the morals of the country. Movie stars like Rudolph Valentino and Claire Bow, the "It" girl, exuded sexuality on screen. The public flocked to movie theaters in record numbers. When Valentino died in 1925, after an appendectomy, 30,000 people stormed Campbell's Funeral Church in New York City to view the body. By the time Al Jolson, another graduate of St. Mary's, made the first talking picture, "The Jazz Singer," in 1927, over 100,000,000 people were attending movies every week.

Prohibition, which banned the manufacture and sale of alcoholic beverages, instead of curing the country of the ills of alcohol, drove it to new heights, and in the process, led to the rise of gangsterism in the United States.

Before the ink was dry on Amendment #18, crafty racketeers, ready to take advantage of every opportunity, were making arrangements to obtain illegal alcohol from other countries, and from illegal manufacturing operations (known as moonshiners), inside the country. Other mobsters were opening secret nightclubs, called "speakeasies." It was the beginning of "The Roaring Twenties."

The atmosphere in the country was fueled by the passage of Amendment #19 to the United States Constitution, the law that gave women the right to vote. The female sex was becoming more independent and was beginning to establish its own identity in the country.

Speakeasies contributed to the lawlessness in the country in another way. In illegal night clubs, there was no "legal" drinking age. If you were big enough to reach the bar, you were big enough to drink. And the booze flowed freely, much of it coming into the country on fast motor boats from the West Indies. Other sources of supply included Mexico and Canada. People also brewed their own liquor at home. It was called Home Brew or Bathtub Gin.

A significant amount of the illegal alcohol came from industrial alcohol that was diverted to making synthetic liquor. In 1926 alone, it was estimated that 60 million gallons of industrial alcohol were diverted for illegal uses.

The Roaring Twenties were a time of fun and games. The new jazz music filled the speakeasies with a sensual, rhythmic beat. Combined with the effects of alcohol, it produced wild orgies in thousands of clubs across the country. Unconventional young women in short dresses, known as flappers, danced away the nights, drinking and behaving wildly. The men followed suit. Rich, old men, known as "Sugar Daddies," took advantage of the situation to latch on to young, willing, companions. The attitude seemed to be "eat, drink, and be merry, for tomorrow we die."

Throughout the twenties the nation partied, and Babe Ruth was right in the middle of it. The Babe could drink and party with the best of them, even before 1920. In fact, manager Bill Carrigan of the Boston Red Sox, tipped off by a hotel employee that Ruth didn't get back to the team hotel until 6 A.M. one morning, broke into the Babe's room and found him under the covers fully clothed. After several arguments and a suspension, Babe agreed to leave a note on Carrigan's door telling him when he got back to the hotel every night. Carrigan, for his part, said he would never check on Babe again, as long as Ruth did not lie to him. Sure enough, the Red Sox manager would find a note on his door every morning that would say something like, "Bill. Got back at 3 A.M. Babe." Babe never lied, and Carrigan never checked on him again. He was satisfied as long as Babe's night life didn't affect his performance on the field.

Prohibition proved to be a monumental disaster for American society. Instead of eliminating the consumption of alcohol, it actually resulted in an increase in consumption, because of the inability to monitor the drinking age. Other results of prohibition were an increase in prostitution, an increase in arrests for drunkenness, a rise in alcoholism, an increase in deaths from poisoned alcohol, and the growth of organized crime. Crime figures like Al Capone and Lucky Luciano got their starts bootlegging during "The Roaring Twenties," eventually expanding into racketeering and protection.

Prohibition was finally repealed by the passage of the 21st Amendment to the Constitution, on November 7, 1933. Laws against drinking however, remained in effect in some localities across the country. Throughout the remainder of the twentieth century, drinking was regulated on a state by state basis, or by a town or a county within a state.

After the 1920 season ended, Babe Ruth joined a New York Giants team managed by John McGraw, on a barnstorming tour of Cuba. The Giants with Ruth won six of nine games against the Havana and Almendares teams, with the Bambino hitting a respectable .345 with two home runs. Cuban strongman Cristobal Torriente however, outhit the Yankee slugger. He pounded New York pitching for three home runs and a .400 average.

Ruth's vacation turned out to be more expensive than he expected. Even though he received $20,000 for the exhibitions, plus expenses for his wife and his agent, he went home broke. The 25-year-old superstar loved to gamble, and he lost thousands of dollars at the Jai Alai Fronton and the Oriental Park Race Track. His biggest losses however, according to Angel Torres, came from an expensive game of darts played at the Casa Granda Hotel in Santiago.

Once back in the states, Ruth retreated to his home in Sudbury, Massachusetts, to relax and to enjoy the life of a gentleman farmer. He also worked out on a regular basis to stay in shape.

When the 1921 season rolled around, Babe Ruth was ready. Baseball fans across the country held their collective breaths, wondering what the Sultan of Swat would do for an encore. The first thing he did was fascinate the people who visited the Yankees' spring training camp. The Babe was an extrovert, and he loved to entertain the fans, both on the field and off, and he spent hours signing autographs whenever he had the time. Over the years, Babe Ruth probably signed more autographs than any other sports figure. And he loved the kids most of all. His close relationship with kids went back to his years in St. Mary's where, as a teenager, he defended the little kids from the school bullies, remembering how tough life was for him when he was little.

The New York Yankees of 1921, unknown to them at the time, were about to embark on a memorable, record-setting journey. Their pennant victory would be the first of 35 such trophies over a period of 78 years, an extraordinary achievement unmatched in the annals of professional sports. Two years later, the Bronx Bombers would win the first of their 24 World Championships. Babe Ruth anchored the attack for the first seven American League pennants and the first four World Championships.

The Yankee team, who by this time had obtained pitcher Waite Hoyt and catcher Wally Schang from their supply house in Boston, started the season in fine fashion, blasting the last-place Philadelphia Athletics, 11–1. Babe Ruth led the attack with five hits, including two doubles. Three days later, on April 16, the Sultan of Swat banged out his first homer, as Miller Huggins' boys took the A's in tow once more, this time by a score of 3–1.

New York struggled during the first month of the season, but by mid–May they were cranking on all cylinders, and moved into second place behind the defending World Champion Cleveland Indians. Through the summer and into September, not more than two games separated the two combatants.

Ruth's home run count reached 14 by the end of May, 26 by the end of June, and 36 by the end of July, leaving him about even with his 1920 pace. The Yankees trailed the Indians by a mere one game.

On August 11, New York beat the Chicago White Sox to move into first place by one percentage point. The dogfight was on. The lead changed hands several times over the next five weeks, as the two teams jockeyed for position. Ruth's cannonading continued unabated through August and into September. On September 9, in Shibe Park, the Bambino tied his own home run record when he unleashed a mighty wallop against the A's. One week later, in the cozy confines of the Polo Grounds, he hit #55 against the St. Louis Browns.

The pennant race finally reached its climax on September 26, when Tris Speaker's Cleveland Indians, trailing the Yankees by ½ game, invaded New York for a crucial four-game series. With the two teams tied at one game apiece, the Yankee bombers unloaded on the hapless Cleveland pitchers. In game three, they completely destroyed the visitors to the tune of 21–7. In the finale, the Sultan of Swat, with two home runs and a double drove in five runs as the Yanks prevailed 8–7. They clinched the pennant on October 1.

The Bambino hit his record setting 59th home run on October 2, in the last game of the season. He hit it in the Polo Grounds with two men on base, as the Yanks edged the Boston Red Sox, 7–6. It was a record-setting season all around the major leagues. Home run totals increased from 630 in 1920 to 937 in 1921, a jump of 49 percent. Still, Babe Ruth was in a class by himself. His nearest competitor in the American League was teammate Bob Meusel with 24 homers. The National League champion, George Kelly of the Giants, hit 23.

Once again, the kid from Baltimore showed himself to be a superstar of immense proportions. His season was arguably the greatest of his career, even better than his fabulous 1920 season. In addition to his 59 home runs, Ruth led the league with 177 runs scored (still the all-time major league record) and 171 runs batted in. His 204 base hits included 44 doubles and 16 triples, good for a .378 batting average. His 16 triples, along with 17 stolen bases, were indicative of his exceptional speed on the bases.

Two "firsts" were set when Miller Huggins' Yankees met John McGraw's Giants in the World Series. It was the first time two teams that shared the same home ballpark met in the Series. It was also the first World Series broadcast on radio. Station WJZ in Newark, New Jersey, covered the game, with legendary sports commentator Graham McNamee doing the play by play. Unfortunately, the Yankees dropped the best of nine series, five games to three. The Yanks got off fast, taking the opener 3–0 behind Carl Mays' five-hitter, and capturing game two, 3–0 on a brilliant two-hitter by Waite Hoyt. Then it was downhill, with the Giants taking five of the last six. Injuries kept Ruth out of the lineup for the last three games, all of which the Giants won.

Babe Ruth's years in New York were hectic and turbulent ones. He always resisted authority, and had continual run-ins with manager Miller Huggins, owner Jacob Ruppert, and Baseball Commissioner Kenesaw Mountain Landis. He even punched an umpire in the jaw one time, resulting in one of his dozen or more suspensions. Those incidents never hurt his popularity however. He was an idol to the fans, young and old alike, and he also had an excellent rapport with the newsmen.

After the Series ended, Ruth and Bob Meusel received offers to go barnstorming around the country. In spite of a warning by Commissioner Landis that such actions would not be tolerated, the Ruth All-Stars hit the road for Buffalo and Scranton and other way stops around the northeast. The Babe cancelled the tour after only a week on the road after Yankee co-owner, Tillinghast Huston told him he was hurting the Yankees. But the damage had been done. Landis immediately suspended Ruth, Meusel and another player for 39 days after the 1922 season got underway.

Although the Yankees had won the pennant in 1921, owner Jacob Ruppert once again visited his favorite supply house, Harry Frazee's Boston Red Sox. This time he picked up pitchers Sad Sam Jones (23–16 for Boston in 1921) and Bullet Joe Bush (16–9), along with shortstop Everett Scott and third baseman "Jumping Joe" Dugan.

New York went on to take the American League pennant again, this time beating a strong St. Louis Browns team by a single game. But Ruth personally had a difficult year. He allowed himself to get out of shape during his suspension and performed poorly when he finally got back into the lineup. The boos of the crowd made him testy, resulted in frequent altercations with the umpires, and brought about four more suspensions. The frustrated slugger was also removed as the Yankee captain after he chased a jeering fan through the stands. And he lost a one-sided fight to teammate Wally Pipp to boot.

Babe Ruth's season statistics were not something he was proud of. He played in only 110 games, hit 35 home runs, batted in only 99 runs, and hit a sub par .315—a career season for some players, but an embarrassment for an icon like Ruth.

The New York Yankees met the Giants in the World Series once again. This time they were swept in four games, much to the chagrin of Miller Huggins and Jacob Ruppert. The Yankees were a lesson in futility, scoring only 11 runs in five games (one game ended in a tie) and never scoring more than three runs in any game. Babe Ruth hit a paltry .118, with just one RBI in the Series. Bob Meusel at .300 and Wally Pipp at .286 were the only Yankee batters to hit over .250.

Over the winter, Babe Ruth worked hard to get in shape for the 1923 season, determined to redeem himself in the eyes of the New York fans. Meanwhile Ruppert dipped into the Boston well one last time and came up with southpaw pitcher, Herb Pennock. The slender six footer went on to win 164 games for the Yankees over a period of 12 years.

The year 1923 was a memorable period in New York Yankee history. Yankee Stadium, known as "The House That Ruth Built," opened on April 18. Fittingly, the "Sultan of Swat" responded in typically heroic fashion. He slammed the first stadium home run, a three-run shot into the right field stands in the third inning, as the New Yorkers won, 4–1, behind Bob Shawkey. The Yanks went on to capture their third successive American League pennant, this time leaving the rest of the league in their dust and finishing a comfortable 16 games ahead of the Detroit Tigers. They capped off their spectacular run with a six-game victory over their arch rivals, the New York Giants, in the World Series.

Babe Ruth had a great season all around. He led the league in home runs again, this time with 41. He also led in runs scored (151) and runs batted in (131), and he hit a career high .394. In the Series, he ripped Giant pitching for three home runs and a .368 batting average.

Another of the great sports idols had a memorable year in 1923. Jack Dempsey, perhaps the most charismatic and popular athlete in America after Ruth, scored a sensational second round knockout of Luis Angel Firpo of Argentina, in one of the most famous fights in boxing history. In fact, if Firpo had reacted more quickly in round one, he might well have snatched the heavyweight championship belt away from Dempsey. But he missed his chance, and "The Manassa Mauler" came roaring back to retain his title.

Jack Dempsey, a vicious fighting machine swarmed the challenger in round one, knocking him down seven times in a wild two-minute barrage of punches. As the champion closed in for the kill, the "Wild Bull of the Pampas" struck out with a right hand that caught Dempsey flush on the jaw, putting him on the canvas. As soon as the dazed champion got to his feet, Firpo banged him again, knocking him completely out of the ring. The slow-moving Firpo was unable to capitalize on his advantage however, and the champion was saved by the bell.

Dempsey regained his senses during the break and came out for round two on the attack again. A devastating right put Firpo on the deck just seconds after the round began. A second right put him down again. Then a left hook to the jaw paralyzed the Argentinean, and a chopping right finished the job. Ninety thousand screaming fans in the Polo Grounds witnessed the four-minute, 57-second massacre. It was the kind of fight that legends are made of. And a legend was born on that night.

Babe Ruth continued his sensational slugging through the 1924 season. Even though the Yankees fell to the Washington Senators in the pennant race, the Bambino won his only batting championship, with a sizzling .378 average. He led the league in runs scored with 143 and home runs with 46. And he also drove in 121 runs.

The Senators' pennant victory was a popular one because 36-year-old Walter Johnson, nearing the end of his illustrious career, racked up a 23–6 record on the mound, leading the league in victories and ERA. "The Big Train" was also the hero of the World Series, trudging out of the bullpen in the ninth inning of game seven to stifle the New York Giant bats for four innings. He came away a 4–3 winner, in 12.

Babe Ruth spent the winter enjoying life in the big city. Since he came to New York in 1920, the big guy fell right into the New York night life. He loved to party, and every night was party night in New York. Whether the flappers and Sugar Daddys were dancing the night away in some speakeasy, or college kids were eating goldfish and crowding into telephone booths, or outrageous adults were engaging in dance marathons, the good times went on around the clock. Whether the people were trying to forget World War I or the devastating flu epidemic of 1920, it was "life on the edge" during the 20s.

When he partied, Babe Ruth drank a lot and ate a lot. His teammates claimed he could eat continuously, 24 hours a day. His favorite meal was hot dogs and beer. It was rumored he once ate a breakfast consisting of an 18 egg omelet, three slices of ham, six slices of buttered toast, a gallon of chocolate ice cream, and a lot of beer.

Babe Ruth's eating binge continued into spring training. He arrived in Florida weighing a flabby 256 pounds, about 40 pounds over his playing weight. As the 1925 season approached, the Bambino was still overweight and out of shape. It finally caught up with him as the team headed north. He collapsed on the train platform in Asheville, North Carolina, and was rushed back to New York for medical treatment. He was operated on for an intestinal abscess, putting him out of action for seven weeks. Newspapers popularly reported the incident as "The Bellyache Heard Round the World."

Ruth returned to the Yankee lineup on June 1, but he never did regain his batting form. He hit below .250 most of the summer but continued to enjoy the night life all around the American League. Finally, in desperation, manager Miller Huggins fined his star $5000.00 and suspended him indefinitely. After the usual threats to quit the team, Ruth recanted, apologized to Huggins, and was eventually reinstated.

His return couldn't help the Yankees however. They struggled through a disastrous season, finishing in seventh place. Their 69–85 record left them a distant 28 games behind the Washington Senators. Ruth played in only 98 games, batting .290 with 25 homers and 66 RBIs. Bob Meusel was the only bright spot on the team, leading the league in home runs with 33 and runs batted in with 138. Rookie Lou Gehrig hit a respectable .290 with 20 homers and 68 RBIs.

The embarrassed Sultan of Swat punished himself over the winter, determined to get back into playing condition. He worked out religiously at Artie McGovern's gym on 42nd Street and Madison Avenue. The regimen paid off. He dropped 42 pounds in five months and arrived at spring training camp in St. Petersburg weighing a svelte 212 pounds. The camp was upbeat as the proud New Yorkers were determined to atone for their dismal showing the previous year.

Miller Huggins' boys got off the mark quickly in 1926, anchored by a new double play combination of Tony Lazzeri at second and Mark Koenig at short. Lou Gehrig at first, with one full year under his belt was about ready for stardom. The Yankees opened the season on April 13, with a 12–11 triumph over the Red Sox in Boston. A 16-game winning streak in May left them with a 30–9 record and a healthy 14-game lead over the Philadelphia Athletics.

A late-season slump by the Yankees and a surge by the Cleveland

Indians closed the gap by the end of the season, but New York still took the pennant by three games. Unfortunately they lost the World Series in seven games, to the St. Louis Cardinals, when grizzled veteran Grover Cleveland Alexander came out of the bullpen in the seventh inning with the bases loaded, two out, and the Cards clinging to a slim 3–2 lead. "Old Alex" fanned "Poosh 'em Up Tony" Lazzeri to end the threat, then protected the lead over the final two innings to give the Cards the World Championship. Babe Ruth, who walked with two out in the bottom of the ninth, was thrown out attempting to steal, ending the Series.

Overall, the Bambino had performed brilliantly, both during the season and in the Series. Playing in 152 games, he once again led the league in runs scored (139), home runs (47), and runs batted in (145), while rapping the ball at a .372 clip. In the World Series he smashed four home runs in seven games, while walking 11 times.

One of the legendary Babe Ruth tales took place during the World Series. The day before the Series got underway, Babe traveled to Essex Falls, New Jersey, to visit Johnny Sylvester, a critically ill 11-year-old boy who idolized him. He gave Johnny an autographed picture of himself, then promised to hit a homer for him in the Series. Babe went without a homer in the first three games, but he exploded for three homers in game four. Johnny was thrilled. He eventually recovered.

Babe Ruth's love of children surfaced hundreds of times over the years. He visited them in hospitals, and even in their homes, but without any publicity. He brought joy and hope to untold numbers of kids suffering from serious, sometimes terminal illnesses.

In 1927 George Herman "Babe" Ruth achieved the pinnacle of his career. At 32 years of age, he was beginning to settle down, take his conditioning seriously, and limit his evening escapades. After a winter of vigorous training, he arrived in Florida ready for action. It was reported that he took young Gehrig under his wing, and told Lou he could hit 40 to 50 home runs a year if he held his bat down at the end and swung with bad intentions. He also suggested that Gehrig try to pull the ball more to take advantage of the short right field porches in most American League parks. Coincidentally or not, Lou Gehrig suddenly blossomed into a feared slugger, increasing his home run production from 16 in 1926 to 47 in 1927. His output in Yankee Stadium jumped up from four homers in 1926 to 24 homers in 27, indicating he did in fact learn to pull the ball. Gehrig went on to average 37 home runs a year over the next 11 years.

The 1927 New York Yankees, who would forever be known as "Murderers Row," and may have been the greatest team of all time, opened their season in Yankee Stadium against the Athletics, before 72,000 fans. Their 8–3 victory gave them a share of first place. They never lost it. By the end of April, they held a one-game lead, and Ruth had just four home runs.

Both Ruth and the Yanks picked up the pace in mid–May. The Yankee slugger began the month by hitting two homers at home, against the A's, on May 1. Then he had a dry spell of eight days before slamming #7 against Milt Gaston of the St. Louis Browns. Gaston became a favorite target of Ruth's during the season, yielding four of Babe's 60 home runs. Southpaw Rube Walberg of the A's also gave up four homers to the Yankee bomber. After a 10–3 streak mid month, the Yanks 23–10 record gave them a 4½ game lead over the Chicago White Sox. On May 22 in Cleveland's League Park, the Sultan of Swat hit his tenth homer, a tape-measure job, off journeyman right-hander Benn Karr.

Another American hero broke into the headlines on May 21. Aviator Charles Lindbergh made the first solo nonstop flight across the Atlantic Ocean, landing in Paris, 33 hours, 29 minutes and 30 seconds after taking off in the rain from New York. "Lucky Lindy" who was welcomed to France by 100,000 deliriously happy fans, was quoted as saying, "At one time there was considerable ice on the bow of the plane, and I was a little concerned. But it cleared up." The city of New York planned a ticker tape parade for the courageous pilot on his return to the U.S.

Both Babe Ruth and the Yankees got into a comfortable rhythm during the summer. Babe had nine home runs in June, including two two-homer days. He pounded out two home runs against lefty Garland Buckeye of Cleveland, in Yankee Stadium, on June 11, then duplicated the feat in Boston, against Hal Wiltse, on the 22nd.

On June 13, Babe hit #21 in Cleveland. Following a habit he established at the start of the season, as reported by Bill Koenig, he put a notch around the trademark of his favorite bat, a model R43, 40-ounce, 35" Louisville Slugger. Notch #21 was the last notch he put on the bat. He broke the bat before hitting #22.

The New York team continued to terrorize opposing pitchers with their long ball attack. In addition to Ruth and Gehrig, Bob Meusel and Earl Combs were stroking the ball at a better than .330 pace, and Tony Lazzeri was over .300 for the New York wrecking crew that was averaging more than six runs a game.

During the heat of the summer, according to Samuel Fuller in Cult Baseball Players, Babe Ruth swaggered into the City Room of the New York Journal one day, announcing to the reporters, "Gentlemen, that bathtub gin is poison," pointing to the half dozen water coolers around the room that, in fact, were filled to the brim with homemade prohibition gin. Ruth was followed into the room by six uniformed cops, carrying six cases of genuine whiskey. Typewriters were left silent and telephones were left ringing as Ruth, the reporters, and the cops drank to each other's health from paper cups.

The Babe hit nine more homers in July, as the Yankees widened their lead in the American League pennant race. After sweeping Bucky Harris' Washington Senators by scores of 12–1 and 18–1 on the fourth of July, their lead mounted to a hefty 11½ games. Lou Gehrig had two homers in the sweep giving him the home run lead over Babe Ruth, 27–26. Babe kept the pressure on however, hitting a homer off Don Hankins in Detroit on the 8th of the month, then following that with two homers off the Tigers' Ken Holloway the next day. He also hit two more off his "cousin" Milt Gaston of the Browns, on July 26. He finished the month with 34 home runs, still in a neck and neck race with his teammate Lou Gehrig.

The Senators stayed hot through July, but when they slumped in August, the Tigers and A's jockeyed for second place, a good 16 games behind the league-leading Yankees. Lou Gehrig, or Larrapin' Lou as he was called, kept pace with Ruth through the dog days of August. On August 10, Lou was in the lead 38 homers to 35. The Sultan of Swat connected for #37 in Chicago on the 16th, becoming the first player to hit a ball out of the remodeled double deck Comiskey Park. He got even with Gehrig on August 22 when he victimized "Lefty" Joe Shaute in Cleveland, smashing his 40th home run of the season. Babe hit nine home runs in August, finishing the month with a total of 43 homers.

Gehrig jumped out in front of the "Sultan of Swat" again, 45 to 44, on September 5. The Yankee lead at that time was a comfortable 15 games. On September 6, Miller Huggins' crew visited Boston to play the

last-place Red Sox. Facing Tony Welzer, the Bambino launched two home runs, giving him 46 for the season. He hit #47 later in the game against Jack Russell, moving in front of Gehrig by two. The following day, the big slugger punished Boston pitching for two more homers, increasing his season total to 49. When he homered off Gaston of St. Louis, in New York on the 11th of the month, it gave him an even 50 home runs with just 17 games left in the season.

The New York Yankees clinched the pennant on September 13 when they swept the Cleveland Indians by identical scores of 5–3. Ruth homered in each game, giving him 52 for the season. The New York triumph was the earliest pennant clinching in American League history. Now the only race of interest for the fans was the home run race, and the race was over as far as Gehrig was concerned. He hit just two more home runs after September 6, finishing the season with 47. Now it was just Babe against Babe.

Babe Ruth was in an enviable position as he chased the record. He was chasing himself, so there was no pressure on him to break someone else's record. There were no radio or television interviews to contend with and no combative newspaper reporters prying for sensational personal exposes.

In Ruth's time, the major leagues were confined to a relatively small geographical area that stretched from Boston in the north to Washington, D.C. in the south, and St. Louis in the west. Travel was less hectic than it is today. Trains carried the New York team to Boston or Washington in three hours. The longest trip of 976 miles to St. Louis was a comfortable overnight ride in a sleeper car.

The New York newspaper reporters traveled with the team when they were on the road. They shared sleeping and eating accommodations with the players, on the train, and they spent their free time playing poker and shooting the breeze with them. They also hung out with the players in the hotel, the restaurants, and the local nightspots. For all intents and purposes, the reporters were just one of the boys. Their reporting was restricted to events on the baseball field. They did not pry into a player's private life or report on any negative off-field incidents.

Opposite: **Babe Ruth dominated the American League for 16 years with his spectacular home run feats. (Brace photo)**

Future home run challengers were not so lucky. They would come under intense media scrutiny, both before a game and after a game. Their private lives were fair game, their indiscretions laid bare for all to see. Future home run challengers lived life in a goldfish bowl.

Babe still trailed his 1921 record pace of 59 home runs as the month approached its final two weeks. When he put #55 in orbit against Sam Gibson of Detroit in Yankee Stadium on September 21, he was still five games behind '21. He was still three homers behind with just four games to play.

According to Robert W. Creamer, when Babe hit his 56th homer he carried the bat around the bases with him. A kid rushed onto the field and grabbed the bat as Babe rounded third, but Babe continued on, crossing the plate, dragging the bat and the kid behind him.

He smashed his 57th home run, a grand slam, off future Hall-of-Famer Lefty Grove at the stadium, in game #151. Two days later, on September 29, playing against the Washington Senators at home, the Sultan of Swat propelled more two balls into the stands, tying his own record of 59 home runs. His first homer came with the bases empty in the first inning. His second homer was a grand slam in the fifth as the Yankees romped 15–4.

Babe Ruth had two more games in which to break his own record. He needed only one. On Friday, September 30, the Washington Senators were in town to close out the season. Tom Zachary, a 6'1", 187-pound curve ball artist was chasing his ninth win of the season, opposed by 18-game winner, Herb Pennock. The two southpaws locked up in a pitchers duel, with the score knotted at 2–2 after seven innings. Ruth had singled and scored both Yankee runs, one in the fourth and one in the sixth, to offset a two-run fourth by Washington. In the eighth inning, Mark Koenig tripled with one out, bringing Ruth to the plate again. The Babe had a perfect day at that point, with two singles and a walk. With a count of 1–1, Zachary uncorked a low, inside fast ball, and Babe jumped all over it. He sent a sizzling line drive down the right field line, barely fair. The ball came to rest about half way up the stands, with the umpire signaling a home run. Tom Zachary argued that the ball was foul, but to no avail. Babe rounded the bases to the cheers of the screaming New York fans. Hats and torn scraps of paper floated down on the field as the wild celebration continued for another ten minutes.

Babe's 60th also turned out to be the game winner as Pennock shut down the Senators in the ninth to win 4–2. During the clubhouse celebration following the game, the Babe exulted, "Sixty. Count 'em, sixty. Let's see some other sonofabitch match that."

Curiously, only 10,000 fans turned out to witness history in the making. Apparently it was no big deal to the blase New Yorkers, who had already seen Babe Ruth set two home run records. They thought he would continue setting records for years to come. So #60 was nothing special to them. That mentality would change drastically as the years passed.

Babe Ruth's glorious season, in addition to his 60 home runs, included a league-leading 158 runs scored, 164 runs batted in, and a .356 batting average. Once again he outhomered every team in the league.

Ruth, Lou Gehrig, and the rest of "Murderers Row," continued their cannonading through the World Series. They swept the timid Pittsburgh Pirates in four straight but, truth be told, they probably won the Series even before the first pitch was thrown. The day before game one, during batting practice, manager Miller Huggins told his charges to see how many balls they could put out of Forbes Field. The bombardment that followed completely demoralized the Pirate players who were outscored 23–10 in the Series.

Nineteen twenty-seven was by no means Babe Ruth's swan song. He hit 54 home runs in 1928, followed by 46, 49, 46, and 41 the next four years.

He continued to play major league baseball until 1935, retiring after a short stint with the Boston Braves. Three other Babe Ruth stories bear repeating because they reflect the stature of the man. In 1930, in the aftermath of the tragic stock market crash of 1929, Babe Ruth signed a New York Yankee baseball contract for the unheard of sum of $80,000. When someone asked Ruth if he thought he should be making more money than President Herbert Hoover, Ruth replied, "I think I should. I had a better year than he did." In the 1932 World Series against the Chicago Cubs, Ruth allegedly called his shot just before hitting a home run. While batting against the Cubs' Charlie Root, in the fifth inning of game three, with the Series tied at one game apiece, Ruth took the first two pitches for strikes. After the second strike, Babe pointed his bat to the center field stands, supposedly telling Root where he was going to park the next pitch. Testimony is contradictory, but two facts are indisputable. Movie films of the incident definitely show Ruth pointing his bat toward center field after the pitch. And Ruth did park the next pitch over the bleacher screen in deep center field, 440 feet from home plate. He went on to hit .333 for the Series with two home runs, and the Yanks won the Series in a sweep.

In 1935, the 40-year-old Babe Ruth played for the Boston Braves, in hopes he might become a team vice president. He retired after 28 games, hitting a feeble .181, but he did have one last moment of glory. On Saturday May 25, in Pittsburgh, he brought back memories of his youth by slamming Pirate pitching for three home runs and a single, driving in six runs in an 11–7 Braves loss. The last home run cleared the right field roof at Forbes Field, coming to rest in Schenley Park across the street. The hit that some observers called the longest ball ever hit in Forbes Field was the first home run to leave the park.

4. The 1930s, 40s, and 50s—An Historical Perspective

On October 29, 1929, a day that would go down in history as "Black Friday," the stock market crashed, wiping out the financial assets of millions of investors and starting a depression that would last for ten years. The 1920s had been a glorious decade for investors and speculators as the business economy boomed. Much of the prosperity, according to "News of the Nation," was built on credit. Stocks were bought with low down payments and with speculators borrowing to get on the bandwagon.

When the stock market lost 50 percent of its value from September 3 to late October, small investors lost their life savings, even their homes. The resulting depression continued through much of the 1930s. By 1933, 12 million people, or 25 percent of the workforce, were unemployed. The new president elect, Franklin Delano Roosevelt, promised to wage war on the depression by instituting government programs to get the people back to work. One such program, the WPA, employed thousands of men to build roads, bridges, and national parks.

Naturally, baseball attendance dropped precipitously during the depression, falling from 10.1 million fans in 1930 to a low of 6.1 million fans in 1933. The game survived, however, and got even stronger with the introduction of the All-Star Game in 1933 and with a bumper crop of bonafide new sluggers filling the rosters of the big league teams. When Babe Ruth retired in 1935, he left a legacy of awesome power unmatched in the annals of professional baseball. His long ball-hitting exploits have since been passed down from one generation to the next. Rawboned sluggers, arriving on the scene periodically, have taken dead aim on his slugging records. Some records have been broken over the years, but others will probably never be broken. The legend of Babe Ruth lives on.

Ruth's impact on major league baseball was not immediate. Many of his contemporaries, who had played major league baseball during the dead ball era, were too set in their ways to change. They continued to choke up on the bat and slap at the ball rather than taking a full cut. It was the mentality of the day when it was considered a disgrace to strike out. A few players like Rogers Hornsby, Tilly Walker, and Ken Williams changed their batting grips to go more for distance, and their home runs increased dramatically. But, for the most part, the change to a Babe Ruth–type long-distance mentality took a generation or more to complete.

One of the first major leaguers to emulate Ruth and go for the fences was a young Maryland farm boy. His name was James Emory Foxx. He was born in the tiny farming community of Sudlersville, on October 22, 1907. A life of hard physical labor on the farm gave young Foxx the rugged physique of a body builder, with bulging biceps and a powerful chest. He was discovered playing for a local team by former Philadelphia Athletics third baseman, Frank "Home Run" Baker, who quickly signed him to a professional baseball contract.

Sixteen-year-old Jimmie Foxx, who was influenced by the awesome slugging feats of Babe Ruth, began his career as a catcher for Easton, Maryland, in the Class D Eastern Shore League. He was already a formidable presence on the diamond, standing 6' tall, and weighing a brawny 195 pounds. Like Ruth, he held his bat at the end and swung from his heels. He punished opposing pitchers in his rookie season, driving out 31 extra base hits, including ten home runs, in just 260 at bats. Defensively, he led league catchers in assists with 73.

The following year, after playing 41 games for Providence in the International League, Foxx was called up to the A's. He appeared in ten games, and batted a sensational .667, with six hits in nine at bats. The 17-year-old strongman was a major leaguer.

The handsome, genial slugger impressed everyone who saw him.

Opposite: **Jimmie Foxx slugged 534 home runs during a brilliant 20-year career. (Brace photo).**

Bill Dickey, the great Yankee catcher, once said he could tell when Jimmie Foxx was at bat, even blindfolded. "He hit the ball harder than anyone else."

Jimmie Foxx was converted to a first baseman by manager Connie Mack because Mack already had future Hall-of-Famer Mickey Cochrane behind the plate. Foxx learned the new position well, leading the league in fielding percentage five times during his career. He is generally regarded as one of the two greatest first basemen in baseball history, the other being Lou Gehrig.

The Maryland strongboy was known affectionately as "The Beast" during his playing days, because of his muscular build and because of the raw power in his swing. Over the years, Foxx was credited with some of the longest home runs in major league history. He cleared the double deck stands in Comiskey Park, hit a tremendous homer over the double-decked stands in Shibe Park, broke a seat in the upper left field stands in Yankee Stadium, and set distance records in Detroit, Cleveland, and St. Louis.

Old "Double X" was not just a power hitter. He could hit for average, had decent speed (125 lifetime triples and 87 stolen bases), and was a good fielding first baseman.

Foxx led the American League in home runs four times, in runs batted in three times, and in batting twice. He was voted the Most Valuable Player in the American League three times, tying the major league record. He batted over .300 in 13 of his first 15 seasons in the majors, including four years over .350. In 1933 "The Beast" won the triple crown, batting .356 with 48 homers and 163 RBIs. The previous year, he just missed the triple crown. He led the league in homers with 58 (a major league record for right handed batters until McGwire and Sosa broke it in 1998), and in RBIs with 169. His .364 batting average was only three points below the league leader.

Foxx's 58 home runs in 1932 came within two of tying Babe Ruth. In fact, if Foxx had played under the same conditions that Ruth enjoyed in 1927, he might have hit as many as 66 home runs. "The Beast" hit five balls off the right field screen in St. Louis and three balls off the left field screen in Cleveland. Neither screen was in place when Babe hit his 60.

Jimmie Foxx was one of the greatest power hitters ever to play baseball. When he retired, he held the record for most career home runs by a right-handed batter (534) and was second to Babe Ruth overall. He still ranks #9 in career home runs, #6 in runs batted in, and #6 in runs batted in per game. His home run frequency of 36 homers a year ranks #7.

Another big right-handed slugger surfaced in the early 1930s. Hank Greenberg, a powerfully built 6'4", 215-pound first baseman from New York City, starred in the majors for 13 years. He missed an opportunity to go down as one of the greatest sluggers of all time when he missed one full season because of an injury and four other seasons in the U.S. Army during World War II. He returned from the war in 1946, played two more years, then retired at the relatively young age of 36.

"Hammerin' Hank" arrived in the American League as a fuzzy cheeked 22 year old in 1933. Two years later with the Detroit Tigers, he led the league in homers with 36, in runs batted in with 170, and batted a solid .328. In 1938, Greenberg came within a whisker of catching Babe Ruth in the home run race. He had 58 home runs with five games to go but went homerless the rest of the way. In two home games against the St. Louis Browns, Greenberg was held to one single in nine trips to the plate. Then, in three road games in Cleveland, the best he was able to do was hit a double off Bob Feller.

Hank Greenberg was a fearsome major league hitter for 13 seasons. In addition to home runs, he also hit more than his share of doubles and triples. He led the league in doubles with 63 in 1934 (fourth highest all time), and 50 doubles in 1940. His extra base hit percentage of .150 trails only Babe Ruth. Greenberg was one of the most efficient run producers ever to play the game. His 183 runs batted in, in 1937, is the third highest RBI total ever, trailing only Hack Wilson's major league record of 190 and Lou Gehrig's American League mark of 184. His career average of .915 RBIs per game (1,276 RBIs in 1,394 games) is #2 all time, just .005 points behind Lou Gehrig's .920.

While Greenberg was playing out his career with the Pittsburgh Pirates in 1947, he tutored a young slugger named Ralph Kiner. Kiner, who was born in Santa Rita, New Mexico, on October 27, 1922, was a 6'2", 195-pound right hander who had led the National League in home runs in his rookie season with a modest 23.

Pittsburgh management, in an attempt to increase Kiner's home run output, constructed a chicken wire fence from left field to left center

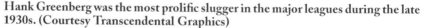

Hank Greenberg was the most prolific slugger in the major leagues during the late 1930s. (Courtesy Transcendental Graphics)

field, reducing the home run distance in left from 365 feet to 335 feet and in left center from 406 feet to 355 feet. The 24-year-old slugger responded with 51 home runs in 1947. He went on to lead the National League in homers his first seven years in the league, including a 54 home run season in 1949. Kiner, like Greenberg, retired early, putting his spikes away when he was just 32 years old. His average of 39 home runs for every 550 at bats is third all time, trailing only Babe Ruth's 50 and Mark McGwire's 49 (through 1998).

Ralph Kiner's career had a profound impact on future baseball players. His statement that "Home run hitters drive Cadillacs. Singles hitters drive Chevys," influenced a whole generation of hitters. Young boys who dreamed about playing major league baseball began gripping the bat down at the end and swinging for the fences.

There was one notable minor league slugger that deserves mention here. Joe Bauman was a big, strong, left-handed bomber who stood 6'5" tall and weighed 235 pounds. Playing for Artesia in the Class C Longhorn League, Bauman hit 50 homers in 1952 and 53 more in 1953. The following year, he moved to Roswell, New Mexico, and made baseball history. In 139 games, Joe Bauman hit 72 home runs, a professional home run record that has never been broken.

During the 1920s, after the introduction of the lively ball, and while Babe Ruth was demonstrating his home run prowess to his contemporaries, the average number of home runs per team per season increased from 39 in 1920 to 98 in 1930. The 98 home runs in 1930 was an anomaly. It was the year of the "rabbit" ball, when the entire major league roster of 16 teams had an average batting average of .296. The average number of home runs for the decade was 72. Major league teams would not reach the 98 home run level again until 1947.

During the 1930s, as more and more boys came into the major leagues with a Babe Ruth–type swing, the average number of home runs rose from 72 to 84. The 1940s were not representative of major league baseball because the able-bodied men were away fighting a war from 1941 through 1945, and the players who filled the major league rosters were not up to big-league standards. The average number of home runs per team per year plummeted to 62 during that time.

The decade of the 1950s was influenced by two factors. First, there was the "Kiner syndrome," which attracted hundreds of free swinging sluggers to professional baseball, players intent on "driving Cadillacs."

Second, integration had a major effect on the batting philosophy of professional baseball players. Integration was the single most significant social change in America in the twentieth century, and it began with major league baseball. Baseball Commissioner Happy Chandler, after seeing black soldiers fight and die side by side with white soldiers during World War II, believed they deserved the right to share equally in the American dream, which included playing organized baseball. When Brooklyn Dodger President, Branch Rickey, approached him in 1945 with his intention of signing a black player to a Brooklyn contract, Chandler gave Rickey his full support. Jackie Robinson subsequently broke the color barrier that had existed for more than 45 years, opening the door for other black players to walk through.

From 1947 until 1959, over 100 former Negro league players made the transition from the Negro leagues to the major leagues. Some of the greatest sluggers in baseball history made their major league debuts during this period, established Negro league sluggers like Roy Campanella, Luke Easter, Larry Doby, and Monte Irvin, as well as young budding Negro league superstars like Hank Aaron, Willie Mays and Ernie Banks.

The 1950s are often called the "Golden Age" of major league baseball, and that is probably true. Certainly, with integration the quality of play in the major leagues was far superior to the quality of play prior to integration. Negro league legends like Josh Gibson, a slugger of the ilk of Babe Ruth, Satchel Paige, one of the greatest baseball pitchers ever, pitchers "Smokey Joe" Williams, Martin Dihigo, and "Bullet Joe" Rogan, shortstops John Henry Lloyd and Willie Wells, third baseman Ray Dandridge, and outfielders "Cool Papa" Bell, Turkey Stearnes, and Oscar Charleston, were prevented from playing major league baseball during the 1920s, 30s, and 40s because of their color.

Over the last 40 years, the quality of major league baseball has once again deteriorated, probably due to several factors, such as the dilution of talent caused by athletes participating in other professional sports like basketball and football, major league expansion, and an improved economy which attracts more and more young men to a business career, rather than a career in professional sports.

The mentality of hitting has also undergone a drastic change from the hitting philosophy of the first half of the twentieth century. Until the 1950s, most hitters were taught to wait on a pitch until the last moment, then when they could identify what kind of pitch it was and where it would cross the plate, they would commit their swing. Beginning in the 1950s, batters began guess hitting—guessing what kind of a pitch would be thrown, and where it would be thrown—and they would start their swing as soon as the pitcher released the ball, hoping they had guessed correctly. Batters became guess hitters in the mistaken belief they would hit more home runs that way. Statistics show that guess hitting does not result in more home runs. It only increases strikeouts and lowers batting averages.

From 1950 to 1960, home runs increased by just 2 percent, while strikeouts shot up 34 percent. From 1950 to 1988, home runs actually decreased by 12 percent, while strikeouts were up 33 percent. Big swingers like Reggie Jackson (35 homers, 145 strikeouts, and a .262 batting average), Mike Schmidt (36 homers, 124 strikeouts, and a .267 batting average), and Dave Kingman (36 homers, 150 strikeouts, and a .236 batting average) glorified the new mentality.

The old-time sluggers, like Babe Ruth (50 homers, 87 strikeouts, and a .342 batting average) and Jimmie Foxx (36 homers, 89 strikeouts, and a .325 batting average), belie the modern hitting philosophy however. And Ted Williams, who wore out opposing pitchers from 1939 until 1960, remains the epitome of batting excellence. He combined a sharp batting eye with world class power. The "Splendid Splinter" averaged 37 homers a year during his career while batting a torrid .344, the sixth highest career batting average in baseball history. He accomplished these outstanding feats while striking out only 51 times a year, proving that truly great sluggers can hit for both average and distance without piling up a lot of embarrassing strikeouts.

Roger Maris, who arrived on the major league baseball scene in 1957, although not the possessor of a high batting average, showed the world it was possible to hit for distance without whiffing every third or fourth time at bat. Maris averaged 30 homers a year during his career while striking out only 79 times.

5. Roger Maris— The Early Years

Babe Ruth's single season home run record of 60 home runs stood for 35 years. He was actually the single season home run champion for 43 years, going back to 1919 when his 29 home runs broke the all-time record set by Ned Williamson of the Chicago White Stockings in 1884. He subsequently broke his own record three times, with 54 homers in 1920, 59 homers in 1921, and 60 homers in 1927.

The man who would break the Bambino's record was born Roger Eugene Maras on September 10, 1934, in Hibbing, Minnesota, a town of about 15,000 people located in the northeastern part of the state, about 100 miles south of the Canadian border. The family name was subsequently changed to Maris when Roger was a teenager.

When Roger was ten years old, the Maris family moved to North Dakota, eventually settling in Fargo, on the Minnesota border. North Dakota is essentially a treeless, wind-swept plain, with an average temperature of 39 degrees. Summers (and baseball seasons) are short, and winters are long and bitter. Farming is the primary industry with over 85 percent of the land used for agriculture. Wheat, barley, and rye constitute the bulk of the farm production.

Rudy Maris, Roger's father, worked for the Great Northern Railroad, providing his sons with a good, middle-class work ethic. He also gave his sons a love of sports, having been a good athlete himself, in his younger days. Roger and his older brother, Rudy Jr., were both outstanding athletes at Shanley High School, a Catholic high school in Fargo. In football, Rudy led the passing attack in the single wing formation, and Roger, an All-State player, did the bulk of the running.

Young Roger, according to Tim Wendel in *Baseball Weekly*, set a North Dakota state record for most touchdowns in a game—five—scoring on runs from scrimmage of 32 and 88 yards, a 45-yard punt return, a 90-yard kickoff return and a 25-yard interception. Roger, who was a solidly built 180 pounder, was a two-way player. Wendel wrote, "God, he loved to hit," says Kelly, one of his classmates. "Rog was a cornerback, and nobody I ever saw could come up to the line (of scrimmage) as fast as him and just rip people. It got to the point where other teams simply stopped running the ball to his side of the field. It wasn't worth it."

Roger Maris was an all-around athlete in high school, playing basketball and track, in addition to football. He also starred for the Fargo American Legion baseball team for three years, winning the Most Valuable Player award in 1950, and helping the team capture the American Legion state championship in 1951.

During Roger's senior year at Shanley, he was recruited by legendary football coach, Bud Wilkinson of the Oklahoma Sooners. The 18-year-old running back was duly impressed to be recruited by Oklahoma, but after visiting the Norman campus, he changed his mind. He didn't think he had the necessary study habits to survive in college, so he turned down the offer and focused his attention on baseball.

That summer, General Manager Hank Greenberg of the Cleveland Indians signed the young outfielder to a $5000 bonus contract to play professional baseball. He was assigned to play in his hometown, for Fargo-Moorehead of the Northern League. That same year, 1953, he married his high school sweetheart, Patricia Ann Carvel, beginning a 32 year married love affair that was blessed with six children.

The smooth-swinging, left-handed hitter thrived in the Class C Northern League, under the tutelage of manager Zeke Bonura, a former major leaguer with a career batting average of .307. Maris finished the year with a .325 batting average, nine home runs, and 80 RBIs in 114 games. He also proved to be an aggressive baserunner, and an outstanding defensive player. Fargo-Moorehead won the pennant by 13 games over Duluth, and went on to win the playoff as well. And 18-year-old Roger Maris was voted Rookie of the Year.

That year was a historic year in the Northern League. Maris' teammate Frank Gravino smashed a record 52 home runs into the North Dakota sky, outdistancing his nearest challenger by 33 home runs.

Gravino, who hit 56 home runs the following year, was one of the most prolific minor league sluggers ever, averaging 38 home runs a year, over a 12-year career. In fact, only eight other professional players have averaged more home runs during their career than Gravino did—and that includes the major leagues, the Japanese leagues, and the Negro leagues. The stocky, 186-pound outfielder missed an opportunity to play in the majors when he lost three years to military service in World War II.

Maris moved up a notch in his second year in professional baseball, playing with Keokuk, Iowa, in the Class B III League. While there, he was taught to pull the ball by his manager Jo Jo White, a former major league outfielder. Maris learned his lessons well. He deposited 32 baseballs over the fence, on his way to a .315 season with 111 runs batted in.

He also spent many hours refining his defensive skills, learning to hit the cutoff man, to get a jump on batted balls, to play balls off the fence, and to improve the accuracy of throws from his cannon-like right arm.

His climb up the minor league ladder was rapid. He started the '55 season with Reading in the Class A Eastern League and, after being selected for the all-star team, he moved on to Tulsa in the AA Texas League.

In 1956, at the tender age of 21, Roger Maris fine tuned his talents at Indianapolis in the American Association, just one step away from the major leagues. He had an outstanding season, batting .293, with 17 homers and 75 RBIs. The Indianapolis Indians won the American Association pennant by five games over Denver, captured the league playoffs, and went on to win the Little World Series, beating the International League champion Rochester Red Wings in a four-game sweep.

The Denver manager that year was Ralph Houk. Four years later, Houk would manage the New York Yankees, and Roger Maris, his former opponent with the Indianapolis Indians, would be his star right fielder.

Roger Maris became a major leaguer in 1957, settling in right field for Cleveland. He got off to a fast start for the Indians, going three for five against the Chicago White Sox on opening day, April 16, then hitting a game-winning grand slam home run in the 11th inning the next day. Maris played in a total of 116 games for Cleveland, batting .235 in 358 at bats, with 14 home runs and 51 runs batted in.

The next year, he was traded to the Kansas City Athletics with two other players for Vic Power and Woodie Held, just before the June 15 trading deadline. His batting average for the season was still on the low side (.240), but he showed improved power with 28 homers and 80 RBIs. He came back to hit .273 in 1959, with 16 homers and 73 RBIs, in 150 fewer at bats than in '58. After the season ended, he was sent off to the New York Yankees in a seven-player swap, with Kansas City getting Don "No-Hit" Larsen and Hank Bauer as part of the deal.

The 1959 New York Yankees, the defending World Champions, were picked to win their fifth consecutive American League pennant. Unfortunately, the proud Bronx Bombers could not get untracked, and they dropped out of the race by August, limping home in third place, a distant 15 games behind the Chicago White Sox. General Manager George Weiss, realizing the Yankees needed more offense, went into the trade market to get it. His first stop was Kansas City, his favorite supply house. Roger Maris, K.C.'s right fielder, with three years of major league experience under his belt, showed potential, but it was still essentially unrealized. Maris was a superb defensive outfielder, with a sound glove and a strong arm. He had reasonable power (58 home runs in three years), and had raised his batting average from .240 to .273 in 1959. Weiss decided to take a chance on the 25 year old, and the trade was made. It put the Yankees back on track to regain the American League pennant in 1960.

Roger Maris was born to be a Yankee. As Robert Wuhl noted in *Cult Baseball Players*, "Roger Maris had THE perfect Yankee Stadium swing. Short. Quick. Powerful. Left handed." And he was the ultimate team player, ready to sacrifice himself, if necessary, for the good of the team. He was a long ball hitter, and a clutch hitter, but he also knew how to handle a bat. Unlike most sluggers, Maris could bunt or hit-and-run as the situation warranted. He was an outstanding baserunner and slider, and one of the best at breaking up a double play. Many baseball experts consider him the best defensive right fielder ever to play for the Yankees, and according to Mark Gallagher in "The Yankee Encyclopedia," "He often dove into Yankee Stadium's right field seats to rob opponents of HRs."

Opposite: **Roger Maris played for Cleveland and Kansas City for three years before being traded to the New York Yankees in 1960. (Brace photo)**

Usually batting just ahead of Mickey Mantle in the power-laden New York Yankee lineup, the kid from Fargo came into his own in the big city. As spring training wound down, Yankee fans wondered if their team could come back from the 1959 debacle. When they lost the final game of the spring, 2–0 to the Boston Red Sox, it left them in last place in the Grapefruit League standings, with a disheartening 11–21 record.

Al Lopez's Go-Go Chicago White Sox were favored to repeat in 1960. They had one of baseball's all-time great double play combinations in future Hall-of-Famers Nellie Fox at second and Luis Aparicio at short. They had explosive speed on the bases, led by Aparicio who topped the American League with 56 stolen bases, and Jim Landis who had 20. As a team, the Go-Go Sox led the American League in stolen bases with 113. They also had outstanding pitching led by Early Wynn (22–10 in 1959), Bob Shaw (18–6), Billy Pierce (14–15), Gerry Staley (14 saves), and Turk Lown (15 saves).

The Cleveland Indians, with Rocky Colavito (42 homers, 111 RBIs), Minnie Minoso (.302, 21, 92), Billy Martin, and pitchers Cal McLish (19–8), Gary Bell (16–11), and Mudcat Grant (10–7), were also expected to be in the hunt.

The season opener, in Yankee Stadium, on a seasonably warm 62-degree day, was a success all around. The Bronx Bombers pounded Boston Red Sox pitching for 17 hits, en route to an 8–4 thumping of manager Billy Jurges' troops. Roger Maris, batting in the leadoff position, led the New York attack with a single, a double, and two home runs into the right field bleachers.

Big 6'4" right hander Jim Coates, on his way to a fine 13–3 season, was the recipient of the early season barrage. The Yankees raked Boston starter, Tom Brewer for six runs in 4⅓ innings, before 35,162 enthusiastic fans. Ted Williams provided the only excitement for the Boston contingent when he blasted his 494th career homer into the right field seats.

Two weeks later, Coates upped his record to 3–0, in Baltimore, as Casey Stengel's boys bombed the Orioles 16–0, scoring five runs in the first and never looking back. Maris cracked two doubles and a home run (his third), driving in four runs. His cohort, Mickey Mantle just missed a home run by a couple of feet, his long drive off the wall going for a triple. The win snapped a three-game New York losing streak, and sent

33,000 Baltimoreans home sad. As the month ended, the Yanks' 8–4 record gave them a 1½ game lead over the Chicago White Sox and Detroit Tigers, with Baltimore another ½ game behind.

The Yankees treaded water most of May, struggling to an 11–13 record for the month. Maris was one of the bright spots, batting .322 and leading the league in both home runs (11) and runs batted it (30). Big Jim Lemon of Washington was second in home runs with ten, while shortstop Ron Hansen of Baltimore had 29 RBIs. Jim Coates was still cruising along with a spotless 5–0 record, but Mickey Mantle was mired in a horrible slump, hitting only .244.

On May 30, after a doubleheader with Washington, Yankee Stadium fans rushed onto the field and mobbed Mantle as he raced from his outfield position to the safety of the dugout. In the melee that followed, the Yankee star suffered a badly swollen jaw as fans tried desperately to strip him of his hat and glove. They got his hat. He saved his glove.

The next day, right hander Jerry Walker threw eight strong innings, as the O's edged the Yanks 3–2 in Baltimore. With Baltimore up 1–0 in the seventh, Mantle sliced a double to left field, and came around to score the tying run on a line drive single to right by Maris. But that was all the offense the Yanks could muster. The Orioles tallied single runs in both the seventh and eighth innings, off Ford and Duren, then held off a brief New York rally in the ninth, to win.

New York's 19–17 record left them in fourth place, four games behind the front-running Baltimore Orioles. Paul Richard's team was the surprise of the league in the early going. They had finished in sixth place in 1959, with a 74–80 record, and they were not expected to do much better in 1960. Unexpectedly, their farm system sent them three young pitchers, Chuck Estrada (22 years old), Steve Barber (21 years old), and Jack Fisher (21 years old). They already had 21-year-old Milt Pappas on their staff. Between them, the "Kiddie Korps" won 55 games against 41 losses in 1960. They were ably supported by Jim Gentile (.292, 21, 98), a timely acquisition from Los Angeles, Gene Woodling, Gus Triandos, and the incomparable Brooks Robinson.

As the weather warmed up in June, so did the Yanks. The M & M boys, Maris and Mantle both went on a tear, and the Bronx Bombers won 20 of their last 25 games, giving them a 21–10 record for the month, and a 1½ game lead over the O's. The pennant race, which was a five-team affair for two months, was now a four-team race as the Detroit Tigers fell by the wayside.

On a hot 87-degree New York day, the Yankees completed a sweep of the Kansas City Athletics, for their 21st victory of the month. Only 8513 fans witnessed the 10–3 victory, or saw the five New York home runs leave the Stadium. First baseman Bill Skowron banged two homers, his nineth and tenth of the year, while Tony Kubek, Roger Maris, and Mickey Mantle hit one apiece. For Maris, the long drive into the upper deck in right field was his league-leading 25th of the season, and 14th for the month of June. Mantle's round tripper gave him 12 for the month and 18 for the year.

July 4th is the generally accepted halfway point of the season, and the league leaders at that point are considered to be the favorites to win the pennant. In 1960, the New York Yankees held a 3½ game lead over their nearest American League rival, Joe Gordon's Cleveland Indians, while the Pittsburgh Pirates held a similar lead over the Milwaukee Braves in the Senior Circuit. Maris was the home run leader with 25. He trailed Babe Ruth by one.

The Washington Senators ruined New York's holiday by knocking them off, 9–8. Roger Maris was nursing a cold and did not play. Mantle hit a three-run shot in the first, giving Jim Coates (9–0) a quick lead, but Coates couldn't hold it. He was still leading 8–6 when he left the game, after giving up six runs and ten hits in less than six innings, but three New York relievers blew the game. The last Yankee pitcher, Ryne Duren, walked in the winning run with two out in the bottom of the ninth, before 16,913 happy home fans.

Cleveland swept a doubleheader from the Chicago White Sox, by scores of 4–0 and 7–4, reducing the Yankee lead to a mere 1½ games. But that turned out to be the high point of the season for the Indians. They immediately self destructed, losing 18 of their next 25 games and dropping out of the race. Jimmy Dykes was brought in as manager in August, but he couldn't right the ship, winning 26 games against 32 losses the rest of the way.

The pennant race was reduced to three teams with the demise of Cleveland. New York, Chicago, and Baltimore were left to battle it out. The Yankees went into another slump in July, leaving the door open for Al Lopez's White Sox. And the White Sox capitalized on it, winning

20 of 29 games, to move into the top spot, by 1½ games over Stengel's boys, who could manage only 13 wins in 27 games. Baltimore was even worse, going 12–15 for the month.

As July wound down, the Yankees were in Kansas City for a doubleheader with the A's, while Chicago played two with Washington. The White Sox swept the Senators by scores of 5–2 and 9–5, while New York and K.C. split a pair. New York scratched and clawed for single runs in both eighth and ninth to tie game one, but two wild throws by third baseman Hector Lopez gave the A's three runs and the victory. Maris drew the collar in five trips to the plate, while Mantle hit #27. Johnny Kucks pitched a strong eight innings, yielding only two runs.

In game two, the Bronx Bombers righted themselves, winning 9–0 behind Art Ditmar's seven-hit shutout. Mantle (1–3) and Maris (1–4) were not factors in the game.

Roger Maris held on to his top spot in both the home run race and the RBI race. The Yankee right fielder had six homers and 17 runs batted in, in 27 games, while Mantle hit nine homers for the month, giving him 27 for the year, four behind Maris. Bill "Moose" Skowron, with 71 RBIs, trailed Maris by ten.

On August 5, in Kansas City, Art Ditmar edged the A's 4–3, to the disappointment of 28,111 loyal A's fans. Maris hit a two-run homer off Johnny Kucks in the third, giving New York a lead it never relinquished. It was Roger's 33rd of the season, putting him six homers ahead of Mantle.

The next day, the Stengel men routed K.C. 16–4 under stifling 97-degree skies. The 24,039 sun worshippers in the stands saw Roger Maris crack his 34th and 35th round trippers of the year, putting him seven games ahead of the mighty Bambino.

On the 7th, Maris went 0–3 in the opening game of a doubleheader, but Bill Skowron took care of the heavy artillery, bombing a two-run homer in the ninth to win the game, 3–2. Bobby Schantz, with three shutout innings of relief, picked up the win. Kansas City came back to take the nightcap, 15–3, ripping Ralph Terry for three runs on four hits, before he could retire a batter. Bud Daley tossed a complete game for the A's, running his record to 13–9.

The split with Kansas City cut the Yankees' lead to a mere ½ game, and they had to face the second-place White Sox in Chicago. A festive crowd of 48,408 filled Comiskey Park, hoping to see their beloved Sox take over the top spot. They were severely disappointed. The Yankees took the first game 7–4, scoring two runs in the seventh, and three in the eighth, before a deluge flooded the field, causing the game to be called after eight innings. In the big eighth, Mantle led off with a walk, Skowron doubled, and Howard was given an intentional pass to load the bases. Johnny Blanchard hit a ground ball to Nellie Fox at second, but Fox's throw to the plate was bobbled by Sherm Lollar for an error, allowing a run to score. Ground balls by Kubek and Arroyo brought in two more.

The next day, Yankee ace Art Ditmar tossed a two-hitter at Al Lopez's boys, the Yanks winning easily 6–0. The two losses dropped Chicago into third place, 2½ games behind the Yankees, and one game behind Baltimore.

On Friday the 12th, the Bronx Bombers returned home to do battle with the Washington Senators. They should have stayed in Chicago. The game was an embarrassment. New York pitchers issued 11 free passes, and the defense played like high schoolers. Washington won easily, 12–7. Roger Maris was one of the few bright spots in the Yankee lineup. He went 2–4 at the plate, with two RBIs and, in the field, he went over the right field fence into the bullpen in a futile attempt to catch Harmon Killebrew's 18th home run. Berra and Skowron homered for the Yankees.

Whitey Ford got the Yanks back on track the next day, tossing a three-hit 1–0 shutout at Cookie Lavagetto's club. The only run of the game came in the seventh inning, when Maris laced a triple to right center field, and Mantle brought him in with a sacrifice fly to deep right.

The joy was only temporary however, because the Stengelmen took multiple big hits on the 14th. Not only did they drop a doubleheader to the Senators, but they lost their star right fielder for 18 games, in the process. In game one, Maris and Mantle were held to a combined 2–9 (one single each), as Washington routed Bullet Bob Turley with a big five spot in the fifth, to win 5–4. Winning pitcher Camilo "Hot Potato" Pascual took Turley down town with the bases loaded, sparking the big rally.

Washington completed the sweep with a 6–3, 15-inning win in game two. Ralph Terry, who entered the game in the 15th, was touched up for three runs, dropping his record to 5–7. A bigger loss occurred in the sixth inning. With Roger Maris on first base, Mantle hit an infield grounder.

Maris slid hard into Billy Gardner at second base in an attempt to break up the double play. He took Gardner's knee to the ribs in the process, sending him to the Lenox Hill Hospital for observation. Fortunately nothing was broken, but his badly bruised ribs would keep him out of the lineup for almost three weeks. Mickey Mantle's failure to run out the double play ball brought Stengel's wrath down upon him. He was immediately yanked from the game and given an early shower.

The double loss left New York in third place, ½ game behind both Chicago and Baltimore. The pennant race was still nip and tuck as August neared an end. On the last day of the month, New York once again had a doubleheader with their cousins from Kansas City. The weather was a comfortable 78 degrees in New York, but only 14,639 fans turned out to witness the contests. The first game was a pitchers duel between 22-year-old Bill Stafford of New York and Ray Herbert of Kansas City. Mickey Mantle's monstrous triple to left center field in the bottom of the sixth rescued Yogi Berra, who had singled, with he only run of the game. Stafford upped his record to 2–0 since being recalled from Richmond, while hard luck Ray Herbert was saddled with his 14th loss of the year against only nine wins. Herbert's luck changed however, and he racked up a 5–1 record the rest of the way. In game two, 34-year-old Ned Garver, who won 20 games for the last place St. Louis Browns in 1951, and was only one year away from retirement, blanked the Yanks with a four-hitter, 6–0. Mantle's single was the only hit he and Maris had between them, in eight at bats. Right hander Ralph Terry, coming off a two-hitter in his previous start, yielded only two runs on three hits in seven innings this time, but that was enough to beat him.

New York held a slim one-game lead over the Baltimore Orioles on the morning of September 1. They compiled a record of 22–11 during August, compared to Baltimore's 22–14 mark. The White Sox were four behind while the Indians slipped out of the race, 12 games behind.

It was a bad month for Roger Maris. The Yankees' hard nosed outfielder, knocked out of action on the 14th of the month, missed 18 games. He still held his lead in homers (35 compared to Mantle's 31) and RBIs (96), but when he returned to the lineup, he couldn't swing with his old aggressiveness, and his home run total suffered as a result.

In the National League, Danny Murtaugh's Pittsburgh Pirates had opened up a 6½ game lead over the Milwaukee Braves, with the St. Louis Cardinals another ½ game behind.

Casey Stengel's Bronx Bombers turned on the afterburners down the stretch, after a slow start. Through the first two weeks of September, the New Yorkers, the Orioles, and the White Sox, continued to jockey for position. New York, coming off a double loss to the last-place A's, that left them at 7–7 for the month, hosted Baltimore for a critical four-game series. The Yanks and the Orioles were tied for first, with Chicago lurking only two games behind, ready to take advantage of the New York-Baltimore skirmishes. Prior to game one, Casey Stengel was quoted in the New York Times as saying, "The main trouble is that our guys aren't mad at anyone. They like everyone, don't argue with anyone.... We've got to play the best, the hardest baseball we know how, and we've got to do it right now....I'll wrap it up for you. My ballclub is too erratic."

The Yanks got hot just in time. In game one, with 49,217 screaming Yankee fans trying to jump-start their boys, Whitey Ford, "The Chairman of the Board," pumped up by the crowd, threw nothing but zeroes at the O's for eight innings, while New York ran up a 4–0 lead. When Paul Richard's team loaded the bases against the Yankee southpaw with two gone in the ninth, Stengel brought in Bobby Schantz to quell the rally. The Yankee closer was touched up for a two-run single, but settled down to fan Marv Breeding for the last out, with the tying runs on base. The New York crew had scored a single run in the fourth, two in the fifth, and another singleton in the sixth, off Baltimore's 21-year-old rookie, Steve Barber. New York's first run was a wind-blown, opposite field home run by Hector Lopez. The ball actually hit the pocket of right fielder Jackie Brandt's glove, before bouncing into the stands. Roger Maris deposited #39 deep into the right field seats in the fifth, with Bobby Richardson on base after a single. It would be Maris' last home run of the season. He would not homer over the last 14 games. The homer itself was a surprise, since Maris was hitting only .180 against southpaws.

The same day, in Milwaukee, 39-year-old Warren Spahn, the Braves' stylish southpaw, finally realized a dream when he stopped the Philadelphia Phillies 4–0 on a no-hitter. His 20th victory marked the 11th time he reached that charmed circle. He would tie the major league record of 13 twenty-victory seasons three years later. In his no-hitter, Spahn fanned

15 Philly batters. Crandall, Mathews, Dark, and Adcock knocked in the Milwaukee runs.

On Saturday the 17th, a Ladies Day crowd of 49,055 whooped it up all afternoon. The Yanks jumped out in front 2–0 in the first, thanks to a two-run homer into the top deck in right field by Mickey Mantle, following a Lopez single. Baltimore pushed across one run in the fifth, then tied the game in the sixth, on Gus Triandos' long home run into the left field seats. Berra immediately untied it in the bottom of the same inning with a homer. Gene Woodling tried to give Baltimore another tie in the seventh, but Maris robbed him of a homer with a great running catch in front of the New York bullpen in deep right center field. Unfortunately Jim Gentile followed with a titanic shot that Maris couldn't catch. It landed in the upper deck in right field to knot the game once again, at 3–3. In the bottom of the eighth, Yogi Berra reached on a bad bounce single. After Skowron was intentionally walked, Blanchard drew an unintentional walk to load the bases. Bobby Richardson then lined a two-run single back through the middle, and New York was home free, 5–3.

The series closed out the next day with a doubleheader. Stengel got outstanding pitching in both games as New York swept the O's, by scores of 7–3 and 2–0. In game one, the Yanks pummeled 21-year-old Jack Fisher for four runs in the third, on a Kubek homer to right field, singles by Lopez and Maris, a walk to Mantle, and a two-run double by Yogi Berra off reliever Hoyt Wilhelm. Art Ditmar won his 15th game against nine losses.

In game two, Bill Terry (9–8) outpitched another of the Baltimore baby brigade, 21-year-old Milt Pappas (13–11). The Yankees' 24-year-old right hander tossed a two-hitter, fanning six and walking only one, in a complete game effort. Pappas tossed a complete game five-hitter, in the loss. The Yankee runs came in the third and the eighth. Bobby Richardson led off the third with a pop fly to short center field. Shortstop Ron Hansen had the ball in his glove, but he dropped it after colliding with center fielder Jackie Brandt and second baseman Marv Breeding. Richardson was credited with a double on the play, and subsequently came around to score on a sacrifice by Terry and a sacrifice fly to center field by Tony Kubek. In the eighth, singles by Clete Boyer and Richardson, a walk to Kubek, and a sacrifice fly by Berra did the damage.

From there to the end of the season, the Yankees just kept winning. On September 28, Mickey Mantle hit his 40th home run, to take a one-homer lead over Roger Maris, who was still bothered by bruised ribs.

Two days later, New York pushed across three runs in the bottom of the ninth to edge Boston 6–5. Red Sox starter, Bill Monbouquette survived home runs by Tony Kubek in the third and Jesse Gonder in the seventh, and carried a 5–3 lead into the ninth. But the Yanks weren't ready to give up. Singles by Bobby Richardson, Gil McDougald, Hector Lopez, and Roger Maris tied the game, and an infield grounder by Bob Cerv plated the game winner. The two Yankee home runs gave them a new American League record of 192 homers.

New York beat the Red Sox again on October 1, 3–1, with Jim Coates winning his 13th game, in relief. The next day, in the last game of the season, Casey Stengel's crew ran off their 15th straight win, an 8–7 squeaker against Boston (their 15th win against the Red Sox in 22 games). Mantle went 0–1, but Maris had two hits including a monstrous triple to left center field, and three runs batted in. The Yankees scored one run in the eighth and two in the ninth, to win. Dale Long's two-run homer was the game winner.

The final standings showed New York with a substantial eight-game lead over Baltimore, and a ten-game bulge over Chicago. Mickey Mantle captured the home run crown with 40, and led the league in runs scored with 119, and total bases with 294. His sidekick, Roger Maris won the RBI title with 112, and led the league in slugging percentage with .581. First baseman Moose Skowron hit .309 with 26 homers and 91 RBIs. The pitching staff was led by Art Ditmar (15–9), Jim Coates (13–3), Whitey Ford (12–9), and Ralph Terry (10–8). Little Bobby Schantz saved 11 games to lead the bullpen corps. As a team, New York led the league in runs scored with 746, slugging average (.426), shutouts (16), saves (42), and earned run average (3.52).

New York's opponents in the World Series were the Pittsburgh Pirates, whose 95–59 record gave them a seven-game bulge over the Milwaukee Braves. Pittsburgh, like New York, was a high-scoring team whose 734 runs scored led the league. They also led in doubles (236), batting average (.276), and double plays (163). Their 3.49 ERA was comparable to New York's.

The two teams were rated even coming into the fall classic. Danny

Murtaugh's club was led by the immortal Roberto Clemente, a true super-star, Bill Mazeroski, one of the greatest fielding second basemen in history, and all-star shortstop Dick Groat, who could beat you with either his glove or his bat. The outstanding pitching staff included Vernon Law (20–9), Bob Friend (18–12), "Vinegar Bend" Mizell (13–5), and Elroy Face (10–8 with 24 saves).

The 1960 World Series turned out to be one of the strangest World Series ever played. The Yankees set new Series records for runs scored (55), RBIs (54), total bases (142), base hits (91), extra base hits (27), and team batting average (.318). They routed the Pirates in three games by scores of 16–3, 10–0, and 12–0. They outscored Pittsburgh by more than a 2–1 ratio in the Series, 55 runs to 24.

New York was awesome. But Pittsburgh won the Series.

The World Series opened in Pittsburgh on October 5, with Art Ditmar facing 20-game winner, Vernon Law. The Yankees got on the scoreboard first when Roger Maris put a Law pitch into the upper deck in right field. But the Pirates bounced back to rout Ditmar in the bottom of the inning, scoring three runs on a double, two singles, a walk, and an error by Kubek.

Vernon Law was in control throughout the game. He left after seven innings with a comfortable 6–2 lead. Elston Howard's pinch hit two-run homer in the ninth made it close, but Pittsburgh prevailed, 6–4. Roger Maris and Tony Kubek, with three hits each, led the Yankee attack, but three Pirate double plays did them in.

The Bronx Bombers erupted in games two and three, outscoring their opponents by a combined score of 26–3. In game two, "Bullet Bob" Turley and Schantz were the recipients of a 19-hit Yankee attack, with Turley being credited with the 16–3 win. Kubek and Richardson had three hits each, while McDougald, Mantle, Howard, and Skowron chipped in with two apiece. Mantle's two hits were both homers, the last one being a tremendous 475-foot drive over the center field wall.

The next day, in Yankee Stadium, Whitey Ford handcuffed the Pirates 10–0, with a four-hitter. Mickey Mantle once again led the attack, ripping four hits, including a double and a long home run into the left field bullpen. Bobby Richardson's grand slam homer into the left field stands in the bottom of the first, capped a six-run outburst against Pittsburgh starter "Vinegar Bend" Mizell, and Ford coasted from there.

Most other baseball teams would pack it in after being routed by such lopsided scores, but Danny Murtaugh's boys were made of sterner stuff. Game four belonged to Vernon Law again, as he won for the second time. A Moose Skowron home run in the fourth went by the boards in the fifth, when the Buccaneers put a big three-spot on the board. Law was in the middle of the rally, doubling in one run and scoring another. Pittsburgh won 3–2 to even the Series.

Another excellent pitching performance the next day by Harvey Haddix with relief help from Elroy Face brought Pittsburgh home a winner again, 4–2, putting them in the driver's seat, up three games to two, with the final two games to be played in Pittsburgh. Maris thrilled the New York crowd when he hit a towering home run into the third deck of the right field stands in the third inning, but it was not enough.

The vaunted Yankee bats came alive again in game six. Seventeen base hits, including four doubles and three triples, rattled around Forbes Field, much to the chagrin of the 38,580 Pittsburgh fans who came to see their beloved Pirates wrap up the title. Maris, Berra, and Blanchard pounded out three hits apiece, and Skowron and Richardson each had two, as Whitey Ford tossed his second straight shutout, this time a 12–0 laugher.

Game seven turned out to be one of the most exciting and dramatic World Series games ever played. Bob Turley started against Vernon Law. Pittsburgh KO'd Turley early, scoring two runs in the bottom of the first, on a Rocky Nelson homer, and two more in the second on three singles. New York got one back in the fifth on a Skowron homer, then drove Law to cover in the next inning when they pushed across four more runs. A three-run homer by Yogi Berra was the telling blow.

The Stengelmen upped their margin to 7–4 with another deuce in the eighth, but Pittsburgh roared back again. In the bottom of the inning, they put up a five-spot on four singles and a three-run home run over the left field wall by catcher Hal Smith.

Pirate ace Bob Friend came on in the ninth to close it out, but he couldn't get it done. After yielding consecutive singles to Richardson and Long, he was replaced by 35-year-old Harvey Haddix. "The Kitten," as he was called, finally retired the side, but not before New York scored two runs to tie the game.

In the bottom of the ninth, with Ralph Terry pitching, defensive genius Bill Mazeroski hit the second pitch over the left field wall to win the game and the Series. It remains the most dramatic home run ever hit in World Series history.

The Yankees won the battle of statistics but lost the war. They had nine batters who hit .300 or better, led by Elston Howard's .462 average. Mickey Mantle batted .400 with three homers and 11 RBIs. Richardson had 12 RBIs to lead the team. Roger Maris hit .267 but he had two home runs. Whitey Ford had a perfect 0.00 ERA, yielding only 11 hits and two walks in 18 innings.

One month after the Series ended, on November 9, John Fitzgerald Kennedy defeated Richard Nixon in the closest Presidential election since 1886. Of the 69 million votes cast, JFK polled just 112,000 votes more than Nixon.

The next day was a big day in the life of Roger Maris. He was voted the Most Valuable Player in the American League for 1960, edging out his teammate Mickey Mantle by three votes, 225–222. Roger Maris deserved the award. He batted a consistent .283, with 39 homers and a league-leading 119 runs batted in. In addition to his slugging, he was a dangerous baserunner, and a brilliant right fielder with a shotgun for an arm. He was also the ultimate team player, one time, in the middle of the home run chase, squeezing in the winning run, much to the surprise of his teammates.

Roger Maris also captured a Gold Glove for his work in the outfield. Teammate John Blanchard was quoted in *Season of Glory*, as saying "Roger Maris in 1960 was the greatest baseball player I've ever seen."

6. Roger Maris— Home Run Champion

After the 1960 season ended, many players hit the banquet circuit, to earn a little more money, and to bask in the adulation of the fans around the country. Roger Maris, on the other hand, went home to Raytown, Missouri, where he and Pat were raising their family. Pat was pregnant with their third child, and the little ranch house was bursting at the seams. Over the winter, Roger rolled up his sleeves and went to work remodeling the house. He added another bedroom, and built a laundry room and a play room.

The young slugger was a private person, who shunned the spotlight. After he became the home run king, he would say, "I never wanted to be a celebrity. I just wanted to be a guy who could hit 25–30 home runs, drive in 100 runs, bat around .280, and help my team win a pennant."

The winter sojourn also included contract negotiations with the Yankee brass. Mickey Mantle had signed for 1961, for $75,000, making him the highest paid player in the major leagues. Whitey Ford came in at $35,000, and Yogi Berra got $52,000. Maris, who was paid $20,000 for his MVP year wanted a raise to $40,000. After some haggling back and forth, he settled for $38,000, a veritable bargain for GM Roy Hamey.

When spring training began in St. Petersburg, Florida, a serious problem that had been festering for years, finally surfaced. Florida was still a segregated state, with segregated schools, housing and restaurants, as well as separate public drinking fountains and rest rooms, for blacks and whites. Black players were not permitted to stay in the same hotel as the white players. Elston Howard, who joined the Yankees in 1955 as their first black player, had always stayed in a private home during spring training. Now New York had three black players, Howard, Hector Lopez, and Al Downing, and it was difficult to find decent accommodations for them.

Yankee management tried to make arrangements with the Soreno Hotel to allow the black players to stay there with the rest of the team, but the Soreno wouldn't allow it. Accommodations for the black players were finally located in private homes. The next year, the Yankees moved to Ft. Lauderdale, and the entire team was housed at the Yankee Clipper.

Another interesting topic of conversation during the spring was whether or not someone would break Babe Ruth's home run record. It was the beginning of a new era in major league baseball—the expansion era—and baseball experts feared that the expected dilution of talent would cause many of the cherished baseball records to tumble. The expansion era actually began back in 1953 when the Braves pulled up their teepees in Boston and set them down in Milwaukee, the first team to relocate in 50 years. They were quickly followed by the St. Louis Browns who moved to Baltimore in 1954, and were renamed the Orioles, and the A's who moved from Philadelphia to Kansas City in 1955 (and later to Oakland). The game finally became a truly national sport in 1958, when the Brooklyn Dodgers moved to Los Angeles and the New York Giants moved to San Francisco.

The next step in the evolution of baseball was increasing the two major leagues from eight teams each to ten teams. The American League expanded first, adding the Los Angeles Angels and the Washington Senators in 1961. The new Washington team replaced the old Washington Senator team that moved to Minnesota that year and became the Twins. The National League followed suit the next year by adding the New York Mets and the Houston Colt 45's.

With two new teams in place in the American League, baseball experts began discussing the possibility that someone would break Ruth's record. After all, ten times since Ruth set the record of 60 home runs in 1927, players had hit more than 50 home runs in a season, with Jimmie Foxx and Hank Greenberg topping out at 58. The addition of two teams meant that 20 percent of the pitchers in the American League in 1961 would have been minor league pitchers if expansion hadn't taken place.

The two most likely candidates to break the record were Harmon Killebrew of the Minnesota Twins and Mickey Mantle of the Yankees.

The 24-year-old Killebrew was just coming into his own as a big league slugger. He had hit 42 homers in 1959, and followed that up with 31 more in 1960. He was a big, powerful right-handed batter who was capable of hitting tremendous home runs in bunches. Mickey Mantle, the 29-year-old New York slugger, already had a 52 home run season under his belt, and was the favorite to surpass the Babe. Mantle's teammate Roger Maris, who had 39 homers in 1960, was considered a longshot since he had never hit more than 28 home runs in any year prior to '60. Another longshot was Rocky Colavito of the Detroit Tigers, a 27-year-old bomber who had two 40+ home run seasons with the Cleveland Indians in '58 and '59.

New York Yankee manager, Ralph Houk, had other things on his mind, than home run records, however. His team got off to a rocky start in the early exhibition games. As the losses mounted, New York reporters pressed Houk for reasons. The hassled manager, as reported in *Season of Glory*, spouted the typical excuses. "There are things you've got to find out about your players, and spring training is the time to find them out." Houk didn't believe his own explanation—he was as puzzled by the team's poor showing as everyone else—but he couldn't put his finger on the problem. He just hoped it would work itself out by the time the season opened.

Spring training did shake out some of the question marks for Ralph Houk. He decided that Elston Howard would be the catcher, with Johnny Blanchard as his backup. Yogi Berra would be the left fielder. Clete Boyer beat out Deron Johnson at third. And Luis Arroyo, Bill Stafford, and rookie Rollie Sheldon won spots on the pitching staff, Stafford and Sheldon as starters, and Arroyo as the closer.

The Grapefruit League season came to a merciful end in St. Louis, where the Bronx Bombers dropped two games to the Cardinals by scores of 7–6 and 16–12. New York finished the spring with an embarrassing 9–19 record.

Two days later, on Tuesday April 11, a windy and cold day in Yankee Stadium, only 14,607 fans braved the elements to root for their heroes. Pre-game ceremonies included the raising of the 1960 American League pennant, and the presentation of the Most Valuable Player plaque to Roger Maris. The game, unfortunately, followed the same script that was used during spring training. The Minnesota Twins, behind the three-hit pitching of 25-year-old Pedro Ramos, blanked Houk's boys, 6–0. The New York offense consisted of singles by Berra and Skowron, and an infield hit by Whitey Ford. Ford, the Yankee starter, stayed with Ramos for six innings, but couldn't make it through the seventh. With the game still scoreless in the top of the seventh, Bob Allison hoisted a home run into the lower left field grandstand. After Earl Battey doubled down the left field line, Rene Bertoia walked, and Billy Gardner sacrificed both runners along. Ramos then helped his own cause by slashing a single over third for two runs. Bertoia added a two-run homer to left in the eighth.

April was an important month around the world, particularly from a communist standpoint. On April 12, the day after the Twins took the Yankees to task, Maj. Yuri Gagarin, a Russian cosmonaut, blasted off into space, becoming the first man ever to leave the earth's atmosphere. He circled the earth at speeds up to 17,000 miles per hour, before returning to a hero's welcome.

On the 14th of the month, a U.S. backed anti–Castro Cuban invasion force of 1400 men, left Puerto Cabezas, Nicaragua, in seven small boats, and landed at the Bay Of Pigs, Cuba, three days later, hoping to win the Cuban citizens to their cause of overthrowing the communist regime. The attack was a complete failure. Castro's troops wiped out or captured the invasion force in less than two days, leaving the United States a laughing stock around the world.

Three days later, before a chilled group of 1947 Yankee Stadium fans, the Oklahoma Comet unloaded a two-run homer in the first inning, as Whitey Ford pitched a 3–0 complete game. The weather during the month of April was horrible; cold and damp. At one point New York played only three games in nine days.

On the 20th, another chilly day, but at least without rain, New York swept a doubleheader from the Los Angeles Angels. Mantle homered twice in game one, a first-inning shot that landed about ten rows up in the right field grandstand, and a fifth-inning dinger, his second and third homers of the year. Mantle hit another one the next day in Baltimore, giving him four homers in four games. The newspaper reporters were all around him after the game, asking him how it felt to be eight games ahead of Babe Ruth's record pace. It should be noted that, over the years, literally dozens of players have been ahead of Ruth's pace during the season, primarily because Ruth hit only 43 home runs through the month of August. He finished up the year with a flurry, banging out 17 homers in September.

On April 26, a frigid day in Detroit, Roger Maris finally hit his first home run of the year. It came in the Yankees' 11th game, against right hander Paul Foytack. Whitey Ford was staked to a 6–0 lead in the game, but couldn't hold it, being raked for ten runs and 11 hits in 6⅓ innings. He was still clinging to an 8–6 lead in the seventh, when Bob Scheffing's club exploded for five runs. Mickey Mantle hit his sixth home run of the year off Jim Donohue, with a man on, in the eighth inning to tie the game at 11–11, then crushed his seventh homer off Hank Aguirre, into the upper left field deck, with Hector Lopez on base, in the tenth, to win it. The loss ended an eight game Detroit winning streak and increased New York's record to 6–5. It was the eighth time in Mantle's career that he homered from both sides of the plate in the same game. Little Luis Arroyo, the pride of Puerto Rico, hurled two scoreless innings for the victory.

Mickey Mantle was off to a sizzling start, batting well over .300, with seven home runs in 11 games. He was determined to have a big year for his new manager, Ralph Houk, whose strategy was to praise the Yankee star at every turn. It was a different approach than was used by Stengel, who looked upon Mantle as a son, and who constantly nagged the youngster to mature and become a team leader. But growing up in the big city was difficult for the kid from Commerce, Oklahoma. As a member of the unholy triumvirate, along with Whitey Ford and Billy Martin, he saw the inside of every nightspot from Kansas City to Manhattan. Now, at the age of 29, having sown his wild oats for a decade, he was beginning to settle down and become the leader Stengel had hoped for. Unfortunately, from a career standpoint, it was too little, too late. His years of living in the fast lane, and his serious leg problems, sapped his tremendous skills, cutting short a potentially legendary career. The powerful switch hitter had more home runs by the age of 30 (404) than any player in baseball history. Hank Aaron had 366 homers, while Willie Mays had 319, and Babe Ruth just 309. After 1961, Mantle would add just 162 home runs to his total of 374, with just two more years of 30 or more homers.

As April wound down, the Yankees were in the nation's capital for a doubleheader with Mickey Vernon's Senators. On April 30, a crowd of

21,904 Washington fans turned out to root for their team. In game one, Dick Donovan had the Yanks under control 2–1 after six innings, but in the seventh, the Bronx Bombers exploded. Moose Skowron opened the inning with a single, and was moved to third on a line drive single by Clete Boyer. Donovan then bobbled Richardson's grounder to load the bases. Jesse Gonder hit into a force play at second to score one run, and another one came across on a double by Kubek. In the eighth, Skowron doubled and Boyer singled for an insurance run. Ford was the winner, 4–3, raising his record to 3–1.

In the nightcap, Rollie Sheldon pitched a creditable game for Stengel, yielding only two runs on five hits over seven innings, but he came away a loser when Hal Woodeshick limited the New Yorkers to a single run in eight innings. In the New York ninth, the Bombers had Woodeshick on the ropes, but couldn't finish him off. With Washington on top 2–0, Lopez started the ninth-inning festivities with a single and moved around to third on a single to right by Mantle. Skowron punched a single to left, scoring Lopez and sending Mantle to second. At that point, manager Mickey Vernon called on veteran reliever Pete Burnside. The tall lefty quelled the rally quickly. He got Elston Howard to pop up on a sacrifice try, then made both Maris and Boyer hit into force plays at second. For the doubleheader, Maris had only two singles in nine at bats, and Mantle wasn't much better, with two singles in eight at bats.

New York had a 9–5 record for the month, leaving them one game behind Detroit. Mickey Mantle got off to a blazing start, hammering seven homers, driving in 17 runs, and batting .327 for the month. He was three home runs ahead of Babe Ruth, and was already being cornered by the reporters asking him if he thought he could break the record. Mantle, who was now a seasoned veteran, fielded all the queries gracefully and politely, giving thoughtful answers, and always smiling.

Roger Maris, on the other hand, was suffering through a deep slump, with one home run and a .204 batting average. Yankee management called him in at one point and asked him if he was having eye problems. They also inquired as to whether he was having personal problems, to which Maris replied, "That's none of your business."

Hector Lopez was also in a slump, and the pitching was erratic, but Mantle and Elston Howard were keeping the team afloat. As May got underway, the Yankees rolled off eight wins in nine games.

On May 3rd, in Metropolitan Stadium, Minnesota, Maris hit #2, but Mantle whacked #9, a 405-foot blast to center field, in the top of the tenth inning, to break a two all tie. The Mick was now 11 games ahead of Ruth, who had six in the same number of games.

Roger Maris hit #3 off Eli Grba in Los Angeles on May 6, then went another ten days before hitting #4. Beginning on May 17, he picked up the pace and got in the race. He cracked nine home runs over the last 14 days of May, bringing his total up to 12. On the last day of the month, the Yankees piled up 11 hits against Boston Red Sox pitching, quieting Fenway's 17,318 paying customers, and edging their beloved BoSox 7–6. Rookie Rollie Sheldon won his first major league game, with 6⅔ innings of four-run ball. Reliever Luis Arroyo was ineffective, but Danny McDevitt came in to shut down the Sox in the bottom of the ninth. After New York tallied one run in the first, Maris hit his 12th homer of the season in the third inning, a thunderous 425-foot blast into the right field bleachers. Four more New York runs crossed the plate in the fifth, on two singles, an error by Don "Bootsie" Buddin, and a 400-foot homer into the right field bullpen by Mantle.

New York's 19–12 record was an improvement over April, but left them in third place, 3½ games behind the red hot Detroit Tigers, who had a 29–16 record. Cleveland was in second place with 26 wins against 17 losses. Mickey Mantle was hitting .318, and leading the league in home runs with 14. Mick's sidekick, Roger Maris, had his average up to .245, and his home run total up to 12.

New York began June by winning 15 out of 19 games, but Detroit kept pace, sparked by first baseman Norm Cash, who was having a career season. Cash, a lifetime .271 hitter, was on to his way to winning the batting championship (.361), with 41 homers and 132 RBIs. Whitey Ford paced Ralph Houk's Bombers in June, racking up a perfect 8–0 mark, a new American League record. It matched the National League record of Rube Marquard, who compiled an 8–0 record in June 1912, on his way to a major league mark of 19 consecutive victories. Closing out the month, "The Chairman of the Board" whipped the Washington Senators, in D.C., by a score of 5–1, with a complete game five-hitter. Maris and Mantle did most of the damage. Dick Donovan (3–8) was up 1–0 after five innings, but the roof caved in on him in the sixth. Richardson singled through the middle to lead things off. He stole second and went to third on a fly ball to right by Tony Kubek. Maris then smashed a ground rule double into the right field seats, to score Richardson. Mantle followed with a tremendous drive to dead center field. The ball struck the wall just to the right of the 461-foot sign. When it bounced back over center fielder Willie Tasby's head, Mantle turned it up a notch, and circled the bases in record time, for an inside-the-park homer. It was Mantle's 25th of the season, leaving him two behind his teammate, Roger Maris, who had a big month, with 15 homers. New York closed out their scoring in the eighth. Richardson singled and Kubek doubled. Then with the infield drawn in, Maris ripped a ball through the right side for two runs.

As June ended, Roger Maris had his batting average up to .260, was leading the league in home runs with 27, and was third in RBIs with 62. Mantle was hitting .312, and was second in homers.

During June, Maris completed the most extraordinary home run hitting feat in the annals of baseball. Beginning on May 17, when Roger hit his fourth home run of the season, and continuing through June 22, the sweet-swinging lefty pounded out 24 homers in 38 games, an achievement unmatched by any baseball player who ever lived. Babe finished his record season in 1927 with a similar run, hitting 24 homers in his last 41 games.

When the sun came up on July 4th, the standings were:

Detroit 49–27
New York 47–27—1
Cleveland 45–34—5½
Baltimore 42–36—8

Roger Maris was at 30 home runs, putting him eight games ahead of Babe Ruth, while Mickey Mantle was four games ahead of the mighty Bambino. The press was beginning to pay more attention to the home run chase now, referring to the two Yankee sluggers as the M& M boys, but most of the coverage was still on Mantle. He was the favorite of the press, the fans, and even some of the Yankee players and Yankee brass. After all, Babe Ruth had been a Yankee and Mickey Mantle was a Yankee. Roger Maris, on the other hand, was an interloper, a late arrival, and not a real Yankee. From this point until the end of the season, the intense media pressure continued to mount. It was on Mantle initially, but would swing over to Maris in a big way in late August, after he became the first player in history to hit 50 home runs before September 1st.

The July 4th holiday presented New York fans with an important doubleheader between their beloved Yankees and the league-leading Detroit Tigers in "The House That Ruth Built." A crowd of 74,246 people made their way through the turnstiles, the largest crowd to see a game in Yankee Stadium since 1947. They were entertained with two superb games, although the eventual split left them feeling unfulfilled. In game one, Whitey Ford won his ninth consecutive game, a workmanlike complete game five-hitter, liberally sprinkled with 11 strikeouts. A five-run rally in the fifth inning KO'd Tiger starter Don Mossi. In the big fifth, Bob Cerv doubled and continued to third on a throwing error by Rocky Colavito. He scored when Chico Fernandez booted a grounder. Bobby Richardson then singled, and Maris singled for another run. An intentional pass to Mantle loaded the bases, and a booming triple to right center field by Elston Howard unloaded them.

Game two was a tense pitchers duel. Frank Lary, a renowned "Yankee Killer," on his way to a brilliant 23–9 season, pitched nine innings, leaving after giving his team a lead in the top of the tenth. New York, down 2–0 in the eighth, pulled even on a double by Kubek and a line drive home run into the lower right field stands by Roger Maris (#31). Al Kaline made a courageous dive for the ball, but couldn't reach it. Detroit went back in the lead in the top of the ninth, but Houk's troops clipped Lary for another run in the bottom of the inning. Moose Skowron led off with a single. Then, after catcher Mike Roarke and third baseman Steve Boros collided on Blanchard's foul pop up, the Yankee slugger drilled a single to right. Lopez's single scored Skowron. Much to the chagrin of the big holiday crowd, Bob Scheffing's determined bengals got the game winner after two men were retired in the tenth. With Boros on first, Dick Brown whacked a ground rule double, putting men on second and third. Frank Lary brought in the eventual winning run by dropping down a surprise squeeze bunt with two strikes on him.

Roger Maris, after reaching 27 home runs by the end of June, kept up his pyrotechnics through July. He hit #35 on the 15th, putting him a full 20 games ahead of Ruth. Mantle was nine games ahead. Four days later, both sluggers hit home runs in the second game of a doubleheader against the Baltimore Orioles, but the homers were lost when rain washed out the game before the required 5½ innings were played. That same day, baseball Commissioner Ford Frick announced that, in order to break Babe Ruth's record, a batter would have to do it in the same number of games Ruth played, 154. If the record was broken after the 154th game, it would have a "distinguishing mark" after it, to differentiate it from Ruth's record. Poor Frick. He never lived down that ruling. He was known as Mr. Asterisk until the day he died. It was a foolish ruling by any standard. The length of the major league playing schedule has changed periodically since the National League was formed in 1876. That first year, the season was only 70 games long. In 1888, it was increased to 133 games, and in 1904 it was increased to 154 games. Now with a ten-team American League, the season was increased to 162 games. Future expansion could increase the length of the schedule again. Yet, except in the case of Roger Maris, no major league record has ever been identified by an asterisk. If asterisks were used to identify differences between records, Babe Ruth would have had one of the first asterisks after setting the home run record in 1919. Ned Williamson originally set the record at 27 home runs in 1884, during a 112-game season. When Ruth broke the record 36 years later, he did it in a 154-game season. Ralph Houk, when questioned about the asterisk ruling, put it in perspective. "If after 154 games, we're on top, I certainly will tell the commissioner that that's the pennant so far as we're concerned."

Late in the month, manager Ralph Houk was fined $250.00 and suspended for five days, by American League President Joe Cronin, for a run-in with umpire Ed Hurley, the previous week. During the second game of a doubleheader, in which the New Yorkers dropped both games, 4–0 and 2–1, Houk became embroiled with Hurley over a called third strike on Clete Boyer. The Yanks had loaded the bases against Milt Pappas with no one out in the ninth. Boyer then took a third strike on a 3–2 count, causing Houk to go ballistic. When Hector Lopez bounced into a double play to end the game, Houk set upon Hurley, resulting in the fine and suspension.

The Yankees took over the top spot in the pennant race, as the dog days of summer wound down. Their 67–36 record on July 31, gave them a 2½ game bulge over the Detroit Tigers and a 9½ game bulge over the Baltimore Orioles. Cleveland self destructed during the month, losing

16 of 27 games after July 3, to fall out of the race. Twenty-six-year-old Norm Cash, in his first full year as a Detroit regular, was belting the ball at a torrid .365 pace, 14 points higher than Yankee catcher Elston Howard. Roger Maris led the home run race with 40 dingers, and the RBI race with 98 RBIs. Mickey Mantle had 39 homers and 95 RBIs.

Frank Crosetti was acting manager as the Bronx Bombers hosted the Kansas City A's in a twin bill on August 2. In the opener, Whitey Ford, looking for his thirteenth consecutive win, brought a dazzling 19–2 record into the game, but he didn't have his usual stuff on this day. It was not an artistic outing for the stylish lefty, and he left after eight innings, with the score tied at 5–5. He almost pulled off his twentieth win, but it wasn't to be. In the bottom of the eighth, with the bases loaded, Ford punched a single over third for two runs, giving himself a 5–3 lead. But in the top of the ninth, he threw a home run ball to Haywood Sullivan with a man on, to tie the score. After the next batter singled, Luis Arroyo relieved him and retired the side. In the bottom of the ninth, the Yanks loaded the bases with none out, on a single by Maris, a double by Mantle, and a walk to Howard. After Berra popped up for the first out, Cerv hit a bouncer to third, as Maris raced for the plate. Third baseman Wayne Causey pounced on the ball and gunned it home, but Maris, being an old line backer himself, plowed into catcher Joe Pignatano, causing him to drop the ball, and ending the game. The home plate collision was a typical Maris maneuver. He was a hard-nosed player, who put his body on the line on every play. He did whatever it took to win.

The second game was a laugher. Ralph Terry (7–1) saw his team go up 12–0 after five, and they hung on to win, 12–5. New York scored three in the first, two in the third, and seven in the fifth. Mickey Mantle clubbed his 40th home run of the year, and 360th of his career, in the first, a two-run shot into the third deck in right field. His outfield partner, Roger Maris, got hit by a pitch in the third, bruising his leg. He left the game to put ice packs on it, but was back in action the next day.

During August, the home run race heated up as both Maris and Mantle kept the pressure on. Maris had a dry spell after July 25, hitting only one homer over the next 17 games. Then, on August 11 he found his stroke again. He banged out his 42nd home run, and went on to hit ten homers in the next 16 games. Mickey Mantle, who took the lead away from Maris when he hit numbers 41 and 42 on August 5, went into a slump of his own, hitting only one homer between August 13 and August 29.

On the twentieth day of the month, the Yanks swept a twin bill from the struggling Cleveland Indians in Cleveland Stadium, before 56,307 hopeful fans. Ralph Terry won his tenth game against a single loss, throwing a complete game, four-hit shutout, winning 6–0. Mickey Mantle hit his first home run in a week, a three-run shot in the first to give the New York contingent a jump start. Mick also chipped in with two singles and a base on balls. Roger Maris broke out of an 0–13 slump with his first homer in four days, a singleton in the third. It was his 49th of the season, putting him 11 games ahead of Ruth.

In game two, Mantle went 1–2 with two walks, and Maris took the collar in two trips. Rollie Sheldon (9–3) went the distance with an eight-hitter, and the Yanks won 5–2, taking three out of four in the series, and moving on to Los Angeles.

Baseball fans around the country were anticipating Maris' 50th home run as the New York club took the field in Los Angeles, to face the Angels. Wrigley Field's inviting 345-foot power alleys in right and left center field were custom-made for the M & M boys. In fact, more home runs were hit in Wrigley Field in 1961 (248) than any park in major league history.

The media circus began to heat up about this time, and the press started to focus its attention on Roger Maris. Where before, most of the attention was paid to Mickey Mantle, now Maris was in the spotlight. And Maris hated the spotlight. He was a quiet, reserved individual, who cherished his privacy. Under questioning, he gave short answers in a monotonous monotone. He was colorless and emotionless. And he told it like it was, no PR platitudes, no political evasiveness. What you saw was what you got.

Roger Maris loved his time on the playing field. He enjoyed all aspects of the game, the home runs, the squeeze bunts, the stolen bases, the exciting outfield catches. But he detested the claustrophobic interview sessions that would become part of his life for the next five weeks. The media pressure before and after the game would eventually take its toll on his mental and physical health. He would begin to lose his hair by mid–September.

He didn't lessen the media circus with his performance on August 22.

Bill Stafford, the Yanks' 21-year-old rookie, faced off against L.A's crack right hander Ken McBride, before a packed house of 19,930. McBride tossed a complete game six-hitter, but he was saddled with the loss when Yogi Berra cracked his 17th homer in the ninth inning, for a 4–3 Yankee win. The Angels had scored three runs in the first inning, then were shut down the rest of the game by Stafford and a bevy of relievers. Roger Maris, making history, whacked his 50th home run of the season, with a man on, in the sixth inning to deadlock the game and set the stage for Berra's dramatics. With his home run, Maris became the first major league player to hit 50 home runs before September 3rd. Babe Ruth in 1921, and Jimmie Foxx in 1932, both hit their 50th home run on the 3rd of September.

The next night, the Yanks won again, this time 8–6 in ten innings. In the process they routed former teammate Ryne Duren.

The Angels also routed New York ace Whitey Ford, in the fourth. The game went to the tenth inning, tied at 6–6. Then Roger Maris walloped a 400-foot triple to center field to drive in the go-ahead run. He scored minutes later on a wild pitch.

On the 31st, in Metropolitan Stadium, Minnesota, Jack Kralick, a lanky southpaw, toughed out a complete game, 11-hit struggle, to win 5–4. A Ladies Day crowd of 33,709 screamed with delight as Minnesota roughed up Sheldon for all their runs in the third inning. The last two runs crossed the plate on a home run by Jim Lemon, off Jim Coates. Mickey Mantle slugged home run #48 in the fourth inning, after hitting #47 the previous day. Trying to add a little humor to the home run race, Mantle, referring to Lou Gehrig, who hit 47 home runs in 1927, told Maris, "I got my man. Now you have to get yours." Maris was five games ahead of Ruth.

The crucial series of the season took place in Yankee Stadium from September 1 to September 3, as the Detroit Tigers invaded the Yankee lair to do battle with Houk's sluggers. The New York lead, as the series began, was a slim 1½ games. On Friday the 1st, with 65,566 Yankee rooters packing the Stadium, Whitey Ford, Bud Daley, and Luis Arroyo, combined on a shutout, and New York edged the Tigers 1–0 with a run in the ninth. Don Mossi, a slick southpaw, on his way to a 15–7 season, matched the Yankee arms pitch for pitch until the ninth. Then, after retiring Maris and fanning Mantle, he hit the wall. Elston Howard cracked a two-out single, Berra moved him along with another single, and the "Moose," Bill Skowron, drove him in with yet another single. It was a stunning defeat for the Detroit crew, who came into the series with a record of 86 wins against only 47 losses.

In game two, 50,261 fans sat transfixed under an intense sun as Yankee killer Frank Lary (19–8) dueled Ralph Terry (12–2). The Tigers jumped on Terry for two runs in the top of the first. Roger Maris, after doubling in the fourth, ripped his 52nd home run of the year in the sixth, to give New York a 3–2 lead. Then, in the eighth, he smashed his 53rd with a man on, as the Bronx Bombers KO'd Lary with a big four spot. Luis Arroyo, in his 55th appearance of the year, pitched 1⅓ shutout innings. He also started New York's eighth-inning rally with a single.

Manager Ralph Houk sent big Bill Stafford to the mound to face eventual 17-game winner Jim Bunning, in the Sunday finale. This was do or die time for Detroit, who now trailed New York by 3½ games. They couldn't afford to fall any further behind with just 26 games left in the season. Neither pitcher was around at the end, although Stafford pitched a creditable game, giving up only two runs in seven innings. He left the game with the lead, but the Yankee bullpen blew it. Mantle and Berra both homered in the New York first to give their team a 3–1 lead. By the time the ninth inning rolled around, New York was on the short end of a 5–4 score. Mickey Mantle, who was playing despite a strained muscle in his forearm, injured the previous day, slugged his second home run of the game, and 50th of the season, to knot the score at five all. After a single by Berra and a walk to Skowron, Elston Howard stepped to the plate with two men out, and sent the fans home happy by slugging a game-winning, three run-homer.

The New York Yankees were now in a comfortable position, holding a healthy 4½ game lead over Detroit, heading down the stretch. On Labor Day, the Yankees swept a doubleheader from Washington while Detroit took the pipe for the fourth straight time. The following day the Yankees beat the Senators again, and the Tigers dropped two. Ralph Houk's boys were suddenly up by 7½ with just 25 games to go. The Yankee win streak reached 13 before they lost, while the Tiger losing streak bottomed out at 9. When the dust settled, New York had a commanding 11½ game lead, with just 18 games remaining.

The media attention now shifted back to the chase of Babe Ruth.

After every game, anywhere from 15 to 50 newspapermen would pin Roger Maris against the wall and barrage him with questions, while photographers' flash bulbs popped incessantly. Some of the questions were enough to make a grown man retch. One reporter asked him if a right hander's curve ball broke in on him. Maris, not trying to hide his sarcasm, said, "It probably does, since I bat left handed." Another reporter asked him if the ball was livelier this year, to which Maris replied, "No, the players are."

Unlike in Babe Ruth's day, when clubhouse banter was protected, every comment uttered by Roger Maris, every minor complaint and off-the-cuff remark made in the friendly atmosphere of the locker room was boldly reported in the next edition of the New York newspapers. Negative comments made by Maris about an umpire or about the New York fans were the next day's headlines. At one point, a distraught Roger Maris said to Mantle, "I can't take it anymore," to which Mick replied, "You have to."

Once or twice, in self-defense, Maris closeted himself in the safety of the trainer's room, which was off limits to the press.

The media pressure on Maris increased with each passing day. The Yankee slugger banged out homer #55 in game 141, keeping him seven games ahead of Ruth. The post-game questions were the same after each game. "Are you hitting so many home runs because it's an expansion year and the pitching isn't as good?" "How many home runs do you think Babe Ruth would hit this year?" "Do you really want to break Babe Ruth's record? He was a great player."

On road trips, fans mobbed the hotels where the New York Yankees stayed, trying to track down Maris and Mantle for autographs. Some people just wanted to touch the two heroes. Several times, the M&M boys had to sneak down the back stairs to avoid the crowds. It was unpleasant.

Even worse was the public recognition Maris now received as a celebrity. He couldn't go anywhere without being accosted by inconsiderate people looking for autographs. He couldn't frequent his favorite New York restaurant or even attend Mass in peace.

Maris became almost paranoid during the final weeks of the season. He complained about the reporters, the fans in the right field stands, even the Yankee management. He was sure his teammates as well as the

Yankee management wanted Mantle, not him, to break Babe Ruth's record.

The press reported all Maris' negative comments about players, officials, and fans. The comments alienated him from the New York fans, and his complaints about being misquoted, and his refusal to talk to reporters after some games, alienated him from the media. As Robert W. Creamer noted in *Season of Glory*, "If you feel, as William Congreve did, that hell has no fury like a woman scorned, you've never seen a sportswriter scorned." Louis Effrat, a writer for the *New York Times*, wrote "While (Mantle) answered all questions and volunteered information, Maris ... remained in the trainer's room and sulked."

The sweet-swinging lefty, trying to find peace on the playing field, banged out homer #56 against Mudcat Grant of Cleveland on September 9, then went a week before hitting another. After going homerless in three games in Chicago (he had four singles), Maris had just one single to show for nine trips to the plate in a doubleheader win in Detroit. Whitey Ford captured his 24th victory against only three losses, in the opener, and the Yankees won their 100th game of the season in the nightcap. Yogi Berra hit a home run to tie the major league team record of 221 home runs in a season, then Moose Skowron hit one out to set a new record. When the season finally ended 16 days later, the New York Yankees' victory total had risen to 109, and their home run total stood at 240.

Mickey Mantle, by this time, had dropped out of the race. Bogged down by a cold and by an injured forearm muscle, the Commerce Comet hit only four home runs after September 3. On the team's last road trip to Chicago, Detroit, and Baltimore, covering a total of ten games, he was unable to connect even once.

Roger Maris slammed #57 against Frank Lary in Detroit on the 16th of the month, and #58 against the Tigers' Terry Fox the next day. Then it was off to Baltimore, the birthplace of Babe Ruth, where Maris would play games 153, 154, and 155.

In a Tuesday doubleheader, Maris went a combined 0 for 8. Steve Barber, Baltimore's 22-year-old southpaw sensation, bested Whitey Ford in a pitchers duel, 1–0, in the opener. Mantle sat out both games.

Wednesday, game #154, drew only 21,032 paying customers to Baltimore's Memorial Stadium (capacity 49,375), to witness Roger Maris' attempt to catch the mighty Babe. Memorial Stadium had a short 309-foot

Roger Maris set a new single-season Home Run record with 61 homers in 1961. (Courtesy Transcendental Graphics)

foul line in right, but quickly opened up to a distant 380-foot power alley. Center field was a healthy 410 feet from home plate. The Yankees' Ralph Terry (15–3) was opposed by young Milt Pappas (13–9). In the first inning, Maris hit a routine fly to right field. Two innings later, he caught a low fast ball from the Orioles' righty, on a 2–1 count, and put it into orbit. The ball cleared the 14-foot wire fence at the 380-foot mark in right center field and settled into the bleachers for #59, making Roger the #2 man of all time, behind Ruth. Dick Hall, a crafty veteran who relieved Pappas in the third, when the Yanks went up 4–0, fanned the Yankee slugger in the fourth. In the seventh, after smashing a long foul down the right field line, Maris hit a fly ball to right center field, that Earl Robinson hauled in near the fence. The courageous left handed slugger had one chance left, but he had to face Baltimore's butterfly artist, Hoyt Wilhelm. Wilhelm fed Maris nothing but junk in the ninth, and Roger, off balance most of the time, couldn't handle it. He tried to check his swing on an 0–1 count and dribbled the ball down the first base line for an easy out. His wife Patricia, watching the game on television in Kansas City, cried, "What did you swing at that pitch for, Roger?"

Afterwards, in the clubhouse, Maris seemed relieved that it was over. As he said in *Season of Glory*, "I tried … I tried hard all night, but I only got one. I wanted to go out swinging, but I never did get a chance to swing good against Wilhelm." Responding to a question about Commissioner Ford Frick's asterisk ruling, Maris replied, "The Commissioner makes the rules. If he says all I'm entitled to is an asterisk, that's all right with me. I'm happy with what I got."

There was a celebration going on elsewhere in the clubhouse, but with very little media coverage. The New York Yankees had just clinched the American League pennant with their 104th victory of the season, a workmanlike 4–2 four-hitter by Terry.

Ralph Houk's warriors traveled to Beantown for a two-game set against Pinky Higgins' Red Sox after the celebration in Baltimore ended. Mickey Mantle returned to the lineup and socked his 54th and last home run of the year in the first game of the series. Maris was shut out in both games.

The team returned home on September 26th, to play the last five games of the season. On Tuesday night, before a disappointing Yankee Stadium gathering of 19,000, Roger Maris faced off against Jack Fisher (10–13), another of Baltimore's Baby Brigade. In the third inning, he caught up with one of Fisher's fast balls and hit it into the third deck of the right field stands, for #60. Reluctantly, the shy slugger emerged from the darkness of the dugout to tip his hat to the roaring crowd. It was an exciting moment for the 27-year-old outfielder.

An even more exciting moment was yet to come. After sitting out one game, Roger Maris returned to the lineup for the final three-game set with Boston. He was unable to connect against either Bill Monbouquette or Don Schwall in the first two games.

The Sunday finale was his last chance to break Babe Ruth's magic 60 home run mark, even if it was with an asterisk. The temperature was in the low 70s, with some clouds, as the Yanks and Red Sox locked horns for the last time in 1961. An embarrassingly small crowd of 23,154 people took advantage of the weather to come to the park to root for Maris.

Tracy Stallard, a tall, husky right hander, toed the rubber for the Sox. Bill Stafford, gunning for his 14th win, was manager Houk's choice to close out the season. The two teams were scoreless after 3½ innings. In the bottom of the fourth, with a count of 2–0, Maris picked out a waist high fast ball and sent a high fly ball to right field. It came to rest in the lower deck, about 360 feet from home plate, for home run #61. An obviously happy Maris made a triumphant trip around the bases, after finally laying the ghost of Babe Ruth to rest beneath the Yankee Stadium sod. Roger's teammates pushed the smiling slugger back up the dugout steps to acknowledge the screams of the crowd. A smiling Maris doffed his cap to the crowd four times before retreating into the peace and quiet of the dugout. As Joseph Reichler and Jack Clary reported in *Baseball's Greatest Moments*, Maris finally felt fulfilled. "If I never hit another home run," he said with deep satisfaction, "this is one they can never take away from me."

Roger Maris' 61st homer was the only run of the game as New York blanked Boston 1–0.

The powerhouse 1961 New York Yankees, arguably one of the greatest teams of all time, buried the Cincinnati Reds in the World Series, four games to one, and outscored their National League opponents, 27 runs to 13. Roger Maris, obviously physically and emotionally drained after his pressure-packed season, batted only .105 in the Series, with one home run. But the Yanks didn't need him this time. Blanchard (.400 with two home runs), Richardson (.391), Skowron (.353), and Lopez (.333), more than took care of the offense. And on the hill, Whitey Ford (2–0), building on his 1960 performance, tossed 14 consecutive shutout innings. In the 1962 World Series he would throw another 1⅔ innings before yielding a run, giving him a total of 32⅔ consecutive scoreless World Series innings, breaking the record of Babe Ruth, set with the Boston Red Sox in 1916 and 1918.

Roger Maris won his second consecutive Most Valuable Player trophy for his history-making season.

The Yankee slugger had another outstanding year in 1962, batting .256 with 33 home runs and 100 runs batted in, but it wasn't up to his 1961 performance, and the fickle New York fans didn't let him forget that. He played four more years in the big city, then was traded to St. Louis, where he helped the Cardinals win two National League pennants and one World Championship. In all, Roger Maris played in the major leagues for 12 years, hammering 275 home runs and driving in 851 runs, with a .260 batting average. Combining his offensive tools with his exceptional glovework, made him one of the major league's best all around players of his era. His contributions to his teams resulted in seven league pennants and three World Championships in just 12 years.

Roger Maris was a winner.

7. The 1960s to the 1990s—An Historical Perspective

Patriotism blanketed the land during the 1940s. Eager young men entered military service to defend their country from foreign enemies. Their wives and sweethearts kissed them good-bye, then went to work in defense plants. Some women even joined the service themselves, serving as nurses, pilots, and administrators.

After World War II ended, the birth rate exploded as returning veterans and their girl friends (known as "Baby Boomers") got married and began raising families. The feeling of patriotism the country had during World War II continued into the 50s with the Korean Conflict once again uniting the people against a common foe.

Times were good in the United States in the late 40s and 50s. The economy boomed, and the standard of living improved for most Americans. New automobiles, television sets, and homes became accessible, not only to the wealthy, but also to blue collar workers. The G.I. Bill of Rights, available to all military veterans, made it possible for thousands of young men to obtain a college education.

As the 60s approached however, a cloud descended over the country. Psychologists introduced the philosophy of "permissiveness" into the society. Parents were taught that disciplining their children was bad and that reasoning with young children was the only acceptable method of raising a child. Children grew up without adult discipline as their parents concentrated on making money. More and more women joined the work force, leaving the children home unsupervised. Teenage pregnancies and suicides increased dramatically over the next two decades, as the family structure and scholastic discipline both eroded significantly.

The 1960s and 70s were a turbulent period in the country. Civil rights for all people was the top priority for the 48 states in the early 60s. Integration was the law of the land, bringing with it the concomitant white backlash, as well as civil rights demonstrations by blacks demanding equal treatment in all phases of American life.

School integration was a major part of the civil rights program initiated by President John F. Kennedy after his election in 1960. On September 30, 1962, James A. Meredith made history when he became the first black to attend the University of Mississippi. The enrollment was not without incident. Two men died in rioting in the university town of Oxford, while many others were injured. More than 300 Federal Marshals guarding Meredith were attacked with stones and bottles. Federal troops occupied the town.

On June 11, 1963, Alabama governor George C. Wallace stood in the doorway of the University of Alabama, trying to block a black student from entering the building. He lost the fight when President Kennedy called in the National Guard to enforce the integration order.

Violence was the law of the land during the 60s. On November 22, 1963, President John Fitzgerald Kennedy was killed by an assassin's bullet in Dallas, Texas, as he rode through the city in a motorcade. Five years later, civil rights leader, Reverend Martin Luther King was assassinated on a motel balcony in Memphis, Tennessee. Within months, Robert F. Kennedy, the president's brother, was assassinated in a hotel kitchen in Los Angeles, while on a presidential election campaign.

Civil rights demonstrations and riots in black inner-city ghettos dominated the news of the nation in the mid–60s. In 1965, 30 people were killed, over 1000 were injured, and 4000 were arrested in a riot in the Watts section of Los Angeles. In 1967, a rash of summer riots caused havoc in Newark, New Jersey, and Detroit, Michigan. More than 65 people were killed in the two cities, and property damage was in the millions of dollars.

A civil rights "Freedom March," from Selma, Alabama, to the state capitol at Montgomery, went off without incident on March 27, 1965. Twenty-five thousand marchers, both black and white, completed the peaceful demonstration under the watchful eyes of the U.S. Army and the Alabama National Guard.

During the mid–60s, the United States became embroiled in another land confrontation, this one in Vietnam. It was an unpopular action from the beginning, involving the country in a civil war between North and South Vietnam. Anti–war demonstrators, called "Yippies" (Youth International Party), battled police in Chicago during the 1968 Democratic Party Convention. Thousands of young men fled the country rather than allow themselves to be drafted into military service.

Thousands of other young people, children of the Baby Boomer generation, "dropped out" of society, living in communes, falling under the influence of drugs like heroin, cocaine and LSD, practicing free sex and, in general, ignoring the mores of the society. In August 1969, thousands of so-called hippies descended on Woodstock, New York, for a rock concert and a weekend of hedonistic revelry.

Richard M. Nixon was elected the 37th president of the United States in 1968 and was re-elected in 1972. The most positive historic event of his administration occurred on July 20, 1969, when astronaut Neil Armstrong walked on the surface of the moon, completing a space project initiated by John F. Kennedy.

Four years later, President Nixon threw in the towel in Vietnam, agreeing to withdraw American troops and American sympathizers from the country, prior to a North Vietnamese occupation of the country. It was one of the darkest moments in American history.

In 1974, another humiliating event tossed the country into depression. President Nixon, admitting to a coverup of a Republican break-in at the Democratic Party National Headquarters in the Watergate Hotel in Washington, D.C., resigned his office of president rather than face a certain impeachment.

Baseball during the 60s, 70s, and 80s became the legacy of the "Baby Boomer" generation and post–"Baby Boomer" generation. It was and continues to be turbulent and chaotic. Expansion continued unabated. Sixteen major league teams in 1960 became 20 teams in 1962, 24 teams in 1969, 26 teams in 1977, 28 teams in 1993, and 30 teams in 1998.

Some significant rule changes were made to major league baseball during the 1970s. The American League adopted the designated hitter in 1973, but the National League did not follow suit. It is likely that the designated hitter will be discarded in the near future. In 1975, in one of the most disastrous decisions in major league history, Peter Seitz, the chairman of a three-man mediation panel, ruled that players who perform one year without a signed contract automatically become free agents. Pitcher Andy Messersmith of the Los Angeles Dodgers was the first major leaguer to test the free agent market. When he signed with the Atlanta Braves for the 1976 season, his salary jumped up from $115,000 a year to $333,000 a year. Free agency has been a Pandora's box ever since, with salaries skyrocketing into the sublime, then the ridiculous. Babe Ruth was the first $80,000 a year player in 1930. Joe DiMaggio was the first to top $100,000 in 1949. Nolan Ryan, a benefactor of free agency, became the first $1,000,000 man in 1980. By 1998, the top salary rose to $15,200,000 when the Los Angeles Dodgers signed free agent pitcher Kevin Brown. The major leagues are being split into the Haves and Have-nots. The wealthy teams in large markets, such as New York, Los Angeles, and Atlanta, can spend freely to obtain the players necessary to make them contenders. Small market teams, like Montreal and Pittsburgh, cannot afford to spend the money necessary to compete.

Another negative aspect of modern major league baseball has been player-management labor relations. Over the past 20 years, strikes, the threat of strikes, and the threat of lockouts have dismayed the paying public. The situation came to a head in 1994 when the players went on strike, canceling the baseball season after playing just 115 games. The World Series fell victim to the strike also and, when a settlement was finally reached in March 1995, 18 games had to be cut off that season as well. The strike had an adverse effect on attendance as fans, bitter at the greed on both sides of the bargaining table, stayed away from major league parks in droves. It wasn't until Mark McGwire and Sammy Sosa put on their pyrotechnic displays in 1998 that attendance came back to the 1993 level.

The batting philosophy in the major leagues changed after the Maris year. The change actually started with Mickey Mantle in the 50s and 60s. The Mick was the guru of the "new breed" of sluggers, a free swinging group that believed home runs and strikeouts went hand in hand. The handsome Oklahoman averaged 116 strikeouts a year during his 18-year career, with 36 home runs. Prior to that, Babe Ruth was the major league's strikeout king, with 87 strikeouts a year, to go along with 50 home runs. Jimmie Foxx, another early slugger, piled up 89 strikeouts a year, with 36 home runs.

During the 1970s and 80s, sluggers actually carried the Mantle philosophy to the extreme, striking out more, and watching their batting averages plummet as they strove for more and more home runs. Batters waved futilely at pitch after pitch, hoping to make contact. "Guess hitting" became a way of life. Rather than waiting on a pitch, to see what kind of pitch it was, and where it would cross the plate, as the players of previous generations had done, the "guess" hitter committed his swing as soon as the pitcher released the ball, trying to guess the type of pitch and the location. It is a philosophy that has never worked, but it is still popular through the 90s.

Some of the more visible of the guess hitters have been Dale Murphy (28 homers, 120 strikeouts), Bobby Bonds (26 & 144), and Mike Schmidt (36 & 124). The Kings of Whiff are Reggie Jackson and Dave Kingman. Jackson, who patrolled the outfield for several teams from 1967 to 1987, banged out 31 home runs a year, but whiffed 145 times in the process. Jackson managed to hit over 40 home runs twice in his career, with a high of 47 homers in 1969. Dave "Kong" Kingman is the top gun in the group. The 6'6" right-handed hitter put 36 balls a year over the fence, but went down swinging 150 times. Both Jackson and Kingman had an additional problem. They were serious liabilities in the outfield. They not only made every catch exciting, but often put their fellow outfield partners in harm's way during a play.

History has proven that more strikeouts do not mean significantly more home runs. More strikeouts generally mean lower batting averages. Babe Ruth, with 50 home runs and just 87 strikeouts, had a career batting average of .342. Jimmie Foxx, with 89 strikeouts, batted .325. At the other end of the spectrum, Reggie Jackson, with his 145 strikeouts, had a career batting average of .262, and Dave Kingman, with his 150 K's, could hit no higher than .236. No major league player, with a minimum of ten years experience, who struck out more than 100 times a year, has had a career batting average over .300. Most .300 hitters, in fact, have struck out less than 60–70 times a year.

Two of the greatest home run hitters in baseball history played during this period. Hank Aaron is the all-time major league career home run king with 755 career home runs. "Hammerin' Hank" was not one of the elite high home run frequency types, like Ruth or McGwire. He was a five-point player, who could hit, hit with power, run, field, and throw—a true superstar. Aaron played in the Bigs for 23 years, finishing #3 in games played (3,298), #2 in at bats (12,364), #2 in runs scored (2,174), #3 in base hits (3,771), and #1 in home runs (755), runs batted in (2,297), and total bases (6,856). He was consistent and dependable, playing an average of 143 games a year over a 23-year period. He batted over .300, 14 times, retiring with a career batting average of .305.

Hank Aaron hit 40 or more homers in eight seasons, with a high of 47 homers in 1971 (52 based on 550 at bats). His career home run frequency was 34 home runs per 550 at bats. He struck out only 62 times a year.

Sadaharu Oh played with the Yomiuri Giants in the Japanese Central League from 1959 through 1980. He is the all-time world professional baseball career home run champion with 868 circuit blows. Three times he hit more than 50 homers in a season, with a high of 55 in 1964 (a frequency of 64 homers per 550 at bats). Oh's career home run frequency (which would be lower if he played in the major leagues) was 52 homers for every 550 at bats. Sadaharu Oh struck out an average of 78 times per year, while walking an unbelievable 149 times (including 29 intentional walks). The Japanese icon batted over .300, 13 times, retiring with a career batting average of .301.

There were only six 50-plus home run seasons between 1950 and 1990 in the major leagues, including Roger Maris' fantastic 61 home run year. The other historic seasons were Mickey Mantle's 52 homers in 1956 and 54 homers in 1961, Willie Mays' 51 homers in 1955 and 52 homers in 1965, and George Foster's 52 homers in 1977. No one challenged Maris' record until 1994.

8. Sammy Sosa— The Early Years

Sammy Sosa was born in the Dominican Republic, on the eastern half of the island of Hispaniola, located in the Caribbean Sea, about 600 miles off the southeastern tip of Florida. The Dominican Republic was first inhabited by Arawak Indians from South America about 700 years ago. It was later visited by Christopher Columbus on his third voyage of exploration. Santo Domingo, founded by Columbus' brother Bartholomew in 1496, is the oldest European city in the New World. For the next several hundred years the D.R. was in a constant state of flux, with the Spanish and French alternately occupying the country. It eventually became part of the Spanish Empire, while its neighbor to the west, Haiti, became a French colony.

The Dominican Republic became an independent nation in the early 20th century, as a result of the Spanish-American War. In 1930, General Rafael Leonidas Trujillo Molina usurped power and established a dictatorship, which lasted until his assassination in 1961. From that time until the present, the Dominican Republic has had a democratic republic form of government.

During the 19th century, foreign businessmen, many of them from the United States, built large plantations on the island to grow and harvest crops such as bananas, coffee, and sugar cane. The southeastern plains are particularly conducive to growing sugar cane. The land is fertile, and the semitropical climate produces temperatures in the 70s during the winter, rising to the 90s during the summer. Job opportunities in the little country that occupies a land area only 235 miles long and 165 miles wide attracted thousands of workers from other islands in the West Indies, who brought with them their own religion and music.

San Pedro de Macoris, a port city that has grown to 90,000, was founded during this time. It is the center of the sugar-growing region, surrounded by sugar cane plantations and a sugar processing plant. In the nineteenth century, it grew into a luxurious and wealthy city, with a magnificent cathedral and an opulent opera house. Known as "The Sultana of the East," it was one of the jewels of the Caribbean, attracting visitors from Cuba, Mexico, and Central and South America. Modern San Pedro is the home of Eastern Central University with a universally recognized School of Medicine.

The port of San Pedro de Macoris is one of the major ports in the country. Shipping traffic is heavy, with food, medical supplies, and luxuries such as automobiles and television sets coming into the country, and products such as sugar, tobacco, alcohol, textiles, and soap being exported, primarily to countries in the western hemisphere.

Baseball was introduced into the island in the 1870s by refugees from Cuba's Ten Years War. The game was promoted by the plantation owners as a way of keeping their employees occupied and happy during the growing season from October to February. Baseball leagues were eventually formed throughout the country, with teams representing various sugar cane plantations, tobacco manufacturers, and oil companies. Tournaments were held at the end of the season to determine a national champion.

During the 1920s and 30s, touring professional baseball teams from Cuba and the American Negro leagues popularized the game. In 1937, baseball was the centerpiece of a presidential campaign. President Trujillo and his opponents each supported one of the four teams in a summer league competition. Trujillo's team included Negro league legends Satchel Paige and Josh Gibson, as well as Puerto Rican all-star, Perucho Cepeda, the father of the San Francisco Giants' Orlando Cepeda. Cuban hero, Martin Dihigo, also participated in the league. President Trujillo kept his team under guard in the evening to protect them from the temptations of the city's night life. During the last crucial series of the year, he locked them in jail overnight. Fortunately for Paige and his teammates, they won the championship and made a hasty departure from the island the next morning on the first Pan American Clipper.

Over the years, baseball has become more than a sport to the islanders. It has become a passion, as well as a means of escape. Since integration opened the gates of organized baseball to all men, more than 200 Dominicans have played in the major leagues, starting with Ozzie Virgil, Felipe Alou, Juan Marichal, and Julian Javier. Other notable major leaguers from the D.R. include George Bell, Julio Franco, Joachin Andujar, Pedro Guerrero, and Raul Mondesi.

A Dominican summer league was formed in 1951. After four years, it was replaced by a winter league, which is still in operation. Today, major league organizations send some of their promising minor league players to the D.R. during the winter to refine their skills. Major league players who are citizens of the D.R. often participate in the winter league also, making the Dominican Winter League one the highest rated winter leagues in existence. It is equivalent to the Japanese leagues, a step above the AAA level, and slightly below the major league level.

Samuel (Sammy) Sosa was born Samuel Montero in the sugar mill company town of Ingenio Consuelo, to Bautista Montero and his wife Lucrecia, on November 12, 1968. The family moved to nearby San Pedro de Macoris when Sammy, or Mayki as he was called, was five years old. Their home, which was located on Calle Cincumbacion, in Jarro Sucio Barrio (Dirty Jar district), a poor section of the town, was a cramped, two-room, tangerine-colored, stucco apartment that was part of an abandoned hospital. Sammy slept on a wafer-thin mattress on a dirt floor. The house had no indoor plumbing, so baths had to be taken by collecting rain water in a drum or by washing in the sea. Open trenches and outhouses served as the barrio's sanitary facilities.

The dirt streets and alleys of Jarro Sucio, where the barefooted children played baseball, were strewn with garbage and refuse. Down the street from the Sosa house was a hard-packed dirt baseball field where many Dominican major leaguers began their careers. Along the right field line, across the street from the field, was the local prison.

When Sammy was seven years old, his father, who worked in the fields and on the highways, was struck down by an aneurysm. He died at age 42, leaving the family destitute. Sammy's mother Lucrecia, although a young widow, was a strong-willed, very religious lady, who was determined to raise her six children, ages two to 14, by herself. She worked as a maid, and also sold sandwiches to workers in the nearby factories. The three oldest boys (Luis Emilio age 14, Sammy, and Juan age 12) worked at odd jobs after school to help make ends meet. Sonia and

Raquel helped their mother and took care of two-year-old Jose, called Nino (The Kid). Luis had a fruit stand in Parque Duarte, the town plaza, where he sold oranges for ten cents apiece. Sammy was a shoe shine boy. He lugged his tools of the trade to the plaza, after school, where he shined shoes for about seven cents a pair. Two of his customers were major league baseball players Joachin Andujar and George Bell. He also washed cars occasionally. On a good day, he would bring home about $2.00. One Mother's Day, Sammy tried unsuccessfully to earn money to buy his mother a present. All he came up with was one cent. He used it to buy her one Monte Carlo cigarette. It was probably the best present Lucrecia Sosa ever received. Once, reminiscing about those days, Sosa said, "I never had a childhood. I went from a little boy to a man overnight."

Sammy's mother eventually remarried, changing the family name to Sosa. Two stepsons, Carlos and Nani, were added to the family circle.

During this time, Sammy Sosa met a man who changed his life. Bill Chase, an American businessman who opened a shoe factory in San Pedro, let Sammy shine his shoes one evening. The ten-year-old youngster, already street smart after three years of hustling jobs in the town square, realized Chase was a good payday, so each evening, he and his little brother Jose would track Chase down, asking him for work. Bill Chase and his wife, Debbie, were charmed by the persistence of the happy-go-lucky kids, and they always gave them odd jobs to do. Actually, Sammy did most of the work. Five-year-old Jose entertained the Chases with his acrobatics. Bill and Debbie bought the boys clothes and other items, becoming like a second family to them. Bill Chase gave Sammy's older brother Luis a job in his factory. When Sammy started to play baseball, Chase bought him his first glove. And when he started playing organized ball, the man that Sosa looks upon as his surrogate father, and whom he calls "Papa," became his business manager, helping him invest his money wisely. Little brother Jose lived with the Chases in Florida for a time.

By the time Sammy Sosa was 11 or 12 years old, he had his heart set on a boxing career. He made boxing gloves out of socks stuffed with rags, and he fought with other neighborhood kids whenever he could. He also played baseball but not in an organized league. He played ball in the dirt streets of the barrio, in his bare feet, with a milk carton as a glove, stuffed rags for a ball, and an old stick or sugar cane for a bat.

Lucrecia and Luis, watching Sammy play baseball, realized that his exceptional baseball talent could carry him to a successful professional career if he could channel his energies in the right direction. At the age of 14, the eighth-grade dropout (education was mandatory only until the age of 14 in the Dominican Republic), urged on by his big brother Luis, began his baseball education. His first teacher was a former member of the Dominican Junior Team, 21-year-old Hector Paguero. The dirt expanses of the field known as "Mexico" became Sammy's school for the next two years, as he struggled to master the fundamentals of hitting. It was the same baseball field that had nurtured such major league talents as Julio Franco, Alfredo Griffin, and George Bell. San Pedro de Macoris, strangely enough, has sent more baseball players to the major leagues, per capita, than any city in the world. At one time, during the 1980s, six of the 26 major league shortstops were born in San Pedro de Macoris. A sign on the outskirts of the city reads, "San Pedro de Macoris, the Birthplace of Major League Shortstops."

Sosa and Paguero worked on Sammy's game four to six hours a day. The first thing Paguero taught Sammy was to swing big, and swing with bad intentions. The big, looping swing Sammy developed was full of holes, but it did make him into a long ball hitter which, in turn, attracted professional scouts.

Luis and Juan played Jiminy Cricket to Sammy's Pinochio. They always made sure Sammy knew whenever a tryout camp was to be held in San Pedro. They constantly pushed Sammy to keep appointments, get to the park on time, and concentrate on baseball. Sammy attended a Philadelphia Phillies tryout camp in 1984 and so impressed the scouts that they waved a professional baseball contract under his nose. The eager 15 year old quickly put his name on the dotted line, but the contract was subsequently voided by baseball officials because Sammy was under age. By the time he was 16, Sammy was playing professional baseball in Estadio de Beisbol Feliberto Pena in San Pedro.

Omar Minaya, a scout for the Texas Rangers, stationed in Florida, received glowing reports about the young slugger, and invited him to a tryout camp in the northern port city of Puerto Plata. Sammy Sosa arrived in camp, after a four hour bus ride, wearing a borrowed uniform and borrowed shoes, determined to impress Ranger officials with his superior baseball abilities. Although Sosa's skills were crude and unrefined, and even though he looked badly undernourished, the 5'10", 145-pound dynamo had certain qualities that caught Minaya's eye. He was outgoing, energetic, aggressive, and optimistic. He gave 110 percent all the time. He had an outstanding throwing arm, a quick bat, and good power. On the negative side, he had only average speed and a looping swing full of holes. He didn't know the slightest thing about baseball fundamentals—he had no concept of the strike zone, didn't know how to run the bases, where to throw the ball on hits to the outfield, how to charge a ball, or how to hit the cutoff man.

Still, on the recommendation of Minaya, the Texas Rangers offered the 16-year-old Sosa a professional baseball contract, with a signing bonus of $3500. He bought himself a bike, then gave the rest of the money, which was almost two years' wages, to his mother. The Rangers, in order to prepare young Dominicans for the culture shock of living and playing baseball in the United States, had them attend a baseball academy at the University of Santo Domingo during their first year. Sammy and the other boys played baseball at the academy, learned rudimentary English, and were taught hygiene, how to use a knife and fork, and other intricacies of everyday living in America.

The next year, 1986, Sammy was assigned to the Sarasota Rangers in the Gulf Coast League. When he arrived in Florida, he still didn't know much English, but he knew how to get ahead. First, he latched on to some Puerto Rican players, like Juan Gonzalez, Rey Sanchez, and Bernie Williams, who could help him with his English. Then he followed the American players, like Dean Palmer, to the local fast food restaurants, ordering what they ordered, until he understood the language better.

The Gulf Coast League was a rookie league that played all its games in just two cities, Sarasota and Bradenton. The league consisted of ten teams divided into two divisions, the north and the south. The Rangers finished the season in third place in their division, their 31–31 record leaving them 2½ games behind the front-running Dodgers.

Sammy Sosa had his ups and downs during the season, but overall his debut was a great success. The right-handed slugger batted .275, with a league-leading 19 doubles, four home runs, and 11 stolen bases, in 61 games. His 96 total bases also led the league. By comparison, teammate Dean Palmer, now entering his tenth year in the major leagues, batted an anemic .209 with no home runs. Bernie Williams of the Sarasota Yankees, an eight-year big leaguer and a New York Yankee mainstay, hit .270 with two home runs and a league-leading 45 runs scored in 61 games, and Juan Gonzalez, who has twice led the American League in home runs and has hit more than 40 home runs in a season, five times in ten years, hit .240 with no home runs.

Sosa struck out 51 times in 229 at bats, but as Omar Minaya explained later, "Dominican players know only one way to get to the major leagues, by putting up big numbers. And you can't put up big numbers unless you swing the bat."

Early in his career, Sammy Sosa was known as a "hot dog." He was flamboyant, enthusiastic, overly aggressive, and swaggered when he walked. At the plate, one coach noted, "He never saw a pitch he didn't like." On the bases, he ran with abandon, regardless of the pitch count or the game situation. His selfish pursuit of his own statistics would bring him considerable criticism for almost a decade. But it was all a learning experience for the youngster from the Dominican Republic. And he was still only 17 years old.

In 1987, Sammy Sosa played with Gastonia in the Class A South Atlantic League. The Rangers did not have a very good club that year, finishing fifth in a six-team division. Their record of 52–82 left them 33½ games behind the Asheville Tourists.

Sosa batted .279 with 11 home runs and 59 RBIs in 129 games, and was elected to the mid-season all-star team. He led the club with 73 runs scored, but also struck out 123 times in 519 at bats. Dean Palmer batted .215 with nine homers, while Juan Gonzalez hit .265 with 14 homers and 74 RBIs.

That winter, Sammy Sosa returned home and started playing baseball for Escogido of Santo Domingo, in the Dominican Winter League. Sammy was living with his mother in San Pedro at the time, and had to borrow money for the bus, or hitch rides to get to the games in Santo Domingo, 40 miles west of San Pedro. He was ready to quit the team, but Escogido owner Daniel Aquinas got Sammy an apartment in Santo Domingo. Escogido manager Phil "The Vulture" Regan, a former closer for the Los Angeles Dodgers, saw great promise in the 20-year-old slugger. He liked Sosa's enthusiasm and raw talent, and the excitement he brought to the game. In one game, Sosa shocked his manager by racing from first base to second after a short pop up to the catcher, and sliding in safely under the tag.

Sammy got into just 11 games that first year, batting .287 in 14 at bats, but he did hit his first DWL home run.

The Texas trio of Sosa, Palmer, and Gonzalez stayed in Class A ball in '88, playing with Charlotte in the Florida State League. Sosa's batting average nosedived with Charlotte, as he hit only .229, but he continued to develop in other areas. He showed good power, leading the league with 12 triples, to go along with 13 doubles and nine home runs. He set a personal high with 42 stolen bases, reduced his strikeouts to 106, and was charged with only seven outfield errors. Unfortunately, he was still having trouble taking pitches, as evidenced by his 35 bases on balls. In three years of professional baseball, totaling 1,255 at bats, he drew only 78 walks. Dean Palmer batted .266 with four homers in Charlotte, while Juan Gonzalez hit .256 with eight homers.

Sosa played Winter League ball for Phil Regan at Escogido again, hitting .275 in 56 games, with 12 extra base hits (2 homers), and 28 RBIs. He continued to work on his defensive game, but he was still like a bull in a china shop in the outfield. Blessed with blazing speed, he ran down every ball, regardless of where it was hit, placing his outfield teammates in constant danger of being trampled.

Nineteen eighty nine was a momentous year in the life of 20-year-old Sammy Sosa. He began the year with Tulsa in the AA Texas League and, for the first time, he began to realize his hidden potential. In 66 games with the Drillers, the right-handed power hitter, now a muscular 175 pounds, smashed 33 extra base hits including 15 doubles, four triples, and seven home runs. He drove in 31 runners, and stole 16 bases, while hitting a solid .297. On June 15, Sosa was called up to the big club for his first taste of major league pitching.

It was reported that, when Sammy Sosa received his first major league check of $18,000, he cashed it, threw the money on the bed, and rolled around on it for several minutes. Then he excitedly telephoned his mother in San Pedro de Macoris to tell her the good news. "Mommy, we're rich."

Even though Sosa got off to a good start by pounding out a single and double against Andy Hawkins of the Yankees in his first game, slugging a home run off Roger Clemens five days later, and enjoying a four-hit game, it was obvious he was in over his head. He batted only .238 in 25 games, with just three runs batted in, in 84 at bats, and he struck out 20 times—with no walks. Tom Grieve, the general manager of the Rangers, later admitted they may have called the 20-year-old Sosa up too soon. Texas didn't have the money to buy free agents, so they were forced to try to develop their young players quickly. It was a mistake that probably delayed Sosa's development. He probably should have stayed in the minors another three or four years, to develop his baseball fundamentals, and refine his knowledge of the strike zone.

Texas farmed Sosa out to Oklahoma City in the AAA American Association, for more experience but, after playing just ten games for the 89ers, he was traded to the Chicago White Sox for Harold Baines. Once again, the Rangers, desperate for an experienced bat, traded away one of their top prospects. Tom Grieve thought that his team, after a fourth-place finish in 1989, could make a run at the Oakland Athletics. But it didn't work out for the Rangers. Texas finished in third place, 20 games out of first.

Chicago sent Sosa to their Vancouver farm team in the Pacific Coast League. Sammy played 13 games with the Canadians and whacked the ball at a sizzling .367 clip, prompting the last-place Chi-Sox to recall him. He finished the season in Chicago, the fifth team he had played on, in a hectic, confusing year. In his first game, Sammy Sosa went three for three, with a two-run homer, against the Minnesota Twins. He played in 33 games for Chicago, batting a respectable .273. In 99 at bats, the kid from San Pedro pounded out five doubles and three home runs, with ten runs batted in and seven stolen bases. It was a good debut.

Over the winter of 1989-90, after his dizzying season in the United States, Sosa went home to the Dominican Republic to be with his family and to relax and unwind. He played 37 games for Escogido in the Winter League, batting .285 with two homers and 19 RBIs. One night, while listening to the merengue music at a disco in Santo Domingo, Sammy noticed a beautiful, olive-skinned, red-haired girl across the dance floor, and was immediately attracted to her. Her name was Sonia. She was 17 years old, and was a singer and dancer on Dominican television. As reported by Michael Bamberger in Sports Illustrated, "He had a waiter bring her a note: 'If you will do the honor of having one dance with me, it will be the start of a beautiful friendship....'" She had no idea that

Sammy was a baseball player, but he had other qualities. 'I like guys who are big, tall and dark,' she says. 'I looked at him and said, 'Oh, wow—what a man.'"

That first dance did indeed become the start of a beautiful friendship. In fact, Sammy and Sonia were married within a year. Keysha, born in 1992, was the first addition to the family. Later, Sammy and Sonia were blessed with Kenia (1994), Sammy Jr. (1996), and Michael (1997).

Sammy Sosa spent the entire 1990 season in the major leagues, with mixed results. In spite of optimism in the White Sox camp, the experts still predicted a last-place finish for Jeff Torborg's team. The experts were wrong. Chicago surprised everyone with a second-place finish. They won a total of 94 games, an improvement of 25 games over '89, and just finished nine games behind the Oakland Athletics. The experts also called Sosa an exciting addition to the Chicago outfield. In this case, they were correct. He played in 153 games for the White Sox and, although he batted only .233, he hit 25 doubles, 10 triples and 15 home runs, with 70 runs batted in. He was the only American League player to reach double figures in all three categories. He also stole 32 bases, joining Ivan Calderon (32)and Lance Johnson (36) in becoming the first White Sox trio in almost 90 years, to steal 30 bases in one year.

Back in the Dominican Republic, it was a busy winter for Sammy Sosa. He bought his mother a new house in San Pedro de Macoris, complete with her first telephone and television set. Several years later, when he began making big money, he added a second story to the house and provided her with a chauffeur. He married the beautiful Sonia. And he had a good year with Escogido in the winter League, hitting .328, although he played in only 17 games because of his recent marriage.

Nineteen ninety one was Sosa's worst years in professional baseball. He was in a bad mental state most of the year, primarily because of an unpleasant relationship with Chicago's batting instructor, Walt Hriniak. He couldn't adapt to Hriniak's style of hitting and was berated for his inability to learn. He lost confidence in his ability to hit.

Sosa did get off the mark quickly in '91, pounding out two home runs and driving in five runners, against Baltimore, but by late July his world had collapsed completely. He was batting an anemic .200, with just 51 hits in 255 at bats, and was on his way to Vancouver. Sosa's immaturity may also have led to his downfall. He, like many other young major league players, succumbed to the demon of too much money and too much celebrity, too soon. He slicked his hair down with gel, bought gaudy gold trinkets, and became part of the night scene.

Sosa spent a month in Vancouver, where he played resonably well, then was recalled to Chicago to finish out the season. His final numbers (.203 batting average, ten homers and 33 RBIs) were easily forgettable. He couldn't even find his batting stroke in the Dominican Winter League, hitting just .248. He did, however, lead the league in home runs, with four. Sammy's Winter League career essentially ended that year. He would play just three more games in succeeding years.

Sammy's big break came on March 29, 1992, when he was traded to the Chicago Cubs. It was the real beginning of his major league career. Manager Jim Lefebvre and batting coach Billy Williams were thrilled to get such a talent, and they went to work immediately to restore the young slugger's confidence.

The team got off to a slow start in '92, winning just 12 of their first 31 games, and falling into the cellar. Sosa was one of the reasons for their poor showing, as he hit just .211, with one RBI, in the first 24 games. He finally hit his first Cubs' homer, off Ryan Bowen of the Houston Astros, on May 7. After he was moved down from leadoff man to #6 in the batting order, he started to hit, banging out four homers in ten games, from May 31 to June 10. Then, just when he seemed to be getting untracked, he went down with an injury. On June 12, Sosa suffered a broken right hand after being hit by Montreal's Dennis Martinez.

He was out of action for almost seven weeks. When he returned to the lineup, he jumped on Doug Drabek's first pitch, homering off the Pittsburgh ace. Four days later, he excited the crowd by scoring all the way from first base on a pitchout, when Met's catcher Mickey Sasser threw the ball into center field on a stolen base attempt. Sammy Sosa whacked the ball at a torrid .385 clip (15 for 39), with three homers and nine RBIs after coming off the disabled list, but his season came to a disappointing end in his tenth game back, when he fouled a pitch off his left ankle, fracturing it.

The season was not a complete loss for Sosa. He found a home with the Cubs. He liked his new manager and his new batting coach. And he got his swing back. In just 67 games, the right-handed slugger hit an

acceptable .260, with eight home runs and 25 runs batted in. It was a season to build on. From now on, it would be onward and upward.

In 1993, Sosa began to live up to his potential, although he was still a raw talent. He swung at pitches in the dirt, and pitches over his head. He stole bases at inopportune times. In the outfield, he was still a threat to the health of his teammates. The other outfielders dove for cover whenever Sosa came in their direction. Cutoff men never grew tall enough to reach his throw-ins. And he was still considered to be a selfish player, more interested in his own statistics than in the welfare of the team.

The Chicago Cubs, coming off fourth-place finishes in 1991 and '92, hoped to work their way back to the top, and Sammy Sosa was one of the important cogs in the wheel. Sosa, now wearing #21 on his uniform in honor of his idol Roberto Clemente, got off to a fast start, leading the Cactus League in home runs in spring training. He continued his blasting when the season started. On April 23, the right-handed bomber ripped two homers with five RBIs, as the Cubbies whipped the Cincinnati Reds 7–4. Eleven days later he went 5–6 with two more homers. His three-run, two-out shot in the bottom of the ninth brought the Cubs back from a 10–5 deficit to a ten all tie. The Rockies pushed across four runs in the top of the 11th to beat Lefebvre's cohorts 14–13 in windswept Wrigley Field. Sosa's two-run homer in the bottom of the 11th was too little, too late.

Sammy Sosa had another two-homer game against the St. Louis Cardinals on June 17, then hit two more in San Diego, on the 30th of the month. The big slugger went six for six against the Rockies in hitter-friendly Mile High Stadium, on July 2, giving him nine consecutive base hits, to establish a new Chicago Cubs record. The Cubs won the game 11–8.

Chicago's new hitting sensation was selected as the National League's Player of the Week for June 28–July 4, hitting .538 in six games, with two homers and six RBIs.

The cannonading continued into August and September. He put up another two-homer day against the St. Louis Cardinals on August 6. He

Opposite: **Sammy Sosa played for the Chicago White Sox for three years, before being traded to the Chicago Cubs in 1992. (Brace photo)**

hit his 30th home run of the season on September 2, driving one off Josias Manzanillo of the New York Mets. And he stole his 30th base of the year on September 15th in 3 Com Park in San Francisco.

It was a good year for Sammy Sosa, but not a good year for the Cubs. They once again finished in fourth place, their 84–78 record leaving them 13 games behind the Phillies. Chicago's poor showing spelled finish for manager Jim Lefebvre, who was replaced by Tom Trebelhorn.

Sosa put up some outstanding numbers. He played in 159 games, batting .261 with 33 home runs and 93 runs batted in. His flying feet enabled him to steal 36 bases, making him the Cubs' first 30–30 man (home runs and stolen bases). In the outfield, he improved immensely. His powerful right throwing arm shot down 17 ambitious base runners, making him the #2 man in the National League in assists. He still needed to become more familiar with the strike zone however, as evidenced by his 135 strikeouts in 598 at bats. He drew just 38 bases on balls.

The 1993 season was a satisfying one for Sammy Sosa in many respects, but it was far from perfect. Many people still looked upon him as a selfish player. And his occasional mental lapses brought more criticism from fans and media types alike. One Chicago radio personality called him "Roberto Clemente without a brain." Manager Jim Lefebvre called the comments on his selfishness, jealousy on the part of some players, who could not understand a potential superstar like Sosa. Lefebvre admitted that when Sosa was in a groove, he could hit homers in bunches, but when he was in a slump, he piled up many strikeouts.

In some respects, Sammy's achievements were selfish. It was the Dominican mentality coming to the surface. Sosa believed that the more money he could make, the more money he could send home to his family. And he could make more money by putting up big numbers. In the Dominican Republic, family, which was the most important thing in a person's life, consisted, not only of the immediate family, but also of cousins, aunts, uncles, and assorted other relations. In Sammy's case, his "family" totaled more than 30 people.

There was one thing everyone agreed with. Sammy Sosa came to the ballpark ready to play every day. And he gave his team and his manager a 110-percent effort every day. Sammy's physical game still needed refinement. And Sammy's mental approach still needed to be fine-tuned. But his enthusiasm and his dedication were above reproach.

Sosa, celebrating his outstanding 1993 campaign, arrived at spring training camp in Mesa, Arizona, flaunting a heavy, gold necklace adorned with two crossed bats and a large gaudy "30–30" inlaid with diamonds. The weight of his jewelry apparently didn't affect his swing however, as he picked up where he left off in '93. Although he hit well in spring training, the Cubs' right fielder went into a slump as soon as the bell tolled to start the regular season. He hit a paltry .225 in April and that, along with first baseman Mark Grace's slump, contributed to the Cubs' painful 12-game losing streak. In an attempt to end the jinx, the Cubs brought a lucky Billy Goat onto the field. Manager Trebelhorn also moved Sosa up into the leadoff spot. The Cubs won, and the jinx was lifted—temporarily.

Sammy Sosa went on to have an outstanding month in May. On the 4th of the month, batting leadoff, he homered off Tom Browning of Cincinnati. He tripled in four straight games from May 14 to 17. And he homered again leading off, this time against Tom Glavine of the Atlanta Braves on May 29. For the month, the big slugger batted .317 with 11 home runs and 23 runs batted in.

He batted .339 over the team's last 53 games, before the players went out on strike, ending the season after only 113 games. It was none too soon for Chicago, who finished in the cellar with a sorry record of 49–64.

Sammy's overall totals showed a solid .300 batting average, 25 homers, 70 RBIs, and 22 stolen bases. He struck out 92 times and walked 25 times, in 426 at bats.

The 1995 season was also an abbreviated season, as the strike, which was finally settled in March, reduced the playing schedule by 18 games. When the season finally began in late April, Sammy Sosa was ready—and happy. He had just signed a one-year contract for $ 4.3 million. This would be his "coming out" year, when he would begin to realize his almost unlimited potential. The undernourished kid from a third world country had grown into a 6', 190-pound slugger with immense shoulders and anvil-like arms, and he was ready to explode. Through the first 31 games, Jim Riggleman's overachieving troops racked up a 20–11 record, sparked by Sosa who hit .315 with ten homers.

On May 14, Sosa reached his first milestone when he homered off Trevor Hofman of the San Diego Padres for his 100th career home run.

One week later, the free-swinging Sosa homered in the top of the 13th inning in Los Angeles to give the Cubbies a 2–1 victory over the Dodgers. It was Chicago's 9000th major league victory, going back to 1876.

The Cubs, who had only a few bonafide major leaguers, such as Sosa, Shawon Dunston, and Mark Grace, slowly drifted back into the pack. By July 2, their record stood at 30–31. Sammy Sosa, on his way to his first All-Star game, was hitting .289, with 15 homers and 52 RBIs in 61 games. His strikeouts and walks were still out of whack however, with 56 K's and only 16 walks.

During August, the Cubs' right fielder went on a home run hitting spree. From August 10 to August 24, he smashed nine homers, with 27 RBIs, in 14 games. He hit seven of the homers and drove in 18 of the runs, between the 17th and 24th. In one span, from the 17th to the 20th, he homered in four straight games. From August 13 to September 2, he hit 13 homers in 20 games, driving in 32 runs. Included in the barrage, were a trio of two-homer games. On August 14, he hit a memorable home run off the Dodgers' Tom Candiotti, the 10,000th home run in Chicago history.

When the season ended, the Cubs had settled into third place, with a record of 73–71, a full 12 games out of first. Sammy Sosa, on the other hand, had an outstanding year. He was selected as the National League Player of the Week, twice. He won his first Silver Slugger Award, and was named to The Sporting News National League all-star team.

On September 24th, Sosa stole third base in a 3–2 win over the Pittsburgh Pirates, making him a 30–30 man for the second time. Only five other men in major league history have been 30–30 men more than once.

For the year, Sosa batted .268, with 36 home runs, 119 runs batted in, and 34 stolen bases. Nineteen sixty-five marked the first of four successive years that Sosa would rack up 30 or more homers and 100 or more RBIs. He continued to impress baseball experts with his outstanding arm, as he finished with 13 outfield assists, #2 in the National League. He was also the first Chicago player in the twentieth century to lead the team in home runs and steals in three successive seasons.

Sosa still had many things to work on before he could become a complete player. During the 1995 season, he spent several hours a day with Chicago Cubs batting coach Billy Williams, working on cutting down his swing. Unfortunately, the excitable Sosa would go through periods when he would forget his instructions and would plummet into a deep slump as a result. During his hot streak in August, he developed some bad habits, like overswinging, and he paid the price for it. Over the last 15 games of the season, Chicago's "Franchise" hit a paltry .179 with no home runs. The program to make Sammy Sosa a superstar would continue into 1996. It would be a continuation of the '95 program—cut down the swing—avoid prolonged batting slumps—avoid bad habits. Try to relax more. Be less excitable. Have more peaks and fewer valleys.

During the winter, Sammy Sosa went back to the Dominican Republic and became a benefactor for his country's needs. He bought a new fire truck for the San Pedro de Macoris Fire Department. He bought 250 computers for schools in his country, with 21 of them finding their way into the San Pedro Public School.

He also built a $1.2 million office/shopping building in San Pedro de Macoris, his gift to the city. The "30–30 Plaza" is a three-storied "U"-shaped complex with offices on the top floor, boutiques on the second floor, and a Burger King restaurant and a Baskin Robbins ice cream store on the ground level. The white and aquamarine building has a central patio containing a statue of Sammy Sosa in a Chicago Cubs uniform in the center, and a fountain dedicated to the shoe-shine boys of the city. Coins thrown into the fountain are used for the benefit of the shoe-shine boys.

The "30–30" Plaza includes a discotheque featuring merengue music. "Sammy's Club," is located in the rear section of the building. Sammy's sisters also have businesses in the plaza, with Sonia's Boutique and Raquel's Hair Salon.

Sammy's mother lives around the corner from the plaza, but Sammy, at the urging of his wife Sonia, built a palatial mansion in an exclusive section of Santo Domingo, near Juan Samuel and Melido Perez. The four-room bedroom suite, by itself, is bigger than the entire house Sammy grew up in. The yard, inside a walled enclosure, showcases a tropical garden and a swimming pool. The expansive garage houses several cars, including a red Dodge Viper, a white Mercedes, a yellow Ferrari, a beige Rolls Royce, a Navigator, an Expedition, and a black Hummer. Sammy also owns a jet ski, a speed boat, and a 60-foot yacht named "Sammy Jr."

The Chicago Cubs star funded a baseball academy in San Pedro,

Escuella de Beisbol Sammy Sosa. The academy includes a playing field, locker rooms, free uniforms with "Sammy Sosa" on the front, free room and board, and professional instructors. In effect, everything a boy needs to develop his game.

The big topic of conversation in the States over the winter was expansion. It was announced that two new teams would be added to the major leagues in 1998, Tampa Bay in the American League and Arizona in the National League. Almost immediately, speculation began about the possibility of someone breaking Roger Maris' home run record. In 1994, before the disgraceful players strike almost destroyed the game, several players were on track to challenge the most visible of all records. No fewer than six players, three in each league, were threatening to hit more than 50 home runs, and one player, Matt Williams of the San Francisco Giants was on track to match Maris' record of 61 homers. The other big boomers included Ken Griffey, Albert Belle, Frank Thomas, Jeff Bagwell, and Barry Bonds.

The 1996 season was another step forward for Sammy Sosa, but a big disappointment for Jim Riggleman's Chicago Cubs. The Cubbies, who were hoping to improve on their 73–71 showing in '95, had a more mature, confident Sammy Sosa in right field. The right-handed bomber, now 27 years old, had discarded his flashy jewelry and was concentrating on being a good person, a devoted family man, and a dangerous clean-up hitter.

The Chicago Cubs stumbled coming out of the starting gate. On Monday, May 13, their record stood at 18–20, leaving them, surprisingly enough, in a flat-footed tie with the Cincinnati Reds, for first place in the weak Central Division. The team was mediocre in all aspects of the game. Sosa was hitting a barely visible .233, but he had hit 11 home runs with 27 RBIs, to lead the team in both categories.

On May 16, Sammy Sosa became the first player in Cubs history to hit two homers in one inning. Facing Jeff Tabaka of the Houston Astros in the seventh inning, the Chicago slugger hit a leadoff homer. Later in the inning, he hit a two-run shot off Jim Dougherty.

Three weeks later, on June 5, the pride of the Dominican Republic slammed three home runs against the Philadelphia Phillies, in a 9–6 Cubs victory. He slammed two home runs off Terry Mulholland, and one off Russ Springer. Sosa's second homer was the 150th of his career.

Sammy Sosa, over his career, seemed to like the warm weather. Perhaps it was his Caribbean upbringing. He routinely batted about .235 in March, April, September, and October, while hitting 30 points higher from May through August. Nineteen ninety-six was no exception. He had a ten-game hit streak from June 11 to the 20th and another one from June 22 to July 3. A third ten-game hit streak followed from July 5 to July 18. Over a 32-game skein, the big slugger pounded the ball at a .328 pace with ten home runs.

At the All-Star break, Jim Riggleman's crew had slipped into fourth place, their 41–46 record leaving them five games behind the St. Louis Cardinals. Sammy Sosa, after a slow start, enjoyed the warm weather and had his average up to .258. His 27 homers led the National League, while his 63 RBIs were near the top.

Sosa continued hot during July, winning the Player of the Month Award for his .358 batting average, ten homers and 29 RBIs. He was on his way to a potential 50 home run season when disaster struck. He was leading the league with 40 home runs on August 21, when an errant pitch from Florida's Mark Hutton broke his right hand, shelving him for the balance of the season. The injury ended a consecutive games–played streak of 304 for Sosa.

The Cubs, who had worked their way back into contention in the National League Central Division, could not compensate for Sosa's loss. They dropped 14 of their last 16 games, and finished the season in fourth place with a disappointing 76–86 record.

Overall, Sammy Sosa had a successful year. Even though he missed the last 38 games of the season, he hit .273 with 40 homers and 100 runs batted in. More important, Sonia Sosa gave birth to a baby boy in October, Sammy Jr. He joined sisters Keysha age four and Kenia age two.

When spring training got underway at HoHoKam Park in Mesa, Arizona, in February 1997, manager Jim Riggleman was faced with many problems, not the least of which was to find a strong bat to hit behind, and protect, Sammy Sosa. The search would prove to be fruitless.

The major leagues were coming off a sensational home run explosion in 1996, when the 28 teams hit a total of 4962 home runs, an average of 2.19 per game, and 22 percent higher than 1995. Eight teams hit more than 200 homers. Seventeen players hit 40 or more homers, with Oakland A's slugger Mark McGwire rattling the fences for 52 home runs, and Baltimore Oriole outfielder Brady Anderson topping out at 50. The reasons for the home run surge are many. Colorado's new Coors Field, at an altitude of more than 5000 feet, produced 70 percent more circuit blows than the average major league field. Other reasons given include smaller ballparks, expansion, and bigger, stronger players who utilize weight training to the fullest. The experts continued to focus on the 1998 season when two new expansion teams would be admitted into the major leagues. They felt that Rogers Maris' record would be in jeopardy, particularly from the likes of McGwire, Ken Griffey, Albert Belle, and Frank Thomas. Sammy Sosa's name never came up in the predictions.

The Cubs were picked to finish third in the Central division in 1997. They had strengthened their pitching staff with the addition of closer Mel Rojas and starters Kevin Tapani and Terry Mulholland, but they were still weak offensively, with just three dependable bats—Sosa, Mark Grace, and Brian McRae.

The season opened, fittingly enough, on April Fools Day. Playing in Florida, Chicago dropped a 4–2 decision to Jim Leyland's eventual World Champion Marlins. Terry Mulholland was rapped around for four runs and seven hits in 4⅔ innings. Sosa went 0–4, Grace had 1–3, and McRae was hitless in two at bats. On the 13th of the month, the Cubs were beaten at home by the Atlanta Braves, 6–4, for their tenth straight loss. The team had an anemic .169 batting average and a poor 4.39 earned run average. Sammy Sosa was hitting .200 with one homer and three RBIs. One week later, on the 20th, Chicago met the New York Mets in a doubleheader. They dropped the opener 8–2 as Bobby Jones tossed a five-hitter at them. Sammy Sosa, after another 0-for-four, saw his batting average plummet to .157. Finally, in game two, behind a strong pitching performance by Kevin Foster, Jim Riggleman's embattled troops broke into the win column, with a 4–3 victory. Jose Hernandez, Kevin Okrie, and Rey Sanchez drove in the runs. Reliever Turk Wendell agonized through a two-run Mets rally in the bottom of the ninth, before getting the last out.

The Cubs' 0–14 start was the worst in National League history, topping the ten game skein by the 1988 Atlanta Braves. The Baltimore Orioles hold the major league record with a 0–21 start, also in 1988.

On Friday, April 25, the Cubs' anemic offense finally came to life.

They pounded out 14 hits in an 11–1 laugher against the Pittsburgh Pirates. Sammy Sosa, with three hits including his third home run, drove in five runs and raised his batting average 27 points to .224. The next day they beat Pittsburgh again 7–6, behind another 14-hit attack. Doug Glanville drove in three runs, and Ryne Sandberg hit a homer to pace the attack.

By the end of April, Harry Caray's favorite team had settled into the cellar with a dismal 6–19 record, but May was a turnaround month for the Windy City boys. Sammy Sosa, who was unhappy at the start of the year, partly because he was playing the last year of his contract and negotiations between his agent and Chicago management had dragged on into the season, picked up his offensive production in May. He was named Player of the Week for the week ending May 18, thanks to a .348 batting average, with four homers, two triples and 12 RBIs in six games. On May 16, he went 4–4 with a triple, a home run, and a career high six runs batted in, against the San Diego Padres. Four days later, he slammed two home runs off San Francisco Giant pitching (the 22nd multi-homer game of his career), as the Cubs won 5–3. And on the 26th of the month, he hit his first inside-the-park home run, in Pittsburgh, sparking another Chicago victory, 2–1.

Surprisingly, as May ended, the Cubs were only five games out of first place, their 15–13 month bringing their overall record up to 21–32. For the month, Sammy Sosa scorched the ball at a .339 clip, with eight doubles, two triples, ten homers, and 28 RBIs. Mark Grace was batting .302, Shawon Dunston .301, Jose Hernandez .319, and Doug Glanville .302.

In June and July, two important things happened that would have a significant effect on Sosa's baseball career. On June 27, the Dominican slugger signed a four-year deal worth $42.5 million, making him the third highest player in the major leagues. The signing took a big load off Sammy's mind. As he said, "Talking about a contract in the middle of the season is hard." Manager, Jim Riggleman, in an attempt to get better pitches for Sosa to look at, moved him up to third place in the batting order, just ahead of Mark Grace.

Then, on July 14, batting coach Tony Muser left to become manager of Kansas City and was replaced by Jeff Pentland, a New York Mets minor league batting instructor. Pentland and Sosa grew close over the next few months, and began to work together to fine-tune Sosa's batting style. Pentland basically worked on just two important things with Sosa, a way to shift his weight so he would be ready for any kind of pitch, and a lowering of Sosa's hands, allowing him to be more relaxed when he swung.

The changes in Sosa's batting stance wouldn't be evident until 1998. In the meantime, the 1997 season continued on its downward spiral. The Cubs went 11–17 in June and 11–17 again in July to fall back into the cellar, a distant 16½ games behind the Houston Astros. Sosa was limping along at .251, but had 49 extra base hits including 21 homers and 77 RBIs. His continued disdain for the strike zone (120 strikeouts and only 32 bases on balls) continued to concern Riggleman and Pentland.

There were a few other notable Sosa achievements before the season ended. He ripped his 1000th major league hit against the Florida Marlins' Livan Hernandez on August 20th. And on the 24th, he smashed his 200th major league home run off Montreal's Steve Kline. It was a three-run shot in the eighth inning, giving the Cubs a 12–3 win at Wrigley Field.

The season finally came to a merciful end, none too soon, on September 28, with Chicago dropping a tight 2–1 decision to Tony LaRussa's Redbirds at Busch Stadium. Sosa struck out as a pinch hitter in the ninth, while St. Louis' new addition, Mark McGwire, hit a home run off Steve Trachsel in the sixth inning. It was an omen of things to come for Trachsel. McGwire would hit his record-breaking 62nd homer off the Chicago righty in the same park on September 8, 1998. Sammy Sosa's numbers for the year showed a .251 batting average, 36 home runs, 119 RBI's, and 22 stolen bases. He struck out 174 times, a new Chicago record, while drawing only 45 walks in 642 at bats.

The year 1997 ended on a happy and satisfying note for Sammy Sosa when he took his "Sammy Claus" Christmas tour to schools and hospitals in six cities. The happy-go-lucky Chicago Cubs baseball star visited Washington D.C., New York, Philadelphia, Chicago, Miami, Santo Domingo, and San Pedro de Macoris, distributing joy and presents to needy children. Appropriately enough Sammy Claus was attired in a bright red Santa Claus suit and hat, as he handed out more than 7000 gifts to the children of two countries. At Washington's Lincoln School, a mixed school where Spanish is spoken as much as English, the kids mobbed their hero. In addition to gifts, Sosa also gave out hundreds of autographs. The Chicago Cubs slugger, who received more then he gave, said, "I love this season." He hopes to visit other countries, including some in Asia, in future years, and intends to distribute up to 50,000 gifts within four years.

One other miracle visited the Sosa family in 1997. Sammy and Sonia were blessed with another addition to the family. Baby Michael brought their brood up to four.

9. Mark McGwire—
The Early Years

Mark McGwire was a big kid who grew into a big man. The entire family was big. His father stood 6'3" tall, and his four brothers went between 6'3" and 6'8". John McGwire, the family patriarch, had his dreams of athletic excellence snatched away from him when he was just seven years old. He collapsed at his home in Spokane, Washington, one day in 1944, with poliomyelitis. It was ten years before the Salk polio vaccine was available, and the disease was thought to be contagious. John spent seven months isolated in a hospital ward. The only contact he had with his family was when a hospital attendant would roll his bed over to the window so he could look out and wave to them. It was a torturous time in the life of a young boy.

Polio was a setback for John McGwire, not a defeat. He grew into a strong, 225-pound athlete, who became a top bicyclist and an outstanding golfer who, at one time, had an eight handicap. His stepfather, Tom Lynch, was a former professional boxer, and he taught John the fundamentals of the sport. John subsequently boxed in college. According to some reports, he could chuck a football some 70 yards, and was a first-rate softball hitter.

John attended the University of Washington in Seattle, where he studied predentistry and met his future wife. Ginger was a nurse for two university doctors.

John and Ginger McGwire settled in Claremont, a small community of about 35,000 people, 35 miles east of Los Angeles. John opened a dental office in Claremont, while Ginger became a homemaker, mother, and community volunteer. She, like many women of her generation, was the backbone of the family, inspiring, healing, disciplining, instructing,

133

or just listening, as the situation warranted. She also utilized her nursing skills working as a visiting nurse for hospice in Claremont and caring for her dying mother.

Ginger, like her husband, was a sports enthusiast. She won several swimming medals in high school in Seattle and also played basketball and volleyball. Her other athletic activities included skiing, golfing, and tennis.

Mark David McGwire was born in Pomona, California, on October 1, 1963. He was the second of five McGwire boys. The oldest boy, Mike, played soccer and golf at Claremont High School, and was an Eagle Scout.

Bobby played soccer and golf at Damien High School in La Verne, and starred for the Citrus Community College golf team in Glendora.

Dan, who was born in 1978, the biggest of the McGwires at 6'8", and 243 pounds, was the football star in the family. As a quarterback, he led Damien High School to a 36–3–1 record in his four years there, tossing 65 touchdown passes. He was offered a football scholarship at the University of Iowa, but chose to stay closer to home, attending San Diego State. He was the #1 draft pick of the Seattle Sea Hawks in 1991, but never achieved stardom in the National Football League. He retired in 1995 after spending three frustrating years with Seattle and another with the Miami Dolphins.

J.J. was the baby of the brood and, according to his mother, the most talented athlete in the family. In high school, he was an outstanding pitcher, a star basketball player, and an aggressive linebacker. Sadly, J.J., like his father, had his athletic career taken away from him. Playing a game of war with his buddies when he was 15 years old, J.J. took a BB in the right eye, blinding him. After trying unsuccessfully to continue his baseball and basketball careers, he switched to weight lifting and bodybuilding in college. Years later, he would move in with Mark as his personal trainer.

Mark was a big, pudgy kid when he was 8–12 years old. He had thick glasses, red hair, and freckles. Although his size made him look threatening, he was actually a gentle, shy boy who wanted everyone to like him. Since the five McGwire boys lived on a cul-de-sac, all the neighborhood kids hung out at their house, rapping and watching TV inside, and playing games like tennis baseball and touch football in the street. Mark, whose size and flaming red locks brought to mind the giant redwoods of Northern California, was called "Tree," a nickname he carried through La Puerta Middle School.

The future home run king played soccer as a kid but switched to baseball when he was eight years old. As reported in "The Mac Attack," John refused to let him play Little League ball at the time, saying, "I'd heard too much about arguing, meddling parents and bad coaches. I didn't want anybody to screw up my son. When I told him he couldn't play, he cried and cried and cried."

Mark played baseball in a less structured youth league in Claremont for two years, with his father as his coach. Since he was bigger than the other kids, he was the pitcher. And over the years, he developed into an outstanding pitcher, with big league speed and excellent control. According to the University of Southern California (USC) baseball coach Rod Dedeaux, Mark McGwire had a live arm that could have carried him to a major league career.

About the time he started playing baseball, John and Ginger McGwire noticed that eight-year-old Mark squinted a lot. He always sat close to the screen when he watched television. He had difficulty reading street signs. And one day, when his father sent him out to play shortstop, he complained that the ball looked fuzzy. Mark was quickly whisked off to an optometrist, who diagnosed his problem as nearsightedness, a condition that would leave his vision at 20/500 by the time he reached the major leagues. The freckle-faced youngster wore thick glasses for five years until contact lenses became popular.

In 1974, his father finally gave him permission to play in the Claremont Little League. In his first official at bat with the Claremont Athletics, the big right-handed basher hit the ball over the 175-foot chicken wire fence in right field, for a home run. His grandmother was there to see the historic blast, but his parents missed it. They were on a cruise. Mark went on to hit 13 home runs in the Claremont Little League, a single season record that stood for 20 years. Although he was a long ball threat, he considered himself to be, first and foremost, a pitcher. Standing almost 6' tall, he was an intimidating presence on the mound. He never lost a game he pitched in Little League, according to his father. Mark was primarily a pitcher for the next ten years, until he was finally converted into a slugging first baseman in his junior year in college.

When he wasn't playing baseball, Mark was watching it on television, and dreaming of the day he could play in the big leagues. He was lying on the living room floor spellbound when Hank Aaron blasted his 715th home run off L.A.'s Al Downing in Atlanta on April 8, 1974. His mother claimed she could never get him to do his chores as long as there was a game on.

Mark McGwire started high school at Claremont High in 1977 but transferred to Damien, a Catholic high school in nearby La Verne, midway through his freshman year, because he thought he had a better chance to play varsity baseball at the smaller school. He was mistaken. He played junior varsity baseball at Damien until his junior year.

In his sophomore year, he pulled a chest muscle and couldn't swing a bat properly, so he switched over to the golf team. McGwire had learned the game from his father when he was five years old, and he could hit the ball a mile. He also had a four handicap. The baby-faced slugger had one memorable golf tournament at Damien in 1979. He shot a 72 to tie for the tournament lead, then won the playoff on the fifth extra hole.

He was back playing baseball as a junior and starred on the Damien team for two years. As a senior, he won five games against three losses, with a 1.90 earned run average. He also banged out five homers and batted .359. During the winter, he played center on the basketball team. Now a full 6'5" tall, he was a force to be reckoned with on the hardwood. Unfortunately, he never reached his potential because he wasn't a good jumper.

He was drafted by the Montreal Expos out of high school as a pitcher, and was offered an $8,500 signing bonus. He was also recruited by several colleges, including Arizona State and USC. He was offered a full baseball scholarship at USC, which he figured was worth about $50,000. He accepted the scholarship.

During the summer months in Claremont, Mark McGwire played on the Claremont American Legion team. Between his junior and senior years at Damien, in a tournament in Laramie, Wyoming, Mark tossed a no-hitter in the championship game. The next summer, he was struck down with both appendicitis and mononucleosis, sidelining him for six weeks. When he recovered, he was in no condition to pitch, so he played first base. He gave an early indication of his offensive capabilities by slugging the ball at a .415 clip, with 14 home runs and 53 runs batted in.

Claremont went all the way to the California State Championship finals where they lost to Santa Maria.

Mark was already known for his titanic home runs, both in high school and on the American Legion team. Tom Carroll, Mark's high school coach, remembered several legendary blasts that topped the 400' mark. The gentle giant continued to hit tape measure jobs at college and with the pre–Olympic and Olympic teams.

Mark McGwire entered the University of Southern California at Los Angeles in the fall of 1981. His primary interest in college was to play baseball and to prepare himself for a professional career. He majored in Public Administration because he thought he might like to be a police officer if he didn't make it in baseball. Mark was an average student, graduating from Damien with a B average, and carrying a C average at USC.

In the spring of 1982, at a pre-season baseball breakfast, Mark met a striking brunette. Her name was Kathy Hughes, and she was one of the team's bat girls. Over the next few months, the big redhead and the beautiful bat girl became an item. Less than four years later, they would be married.

During Mark's freshman year at USC, he got into 29 games for the Trojans, most of them as a pitcher. The big right-hander compiled a 4–4 record, with a 3.04 ERA. He struck out 31 batters in 47 innings. At the plate, he hit only .200 but showed some power with three home runs in 75 at bats.

Mark's biggest asset throughout his career was his dedicated work ethic. He had the talent to become a major league player, and he had the discipline to work hard to perfect that talent.

One of the USC coaches, Ron Vaughn, saw tremendous potential in the big, 6'5" behemoth's bat, so he convinced the youngster to play baseball in Alaska during the summer. Mark joined the Anchorage Glacier Pilots as a first baseman but almost quit before the season started. It was his first long-distance separation from his parents and from Kathy, and he was homesick. Fortunately, Vaughn spoke to Mark's father on the phone, and John convinced his son to stick it out. At Anchorage, under the tutelage of Vaughn and Pilots manager Jim Dietz, McGwire became a slugging first baseman. He led the league in batting with a .403 average, and chipped in with 13 homers and 53 runs batted in. The Glacier

Pilots went to the National Baseball Congress tournament in Wichita, Kansas, and took home the second-place trophy. McGwire said the thing that helped him most in Anchorage was that Dietz let him play through his problems. "He let me work my way out of any slumps. He also made a few adjustments in my swing which gave me a short, fast stroke."

When he returned to USC for his sophomore year, Mark told coach Rod Dedeaux he wanted to play first base. Dedeaux still wanted him to pitch, but after the Claremont Clubber hit a couple of early-season home runs, the USC coach reconsidered and put him on first base. Mark responded brilliantly, with a tough .319 batting average, 19 home runs and 59 RBIs. His 19 homers broke the USC single-season home run record of 17, held jointly by Kent Hadley and Dave Hostettler. After Mark tied the record, he began to press and went into a slump that lasted seven games. He finally broke his 1–12 skid late one Sunday afternoon, in the second game of a doubleheader at Cal. The Cal pitcher tried to put a first pitch slider past the right-handed slugger, but he threw it right down the middle, and Mark got all of it. He drove it over the left field wall for #18. Mark's achievement can be appreciated more when it is put in perspective. In addition to Hadley and Hostettler, several other major leaguers played baseball at USC. Dave Kingman's best single-season home run output at USC was nine, Fred Lynn's was 14, and Steve Kemp's was ten. Between them the trio of Kemp, Kingman, and Lynn hit 878 major league home runs.

Mark's pitching record for the year was three wins against one loss, with a 2.78 earned run average.

During the summer between his sophomore and junior years, Mark played baseball for the pre–Olympic National Baseball Federation team. The team visited Japan and China, and played against Japan and South Korea in the U.S. They also played in the International Cup Tournament in Belgium and the Pan American Games in Venezuela. McGwire slugged the ball at a .454 clip, with six homers in just 33 at bats. The U.S. team came in second in the Pan Am Games, losing to Cuba in the finals, 8–1. Mark's experience in Venezuela was not a happy one. The sheltered middle-class American teenager couldn't eat the food and couldn't adjust to the primitive living conditions in the South American country, causing him to lose almost 15 pounds.

In his junior year, the big redhead's bat sizzled to the tune of .387, with a whopping 32 homers and 80 runs batted in. The 32 homers broke his own USC record and set a new Pac-10 Conference record. It also led all NCAA schools in 1983. His 54 career home runs set a new USC career home run record. His slugging feats earned him the *Sporting News* College Player of the Year award, as well as a spot on the *Sporting News* College All-America team. His three-year totals at USC included 54 home runs in 503 at bats, a frequency of 59 homers for every 550 at bats.

During the summer, Mark tried out for, and made, the United States Olympic Team, a talented team that included future major leaguers Barry Larkin, Billy Swift, Cory Snyder, and B.J. Surhoff. Prior to the Olympics, the team traveled the country, playing a strenuous schedule. They played 35 games in 33 cities in five weeks. They played in several major league parks, including Shea Stadium and Fenway Park. Once again, Mark's bat was on fire. His .391 batting average included 13 doubles and six home runs in 110 at bats. He didn't fare as well in the Olympics however. He was held to four singles in 21 at bats as the U.S. team won the silver medal. After dumping Taipei 2–1, Italy 16–1, the Dominican Republic 12–0, and South Korea 5–2, they came out on the short end of the game with Japan 6–3, after having defeated Japan six times in seven previous meetings.

After the Olympics, Mark decided to forego his senior year at USC and enter the baseball draft on June 4, 1984. He was selected in the first round, by the Oakland Athletics, and received a $125,000 signing bonus. As soon as the draft was over, he proposed marriage to Kathy Hughes. They were married in December.

Mark was sent to Modesto in the Class A California League. It was wakeup time for the immature teenager, and it almost beat him. The A's had a decent team that year, finishing second to the Redwood Pioneers, with an 83–56 record. The young first baseman didn't contribute much however, as he batted a barely visible .200, with three homers and 11 RBIs in 75 at bats. The next year, back with Modesto, he got off to another horrible start. According to Rick Reilly, Mark was ready to give up. Kathy said Mark would often lie in bed in the middle of the night saying, "I can't hit the baseball anymore. I'm done. I've lost it. I've got to quit."

Mark didn't quit however, and he eventually regained his stroke. He finished the year with a respectable .274 batting average, with 24 dingers and 106 RBIs in just 489 at bats.

From there it was onwards and upwards. In 1986, the big slugger started the season with Huntsville in the AA Southern League, moved up to Tacoma in the AAA Pacific Coast League, and was called up by the Oakland Athletics at the end of the season. He hit .303 with ten homers and 53 RBIs in 195 at bats with Huntsville, and followed that up with a .318 average, 13 homers and another 53 RBIs, in 280 at bats with Tacoma.

It was a hectic year for the newlyweds, but they reveled in it. Mark took care of business at the park, and Kathy ran the house. In addition to paying the bills and keeping house, the young bride also made all the moving arrangements.

Mark McGwire became a major leaguer on August 22, 1986. After going 0–6 in his first two games, Mark broke out with three base hits on the 24th. The first two hits, a single and a double, were off Tommy John, and Oakland beat the Yankees 11–4. The next day he clipped Detroit's Walt Terrell for his first major league home run, a 450-foot bomb over the center field wall. He finished the season with a batting average of just .189, but he impressed manager Tony LaRussa with his power, hitting three homers with nine RBIs in 53 at bats.

The 1987 season catapulted Mark McGwire into the national spotlight, but in some ways it was a year he would rather forget. On the field, it was a thrilling introduction to the big time. Off the field, it was a self-destructive descent into hedonism. His baseball career survived. His marriage didn't. Mark had an outstanding spring in Scottsdale, Arizona, but sputtered coming out of the starting gate. He was hitting only .136 after three weeks, with a single home run, but he clocked #2 on April 21 and took off from there.

After finishing April with just four home runs, the 215-pound slugger clocked 15 in May, one less than Mickey Mantle's major league record for the month. He followed that up with eight more in June and another six through the All-Star break on July 14. His 33 homers at the All-Star break were just four behind Reggie Jackson's record 37 set in 1969.

American League All-Star manager, John McNamara of Boston, selected the big first baseman as one of his reserves. The game was played in Oakland-Alameda County Stadium on the 14th, and McGwire played about half the game, going 0–3 against National League pitching. The Nationals won the game on a two-run triple by Tim Raines in the top of the thirteenth inning.

As the second half of the season got underway, the McGwire watch was focused on the rookie home run records. Al Rosen of the Cleveland Indians held the American League mark with 37 homers in 1950, while Wally Berger of the Boston Braves (1930) and Frank Robinson of the Cincinnati Reds (1956) were tied for the major league lead with 38.

Mark finished July with 37 home runs, then went ten days without another one. He finally smashed #38 against Mike Moore of Seattle on August 11, to break the American League record and tie the major league mark. Three days later, he became the major league's rookie home run champion, hitting #39 against curve ball artist Don Sutton of the California Angels.

The new celebrity status had Mark's head spinning, as newspapermen suddenly descended on his locker after every game to question him about his record breaking home run feats. All the attention overwhelmed the claustrophobic slugger, but he bravely confronted it head on. He also received good advice, from time to time, from Oakland coach Reggie Jackson, who had more than his share of media attention over the years.

Mark was less than successful in dealing with his off-field celebrity. He started accompanying his teammates out on the town after games, and was soon engulfed by adoring fans and by groupies of every age and description. The sheltered youngster from Claremont soon succumbed to the fame, fortune, and revelry. From that point on, Mark's marriage began to dissolve as Kathy could not compete with the excitement of the night club scene. Mark would later say that he and Kathy just got married too young, and that, if he knew then what he learned over the next ten years, the marriage would probably have lasted. In 1987, 23-year-old Mark McGwire was too immature to deal with it.

The Oakland bomber slowed down slightly after setting a new rookie home run record, hitting only two more homers over the last 17 days of August. He finished the month with 40 homers, a tremendous achievement for a raw rookie, and he was not done yet. On September 15, Mark hit two homers against the Texas Rangers, bringing his total to 45. He hit #46 at Kansas City on the 20th, then tied Reggie Jackson's Oakland mark with a dinger against the White Sox four days later. The next day he broke Jackson's record with #48 off Chicago's 6'3" closer, Bobby Thigpen. Number 49 left his bat on the 29th, leaving him just one homer short of the magic 50, with five games remaining on the schedule.

He looked like a cinch to become just the 18th player in major league history to hit 50 or more home runs in one season, but fate decided otherwise. Mark's wife Kathy was pregnant with their first child and was due any day. The two of them had discussed the matter in some detail and had decided that if the pennant didn't depend on it, Mark would leave the team to be with her when she went into labor. Mark received manager Tony LaRussa's permission to do just that.

Mark went homerless in the final two games against Cleveland, then accompanied the team to Chicago for the final three games against the White Sox. The big slugger failed to connect in the first two games of the series, and before the last game of the season was played, Kathy went into labor. Mark jumped the next plane west, and the potential 50-homer season went down the drain. But a bigger reward awaited Mark in Oakland when Kathy gave birth to a son. Matthew was a far greater thrill than 50 home runs.

Mark and Kathy tried to salvage their shaky marriage after the birth of Matthew, without success. They separated for a period of time, tried to get back together again during the 1988 season, then split for good just before the '88 World Series.

The year 1987 had been an exciting year for Mark McGwire on the field. He won the American League home run title and tied with Andre Dawson of the Chicago Cubs for the major league lead. And he was voted American League Rookie of the Year by the Baseball Writers of America.

The Oakland Athletics had finished in third place in 1987, just four games behind the Minnesota Twins. The A's strengthened their club over the winter, picking up slugging outfielders Dave Henderson and Dave Parker, as well as 15-game winner Bob Welch. And they inserted rookie Walt Weiss at shortstop. They already had a great nucleus in pitchers Dave Stewart and Dennis Eckersley, and sluggers Jose Canseco and Carney Lansford.

The 1988 season opened on April 7, with Oakland hosting Seattle. Dave Stewart, the ace of manager Tony LaRussa's staff, handcuffed the Mariners for 8⅓ innings en route to a 4–1 victory. Canseco and Henderson sparked the attack with home runs. Mark McGwire hit his first of the season on the 7th as the A's crushed California 8–2. Jose Canseco hit his second.

Canseco had hit 31 homers in 1987 after banging 33 in his rookie season. He and McGwire had become known as the "Bash Brothers" in 1987 for their habit of bashing forearms with their teammates after hitting a home run. They "bashed" 80 times between them in '87 and would do it another 74 times in '88.

Mark McGwire hit his sixth home run of the year on April 27 as Oakland topped the Toronto Blue Jays, 5–3. Dave Henderson chipped in with his third round tripper. Canseco hit his eighth home run on the 30th to finish the month two ahead of McGwire. Oakland had run up a record of 16–7 through April 30, giving them a four-game bulge over the Chicago White Sox.

Dave Stewart dropped a 4–1 decision to the Baltimore Orioles on May 13, saddling him with his first loss of the season after eight wins. Mark McGwire hit a leadoff home run in the second inning in Baltimore on May 15 to give Tony LaRussa's boys a 1–0 lead. Weiss homered in the fifth and Canseco hit one out with a man on in the eighth as Oakland won 7–4. The A's were streaking, their 10–3 record in May good enough for a seven game lead. By the end of the month, after winning nine of the next 14 games, they had opened up a nine-game lead over the Minnesota Twins.

McGwire's big bat went silent in June as he put only two home runs on the board. Canseco struggled to keep the team afloat, but his eight dingers were not enough to protect their lead. It dwindled to five games over the Twins by month's end.

The attack continued to sputter through July 10 when, mercifully, the All-Star break gave LaRussa's boys time to relax and regroup. One of the few bright spots in early July occurred on the 3rd, when the A's outslugged the Blue Jays 9–8 in 16 innings. Mark McGwire belted his 14th homer of the season in the top of the 16th to win the game. But Jose Canseco was the star of the game with three homers and six runs batted in. The 240 pound Cuban left the yard in the first, sixth, and 12th innings.

The A's put five players on the All-Star squad, including Canseco, McGwire, Lansford, Steinbach, and Eckersley. Terry Steinbach was the hero of the game for the American Leaguers, driving in the winning runs with a home run to right field off Dwight Gooden in the third inning and a sacrifice fly to deep left field in the fourth. The final score was 2–1 with Dennis Eckersley picking up the save.

Mark McGwire and his Oakland teammate, Jose Canseco, were known as "The Bash Brothers" in the late 1980s. (Brace photo)

By July 17, the Oakland lead was down to just three games as they dropped three of four to Toronto, with Luis Polonia hitting the only Oakland home run of the series. Dave Stewart, who was shut out 1–0 by Jimmy Key, was 4–8 after his sizzling 8–0 start.

On July 18, the Oakland Athletics met the Cleveland Indians in Oakland. It was just the tonic the A's needed. They took three of four from Doc Edwards' team, with Canseco homering in game one and McGwire going yard in both games of a doubleheader. Big Mac's two-run shot in the bottom of the first inning of game one was the game winner. In game two, his three-run dinger in the fifth brought his team back from a 6–4 deficit, the A's winning 9–6.

By the end of July, the Oakland lead was back up to 5½ games, and by August 14 it was a healthy 8½ games. From July 18 to August 14, the A's won 20 games against only seven losses while the Twins went 14–12. McGwire hit nine homers in 27 games, and Canseco chipped in with 7.

Oakland maintained their lead for the rest of the season, finishing with a record of 104–58, a full 13 games ahead of Minnesota. Jose Canseco was the big story of the year. He hit his 40th home run of the year on September 18. Then, on the 23rd, he stole two bases to become the first player in major league history to hit 40 home runs and steal 40 bases in the same year.

For the season, Canseco led the league with 42 homers and 124 RBIs, while hitting .307. His "Bash Brother" Mark McGwire batted .260 with 32 homers and 99 runs batted in. Dave Stewart won 21 games while Bob Welch won 17. Dennis Eckersley led the league in saves with 45.

The A's swept the Eastern Division champion Boston Red Sox in four games to advance to the World Series. Their opponents in the Series were the improbable Los Angeles Dodgers. Tommy Lasorda's team won the National League west with a .584 winning percentage. They beat the New York Mets in the Championship Series, four games to three, thanks to brilliant pitching by Orel Hershiser and key home runs by Mike Scioscia and Kirk Gibson.

Oakland was an overwhelming favorite to take the World Series against one of the weakest teams ever to play in the fall classic. But in 1988 L.A. was a team of destiny. Kirk Gibson's dramatic home run in the bottom of the ninth inning off Dennis Eckersley, giving the Dodgers a 5–4 victory in game one, set the tone for the Series. The Dodgers went on to win the World Championship in five games. The A's only bright spot came in game three when Mark McGwire picked out a Jay Howell fastball to his liking and deposited it into the left center field stands with two men out in the bottom of the ninth inning to win the game, 2–1. It was Mark's only hit of the Series as he went one for 17. His Bash Brother, Jose Canseco, was just as ineffective, going one for 19 with five RBIs. Jose's only hit was a grand slam homer in game one.

Mark McGwire's life was in the pits as the 1989 season got underway. His marriage was in a shambles, on its way to the divorce courts, and he was having trouble reconciling his new lifestyle with his personal values. His off-the-field problems carried over onto the field, and his career began to slip away before his eyes.

In 1989, the Oakland Athletics repeated as American League Western Division champions, crushed the Toronto Blue Jays in the A.L. Championship Series four games to one, and whipped the San Francisco Giants in the World Series, in a four-game sweep. But for McGwire it was a subpar year. Shortly after the season opened, McGwire pulled something in his back and went on the disabled list for two weeks. There were numerous distractions from the media and the fans hounding him for autographs, all of which carried over onto the field. His batting average dropped 29 points from 1988 to an embarrassing .231, although he still managed to hit 33 home runs with 95 runs batted in. One of his few pleasant moments during the year occurred on July 5 when he hit his 100th major league home run off Charlie Leibrandt of the Kansas City Royals. His 100 homers came in just 1,400 at bats, the second fastest time in major league history. Ralph Kiner hit 100 homers in 1,351 at bats back in 1948.

The next year was more of the same. The A's took the A.L. west by nine games with a record of 103–59. McGwire hit just .235 for the season but slammed 39 home runs and drove in 108 runs. He became the first player to hit 30 or more home runs in his first four seasons. He also won a Golden Glove Award in appreciation of his defensive play around first base. Unfortunately, Mark had another dismal postseason. He was two for 13 with no home runs in the Championship Series as the A's once again routed the Red Sox four games to none. In the World Series, he hit just .214 with no homers and no RBIs as the A's were stunned by the Cincinnati Reds four games to none.

In 1991, the Oakland A's collapsed, and so did Mark McGwire's world. Oakland dropped to fourth place, 11 games behind the pennant-winning Minnesota Twins, and the big first baseman hit rock bottom at the plate, nudging the ball at a barely visible .201 clip, with just 22 homers and 75 RBIs. McGwire's private life was in complete disarray, and he lost confidence in his ability to hit a baseball. He once remarked, "I must have gotten 100 suggestions, and I listened to 90 of them." He got off the mark slowly when the season opened, and by July 26 he was bottomed out at .187. He didn't hit it off with the A's new batting coach, Rick Burleson, either, which added to his confusion. Things got so bad that he asked manager Tony LaRussa to bench him for the last game of the season, in fear that his average would drop below .200.

Mark McGwire's collapse was more noticeable in his batting average than in his other statistics. From 1986 to 1988, Mark averaged 40 home runs a year, with 107 RBIs, while batting .271. In the three-year period from 1989 to 1991, he still hit 35 homers a year with 102 RBIs, but his batting average plummeted 48 points to .223.

When the season ended, McGwire cleaned out his locker and began the 380-mile drive back to his home near Los Angeles. He spent the five-hour drive analyzing his life, and where it had gone awry. He came to the conclusion that he needed outside help, both physically and mentally. He couldn't do it by himself. When he got back to Long Beach, he contacted a therapist, beginning a relationship that would continue through the decade. The therapy not only dealt with his personal life as a bachelor, but also touched on his relationship with the media and the fans. Mark's brother J.J., a physical trainer, moved in with him and began a program to build up Mark's body. The weight lifting, aerobics, and running, combined with a regimen of nutritional supplements, continued daily through the winter.

By the time spring training began in Scottsdale, Arizona, Mark McGwire was ready to resume his baseball career. He was more focused mentally and better able to deal with the off-field distractions. The Oakland A's bounced back also, capturing the Western Division by six games over Minnesota. The big first baseman, now with 20 pounds of additional muscle at 235, crashed 42 homers, drove in 104 runs, and batted a decent .268. His .385 on base percentage was the highest of his career, and his .585 slugging average was his second highest. He reached another milestone on June 10 when he hit his 200th major league home run off Chris Bosio of the Milwaukee Brewers.

Oakland couldn't maintain its momentum in the postseason, losing the Championship Series to the Toronto Blue Jays four games to two. Mark McGwire's two-run homer in the top of the second inning of game one, got the A's off running, and they won the game 4–3. But after that, it was all downhill. The Jays took the next three, on their way to becoming World Champions. Mark McGwire had a dismal series, finishing with a batting average of .150 on a three for 20 performance.

All in all, it was a good year for the man from Claremont. His mind was back on track, and his bat was as quick as ever. Unfortunately, his body was about to self destruct. The 1993, '94, and '95 seasons were three years Mark McGwire would rather forget. He was on the disabled list a total of six times, including the beginning of the '96 season, from March 31 to April 23. He had three surgeries over that period.

He suffered a severe heel injury on May 14, 1993, which was originally diagnosed as a bruised heel. It turned out to be much more serious—a partial tear of the fascia, the tissue that supports the arch. He was on the disabled list for almost four months, returning to action on September 3. He played only 27 games in 1993 and 47 games in 1994. In addition to the foot problems, he was also sidelined with another back injury in 1995.

When he was able to play, Mark McGwire was a terror at the plate. Although limited to a total of 317 games (out of a possible 583 games) from 1992 to 1995, he pounded the ball at a .273 pace, averaging 54 home runs and driving in 133 runners for every 550 at bats. In 1995, in just 317 at bats, the big slugger ripped 39 homers, an average of 68 homers for every 550 at bats. It was the best single-season average in major league history. Using his new J.J.-built muscular frame, his long-distance bombarding gave him an average distance of 418 feet for every home run. His .685 slugging average was his personal best, and his .441 on-base percentage was the second highest in Oakland history.

McGwire's injuries had some unexpected positive results. They made him a better hitter. He put the time on the bench to good use, studying the pitchers, talking to the coaches and scouts, and sitting behind the plate to analyze each pitcher's delivery. He stopped being a guess hitter and started to develop his mental faculties, concentrating on getting into a "zone" prior to going to the plate. The newly acquired mental aspect of his game was one of the primary reasons he was able to break Roger Maris' home run record in 1998.

Mark McGwire hit .333 in 27 games in 1993, .252 in 47 games in '94, and .274 in 104 games in '95, with 9, 9, and 39 homers respectively. In 1996, he played in 130 games and finally began to realize his full potential. Although the A's, who were now in decline, finished third in a four-team division under first-year manager, Art Howe, the rugged red head, now a Bunyonesque 250 pounds, put on one long-distance show after another for the fans around the league.

After coming off the disabled list on April 23, he started to drive the ball with authority. By the end of May, he was hitting a robust .327, with 11 homers and 27 RBIs. It wasn't enough to help the Oakland team, however. They had settled into last place with a 24–27 record. In June McGwire hit .329 with 14 home runs and 25 runs batted in to win the American League Player of the Month Award. On the 25th of the month, he smashed his 300th major league homer off Omar Olivares of the Detroit Tigers.

Some of McGwire's home runs were titanic blasts, such as the one he hit in Toronto's Skydome in late July. It traveled an estimated 488 feet before landing in row seven of the fifth deck of the left field stands.

On September 14th, in just his 119th game of the year, Mark McGwire blasted a home run off Chad Ogea of the Cleveland Indians for his 50th home run of the year. No one in baseball history had ever before hit 50 home runs in less than 140 games. It was a satisfying year for the big first baseman. He played in 130 games and hit a career high .312 with 52 home runs and 113 RBIs.

The good times continued in 1997, although there were constant trade rumors as the Oakland management restructured the team to go with young players. They had brought Jose Canseco back to team up with the 34-year-old McGwire, in hopes that the "Bash Brothers" could lead a young team into the playoffs. Failing that, they intended to trade McGwire to a contender before the end of the season, since he was on the last year of a contract and would become a free agent after the season ended.

When spring training got underway, the veteran slugger was the center of media attention. There was speculation that Roger Maris'

37-year-old single-season home run record would fall by the wayside, based on the fact that home run production was up 30 percent in '96, over previous years' outputs. The most likely candidates to break the record were McGwire (52 homers in '96), Ken Griffey Jr.(49 homers in '96), Albert Belle (50 homers in '95), and Frank Thomas (40 homers in '96).

When asked about his chances to hit 61, McGwire said it was possible, but that it would take a perfect year with no injuries and no prolonged slumps. He also said it was foolish to speculate about it so early in the season. If he entered September with 50 home runs, then he would have a shot at the record.

When the season opened on April 2, McGwire was ready. He had a double and three RBIs in an opening day 9–7 loss to Cleveland, then smashed a double and a homer and drove in two more runs in a 5–4 win over the Indians. By the end of April, the 6'5" slugger had 11 home runs and 25 RBIs, and was hitting a lusty .322. The A's were in third place in their division, 2½ games behind Seattle, with a 13–13 record.

Mark McGwire banged out another nine homers in May, giving him 19 for the year, but the Athletics won only nine games against 21 losses to fall into the Western Division cellar, a full nine games behind the Seattle Mariners. Art Howe's cohorts had more than their share of problems, particularly on the mound. Like 1996, their pitchers were giving up runs at a record pace. No team in the major leagues had a higher earned run average than the A's 5.49. Their offensive production and their defense was in the middle of the pack, but pitching was almost nonexistent.

McGwire and Canseco tried to keep the team afloat, but it was a losing battle. By the end of June, Oakland had sunk 14 games out of first place after going 12–15 during the month. While Canseco was bogged down with 17 home runs and a .240 batting average, the kid from Claremont was hitting a respectable .279 with 63 runs batted in. His 29 home runs in 83 games still had him in contention for the home run title. Ken Griffey, Jr., and Tino Martinez of the New York Yankees also had 29 homers, making it a three-man race through June 30. No one in the National League was even close.

Mark had one memorable home run on June 24. In a game against the Seattle Mariners, facing fireballer Randy Johnson in the fifth inning, he hit a shot into deep left center field, that landed high up in the upper deck of the Kingdome. It was measured at 538 feet, one of the longest home runs ever measured. Johnson said later that McGwire hit it so far, he ought to get credit for two homers.

As the second half of the season got underway, with Oakland's hopes dashed for another year, the trade rumors regarding Mark McGwire heated up. Since the big first baseman had to approve a trade, and since he preferred playing in Southern California if possible, it was expected he would end up in either Los Angeles or Anaheim. But fate ruled otherwise. The Dodgers and Angels took themselves out of the running, while the St. Louis Cardinals moved to the front of the pack. Since McGwire would be a free agent at the end of the season, able to negotiate with all teams, he decided to approve a trade to St. Louis if it could be made. Cardinal general manager, Walt Jocketty, realizing the risk he was taking, felt he could re-sign McGwire once Mark got to know and appreciate the St. Louis management, the team, the city and, most of all, the fans.

The trade was completed just before the trading deadline for postseason play, on July 31. Mark joined the Cardinals on August 1 in Philadelphia and drew the collar in three trips to the plate as St. Louis fell 4–1. By the time the Cardinals returned to Busch Stadium seven days later, McGwire was mired in a 2–25 slump with no home runs. In his first home game however, before a welcoming committee of 38,300 screaming fans, the big red head slammed a one out homer off Mark Leiter of the Phillies in the bottom of the third inning. The Cards won 6–1, and McGwire was on his way to becoming a St. Louis legend.

Unfortunately, the trade may have inadvertently cost the handsome slugger a new home run record. His 35 home runs as of August 8 had him on a pace to hit 52 for the year. He had been on a record pace only three weeks earlier, but the distractions of the trade rumors, followed by the adjustment to the National League, took its toll. He went through a long drought, going homerless over his last 13 games in Oakland and his first seven games in St. Louis. From July 16 to August 8, he went 71 at bats without going yard.

McGwire was happy to be reunited with his former Oakland manager, Tony LaRussa, who took over the Cardinal reins in 1996. And LaRussa was thrilled to have his slugging first baseman back in harness. His St. Louis team was floundering in third place, their 51–57 record leaving them 7½ games behind the Houston Astros. They had scored two runs or less on 43 occasions in '97. They desperately needed some offensive help.

Maris' heir apparent struggled with the bat his first two weeks in St. Louis. After ten games in which the Cards went 2–8, Big Mac was hitting a paltry .088 with just one homer and one RBI. He gradually settled in over the rest of the season. He hit eight homers over the next 15 games and drove in 17 runs in the process. By the end of the month he had his average up to .211.

McGwire continued to punish the ball down the stretch although he couldn't pull the Cards out of the doldrums. On September 10, in San Francisco, he hit a 446-foot blast into the left field stands against southpaw Shawn Estes. It was his 50th home run of the year, making him the only player (other than Babe Ruth) to hit 50 or more home runs in two successive seasons. In the season finale against the Chicago Cubs, he homered in the bottom of the sixth, and the Cards went on to win 2–1. Still, it was just their 22nd victory with McGwire. They lost 33 times. Over his last 41 games, McGwire hit a tough .293, with 23 homers and 41 runs batted in. In all, his Cardinal totals were .253, 24, 42.

His overall record for 1997, with both Oakland and St. Louis, showed a .274 batting average with 58 home runs and 123 RBIs. The 1997 season showed that Mark McGwire had reached a new level in his baseball career. He was now a world class slugger, capable of competing with any of the mythical giants in baseball history, including the mighty Babe Ruth. His 58 home runs in '97 were the most home runs in a season since Roger Maris pounded out 61 in 1961. Since his injury-plagued seasons of '93–'94, when he was forced to sit on the bench and just observe, he had become a much more dangerous hitter. From 1987 through 1994, he batted .250 and averaged 39 home runs for every 550 times at bat. From 1995 through 1997, Big Mac ripped the ball at a .287 clip and averaged a mind-boggling 67 home runs a year!

According to Rick Reilly in *Sports Illustrated*, Manager Tony LaRussa, when comparing McGwire to his Oakland days, said, "He's better now. He's better conditioned. His swing is quicker. His stroke is much more repeatable. Now, he thinks all the time."

During his two-month stay in St. Louis, Mark McGwire came to love the city and its loyal fans. He also felt comfortable with his teammates and with the Cardinal management. He told his agent, Robert Cohen, that he wanted to stay in St. Louis, and instructed him to negotiate a new contract with the Cardinals. General Manager Walt Jocketty, who had taken considerable flak from the press for obtaining a player who would be a free agent at the end of the season, was light-headed when he was contacted by Cohen. An agreement was reached in short order.

On September 16, Jocketty announced that Mark McGwire had signed a $28.5 million contract to play for the St. Louis Cardinals through the year 2001, with an option for a fourth year. McGwire made a simultaneous announcement that he was establishing a new foundation for sexually and physically abused children and would personally donate $1 million a year to the foundation. He celebrated his new contract by slamming a 517-foot dinger into the left center field stands off Dodger ace Ramon Martinez, in the first inning at Busch Stadium. Twenty-seven thousand Redbird fans cheered their new hero, anticipating the exciting years ahead.

10. The Great Home Run Race of 1998

The 1998 baseball season got underway with unbridled expectations on the part of the baseball community. Fans everywhere were holding their collective breaths, wondering, "Will this be the year Roger Maris' home run record will fall?" The media began speculating about that possibility as far back as 1996 when it was announced that two new teams would be admitted into the major leagues in '98. There were indications as early as 1994 that the single-season home run record was in jeopardy.

During that season, several players made a run at the record, only to be derailed by the heinous player's strike. When the season ended prematurely on August 11, Matt Williams of the San Francisco Giants was on track to tie Maris with 61 homers. Ken Griffey, Jr., would have hit 58, with Frank Thomas at 54, and Albert Belle at 52. Overall major league home run production in 1994 was up more than 23 percent over the previous 30-year average.

In 1995, Albert Belle hit 50 homers in another strike-shortened season of 144 games. The next year, Brady Anderson of the Baltimore Orioles hit 50 homers and Mark McGwire banged out 52. In 1997, it was more of the same. Mark McGwire, the new "Monster of the Midway," crushed 58 homers while Ken Griffey, Jr., hit 56. Albert Belle chipped in with 48.

The overall home run output stayed at the new higher level established in 1994. The average home runs per team from 1994 through 1997, calculated on a base point 154-game schedule, was 162. The average home runs per team from 1967 through 1993 was 120.

It seemed to be just a matter of time before the record would fall.

There were many reasons given for the increased home run production, including:

• In 1994, major league baseballs began to be manufactured in Costa Rica. They had been manufactured in Haiti since 1980. The new "Costa Rican" balls seemed to be livelier.

• In 1993, the major leagues expanded from 26 to 28 teams, with the addition of the Florida Marlins and the Colorado Rockies. In 1998, the Tampa Bay Devil Rays and the Arizona Diamondbacks joined the majors.

Every time a new team is added to a league, it dilutes the quality of the pitching by about 7 percent. In 1998, there were approximately two dozen pitchers in the major leagues who would have pitched in the minors under the 1992 alignment.

• The players of the 1990s were bigger, stronger, and better conditioned. Weight training and dietary supplements added extra muscle to the modern-day sluggers.

As soon as spring training opened, writers and sportscasters descended on Florida and Arizona in record numbers, interviewing Griffey, Belle, Thomas, and McGwire, about the home run record. Sammy Sosa was not considered to be a threat to Maris' record at the time. When McGwire was asked if he thought the record would be broken, he repeated what he had said in 1997, it would take a perfect season to do it. He also reiterated that if he could get 50 homers by September 1, he would have a chance. One reporter asked him if he could hit 70, to which McGwire replied, "If I hit 70, I'll retire."

Mark McGwire was the odds-on favorite to break the record since he had hit over 50 homers in each of the two preceding seasons and had averaged 64 homers for every 550 at bats, over the last three years.

Ken Griffey, Jr., six years McGwire's junior, and the son of former Cincinnati Reds star, Ken Griffey, had unlimited potential. A major leaguer since he was 19 years old, he was now a seasoned nine-year veteran, seemingly ready to move to a new level of proficiency. The 6'3", 205-pound slugger had averaged 50 homers a year for the past two years and was the co-favorite with McGwire to set a new single-season home run record.

Albert Belle, another potential superstar, produced big numbers year after year but was temperamental and a divisive force in the clubhouse.

156

Still, the 6'2", 200-pound right-handed bomber had all the weapons, and at 31 years old, had a few years left to chase the record.

Frank Thomas, the Chicago White Sox "Big Hurt," was another monster in the mold of McGwire. The towering 6'5", 255-pound first baseman was capable of hitting 60 or more homers at any time. And he was the premier batsmith of the group. A lifetime .330 hitter, Thomas averaged only 87 strikeouts a year, while walking 129 times. He walked over 100 times a season in each of his first six full years in the majors, leading the league in walks four times.

McGwire and Griffey both got off the mark quickly during spring training. Mark McGwire batted a healthy .328 in the Grapefruit League with seven home runs in 58 at bats. On the other side of the country, Ken Griffey, Jr., crushed the ball at a .377 clip with four homers in 77 at bats in the Cactus League. While the two big names drew all the media attention, Sammy Sosa in the Chicago Cubs camp at Mesa, Arizona, was quietly hammering the ball to the tune of .424 with nine dingers in just 59 at bats.

The 1998 season opened with a bang on March 31, with the Cards hosting the Los Angeles Dodgers, one of the pre-season favorites to win a division title. In the fifth inning of a scoreless game, Mark McGwire stepped to the plate with the bases loaded. He promptly sent a 1-0 changeup from Ramon Martinez into moon orbit. It finally came down and settled into the left field stands, 364 feet from home plate. The grand slam sparked the Cards to a 6-0 opening day victory.

The next day the Dodgers and Cardinals were locked in 5–5 game in the 12th inning when Mighty Mac stepped to the plate again, this time with two on and two out. He crushed a Frank Lankford serve 368 feet into the left center field stands for the game-winning homer.

When McGwire also homered in games three and four, the newspaper headlines said, "McGwire on a pace to hit 162 home runs." His four home runs tied Willie May's record of homering in the first four games of the season.

Ken Griffey, Jr., kept pace with McGwire on March 31 by homering off Charles Nagy of the Cleveland Indians in the fifth inning, but the Indians prevailed 10–9. The smooth-swinging left hander homered again on April 3rd and April 4th, giving him three homers for the year, one behind McGwire. Sammy Sosa hit his first 1998 home run on April 4, a game-winning homer as Chicago beat Montreal 3–1.

The McGwire blitzkrieg continued unabated through the month of April. Number four was a monstrous 430-foot shot off Don Wengert of San Diego; #5 a 424-foot sizzler to left field off Jeff Suppan of the Arizona Diamondbacks, #6 a mini-homer, 347 feet off Suppan again, #7 a titanic 462-foot blast off Barry Manuel of the Diamondbacks, his third homer of the game, #8 a 410-foot drive to left off Matt Whiteside of the Phillies, #9 a long 440-foot homer off Trey Moore of the Expos in Exposition Park, #10 a 410-foot dinger off Jerry Spradlin of Philadelphia, and #11 a 380-foot chip shot into the left center field stands at Wrigley Field. McGwire finished the month with 11 homers and 36 RBIs in 27 games.

Sammy Sosa hit just six home runs in April, but Griffey was on fire, matching the St. Louis bomber homer for homer. He hit three bombs against the Boston Red Sox, two against Cleveland, one each against Minnesota and Kansas City, and one against Mike Stanton of the Yankees, on April 29. When he stroked two out of the park against David Wells in Yankee Stadium on April 30, it gave him 11 for the year. The Maris watchers were ecstatic, since Roger hit only one in April. McGwire and Griffey were a full 30 days ahead of the Yankee record holder and 23 days ahead of Babe Ruth.

Mark McGwire put on a pyrotechnics display in May that left his closest competitor far in arrears. On May 1, in Chicago, the St. Louis slugger took Rod Beck downtown in the ninth inning with a man on base. The 362-foot homer to left center field brought the Cards to within one run of the Cubs, but Beck settled down to retire Gaetti and preserve a 6–5 victory.

Seven days later, McGwire reached another milestone when he crushed his 400th career homer off Rick Reed of the New York Mets. The 358 foot dinger came in McGwire's 4,726 at bat, 128 fewer at bats than it took Babe Ruth to reach the magic plateau. He is just the 26th player in baseball history to hit 400 homers. No other active player has reached that mark.

McGwire's theatrics through the first 34 games brought increased media pressure. His 13 homers put him nine games ahead of Ruth and 13 games ahead of Maris. The baseball world eagerly awaited each day's TV sports news or daily newspaper to see if their hero had hit another one. Writers, reporters, and cameramen, by the dozen, began to descend on the Cardinals' locker room before and after every game to obtain a

Mark McGwire blossomed into the world's deadliest slugger when he joined the St. Louis Cardinals in 1997.

story for the next edition or TV spot. For McGwire, a naturally shy, claustrophobic individual, the interviews affected him emotionally. They would continue to irritate him until Sammy Sosa came to his rescue and showed him how to enjoy the attention.

The off-field difficulties, fortunately, did not carry over onto the field. Mark McGwire was loose and relaxed once the game started.

On May 12, Big Mac hit a towering blast, 527 feet into the upper deck in left center field, a Busch Stadium record. It came in the fifth inning off Paul Wagner of Milwaukee, and gave the Cards a 4–3 lead in a game they eventually won 6–5 in ten innings. Two days later, he hit #15 against Atlanta, and on the 16th he reached the pinnacle. Batting against Livan Hernandez of the Florida Marlins at home, he guessed right on a pitch and crushed it. The ball traveled on a high arc to straightaway center field, finally coming to rest just below the luxury boxes, 550 feet from home plate. As McGwire said later, "I don't think I can hit a ball any better than that."

As the media attention increased, the reporters zeroed in on every one of McGwire's idiosyncrasies and superstitions. When the big slugger played with Oakland, he and his teammates perfected the forearm bash, the signature of the "Bash Brothers," McGwire and Jose Canseco. In St. Louis, his signature is a feigned punch to the midsection. After each homer, McGwire fakes a punch to the stomach of the man in the on-deck circle, then to any teammates who come out of the dugout to welcome him. They fake a punch to his midsection in return. McGwire is supposed to pull the punch but, according to teammate Brian Jordan, who occasionally bats behind McGwire, the big man sometimes gets too rambunctious and sinks his fist into Jordan's breadbasket, leaving the outfielder gasping for air as he walks to the plate.

Mark McGwire has more than his share of superstitions. Food is a big one. In May, after having a cheese pizza for lunch, the big man hit a home run. From then on, it was cheese pizza for lunch every day, much to the dismay of his teammates who accompanied him to the restaurant. For dinner, it's steak, steak, and more steak—washed down with buckets of iced tea.

When the team plays at home, the big slugger often dines alone—on steak—goes shopping at the mall, or watches "The Learning Channel" on TV. Sometimes he hangs out at his former wife's house with his son Matt and Kathy's new husband Tom Williamson.

At the park, Mark McGwire, who is somewhat of a "neatnik" at home, has a definite routine he goes through every day. He arrives at the clubhouse at the same time, visits the trainer's room, does loosening up exercises, puts his clothes on in the same order, and socializes with his teammates. On the field he signs autographs (mostly for children) and takes batting practice. It never varies from day to day. When the game starts, he has other routines he follows, on deck and at the plate—adjustments to his glove, putting rosin on his bat, stretching, digging in at the plate, and staring into space as he attempts to reach "the zone."

McGwire's punishment of opposing pitchers continued through the month. Eleven more home runs left his bat over the next two weeks, including several tape measure jobs. Two days after he punished Livan Hernandez, the right-handed bomber hit a 478-foot shot off Hernandez' teammate, Jesus Sanchez. He went on to hit nine homers in the next eight days. On the 19th, he hit three titanic homers, totaling 1,362 feet, against the Philadelphia Phillies. The first one was a 440-foot jolt against Tyler Green, the second a mighty blast of 471 feet against Green again, and the third a 451-foot zinger against Wayne Gomes. His third homer, in the eighth inning with a man on, proved to be the game winner for the Cards, 10–8.

McGwire hit a 425-foot bomb against Mark Gardner of the Giants on the 22nd and followed that with a two-homer game the next day. Homer #1 was a 366-foot chip shot off Rich Rodriguez, while #2 was a towering drive of 477 feet into the upper deck in left center field at Busch Stadium. As in his three-homer game four days earlier, the Cards needed both of McGwire's homers to win. His second of the game, with two men on base in the fifth inning, was the eventual game winner, 11–10.

When the sun set on May 23rd, Mark McGwire's 23 homers in 47 games put him on a course to hit 79 home runs for the season. He was 13 games ahead of Ruth and 14 games ahead of Maris. He had opened up a big lead on the other challengers. Ken Griffey, Jr., was stuck at 17 homers, having hit just six in May and three in the last 12 games. Surprisingly, Griffey's teammate, shortstop Alex Rodriguez, was McGwire's closest competitor with 18 home runs. The 22-year-old potential superstar had clocked nine homers in each of the first two months. Albert Belle, the White Sox anti-social left fielder, had nine homers, and Frank

Thomas had seven. Sammy Sosa, also with nine homers, was lurking in the back of the pack but was ready to explode.

When the month ended, the tally sheet showed McGwire with 27 home runs, Rodriguez with 20, Griffey with 19, and Sosa with 13.

On May 25th, Sammy Sosa banged out two homers against the Braves in Atlanta, his 10th and 11th of the year. From there, the Cubs outfielder went on a tear, hitting 24 home runs in the next 33 games, over a period of 37 days. His two shots at Turner Field both topped 400 feet. Two days later, he crushed a 460 footer over the left field fence onto Waveland Avenue against Darrin Winston of the Phillies in another two-homer game. The second dinger, off Wayne Gomes, carried 400 feet into the right field stands.

As June got underway, Sosa trailed Big Mac by 14 home runs, but things were about to get interesting. The happy-go-lucky Dominican bruiser tattooed 17 different pitchers for home runs in June to break the record of 15 home runs in June, held jointly by Babe Ruth, Bob Johnson, and Roger Maris, and to break the record of 18 home runs in a single month, set by Rudy York in August 1937.

Sosa started right in on June 1st with a two-homer game against the Florida Marlins. His first homer was a 430-foot blast against Ryan Dempster, the second a 410 footer against Oscar Henriquez, both to left center field. The Cubs won the game easily, 10–2. The 6', 200-pound slugger homered again on the 3rd, the 5th, the 6th, the 7th, and the 8th, bringing his total to 20 in 62 games, not world class stuff, but getting closer.

After hitting his 21st homer in a 10–8 Cubs win over the Phillies on the 13th, Sammy went on another homer spree two days later. In a 6–5 Chicago victory over Milwaukee, he went yard three times, all against the Brewers' Cal Eldred. A crowd of 37,903 screaming Sosa fanatics cheered as he put the first ball into the right field stands, then chipped the next two to the legion of fans waiting on Waveland Avenue. Sammy himself celebrated each homer with his own special routine. First, after the ball left the bat, he hopped sideways toward first base, then skipped before he started his home run trot. After crossing the plate, he touched his lips with two fingers, then his chest, then threw a kiss skyward as he mouthed the words, "I love you momma." Another kiss was sent to mothers in Chicago as well as the Dominican Republic. And he finished with

Sammy Sosa finally realized his "superstar" potential in 1998. (Brace photo)

a "V" for victory sign to his guardian angel, Harry Caray, who died on February 18. Caray had been a beloved figure in Chicago, as well as the Cubs' play-by-play broadcaster for 16 years. His famous oversized glasses and his raspy seventh-inning stretch rendition of "Take Me Out to the Ballgame," are Cubs legends.

Sammy Sosa trailed Mark McGwire by only seven home runs after his demolition of Eldred. The Cardinal first baseman took Jose Lima of Houston downtown on the 17th, but Sosa kept pace with a shot off Milwaukee's Bronswell Patrick. Another multi-homer game against Philadelphia, his fifth of the season, brought his home run total to 27. The next night the amazing 29-year-old slugger ripped two more homers against the Phils, with 39,761 Cubs fans looking on. The first one was a pitching wedge of 366 feet that barely carried into the left field seats. The second homer, off side-wheeling Toby Borland, came in the sixth inning with two men on base and gave the Cubs a 9–4 victory. It was the longest homer of Sosa's career, a 500-foot rocket that disappeared over the left field wall, sailed over Waveland Avenue, and landed on the roof of a three-story apartment building, scattering 60 guests who were attending a party. It was Sammy's 16th homer of the month, which broke the record for home runs in June—and there were still ten days left in the month.

The 6' strong man hit #30 against Tyler Green of the Phils on June 21, pulling him within three homers of Mark McGwire. Now the race was on in earnest. And as he would do several times over the next three months, Mr. McGwire would answer the challenge. First, he punished Jared Wright of the Cleveland Indians with #34, a 433-foot blazer in Jacobs Field. He followed that up with a gigantic shot of 461 feet. The ball would have left the park completely if it hadn't hit a beam attached to the scoreboard. McGwire's 35th was followed by Sosa's 32nd, hit against the Tigers' Brian Moehler. It was Sammy's 12th homer in 13 games.

The Cardinal slugger hit #36 on the 27th and #37 on the 30th to close out the month of June with ten homers for the month, and a total of 37 for the year. Sosa's last blast on the 30th was his 20th of the month and his 33rd of the year. It established a new record for the most homers in a month, breaking the old record by two. Ken Griffey, Jr., was still in the race with 33 home runs of his own after a big month in which he hit 14 homers. Alex Rodriguez had dropped out of contention after hitting for just seven homers in June. Albert Belle with 17 homers, and Frank Thomas with 14, were never factors in the race.

The media circus finally caught up with Mark McGwire in June. After months of literally living in a goldfish bowl, constantly surrounded by cameramen, reporters, writers, and fans of every size and description, he put his foot down, saying he felt as if he was in a cage. The before-and-after game interviews became a thing of the past. For the rest of the season, on the road, the St. Louis slugger would hold a pre-game interview before the first game of the series. No other interviews would be scheduled. At home he would hold a post-game interview, discussing only the day's game. Other interviews would have to be scheduled in advance.

In the pennant races, the Chicago Cubs were hanging tough in the Central Division race. Their 43–39 record had them in third place, just one game behind Milwaukee for the wild card berth. They were seven games behind the front-running Houston Astros. The Cardinals, on the other hand, were 10½ games out of first and 4½ games out of second, despite McGwire's heroics.

With the home run race turning into a three-man contest, the media vultures began to circle the Chicago clubhouse, looking for the Cubs' gift to major league baseball. They began to corral Sosa before and after every game, similar to the treatment being given McGwire. Unlike the St. Louis strongman however, Sosa never saw a camera he didn't like. He reveled in the media attention and, over the course of the summer, developed a routine that fascinated and entertained the viewing public. His one-liners even captivated the writers. His favorite expressions included, "To tell you the truth," "I'm not gonna lie to you," "Believe me when I tell you," "I love this country," and "You don't wanna know, buddy."

Sammy Sosa, like McGwire, had a few superstitions, which the media began to focus on. Before every game, Sammy carried a cup of coffee into the dugout, then proceeded to bless the area around the bat rack, in three equal pours. Several times during a game, the trainer brought Sammy a cup of water, which Sammy splashed on his face to cool down. When he walked up to the plate, he crossed himself, then gently tapped the catcher on the back of the leg with his bat as a sign of respect.

During the summer of 1998, Sammy Sosa and Mark McGwire brought class and dignity back to major league baseball. After years of watching egocentric ballplayers behaving like clowns after hitting a home run, it was refreshing to see two players act professionally on a baseball field, doing what they were being paid to do, without creating a circus atmosphere.

July was a slow month for all the sluggers as they appeared to be getting their second wind for the stretch run. The All-Star break on July 7 gave them a chance to relax for a few days. Ken Griffey, Jr., was the only challenger to hit any home runs prior to the break. He slugged #34 off Mike Saipe of the Colorado Rockies on the first of the month, then punished Darryl Kile of the same team the next day to close within two of McGwire.

When action resumed on July 9, Griffey went downtown again, this time against Pep Harris of Anaheim. The same day, Sammy Sosa lugged his big black bat to the plate against Jeff Juden of the Milwaukee Brewers and promptly sent a 432-foot dinger into orbit at County Stadium for #34. The Chicago bomber hit another one the next day, a 450-foot laser off Scott Karl of Milwaukee. Big Mac didn't hit his first home run of the month until the 11th when he connected for #38 off Billy Wagner of Houston. He added seven more by the end of July to give him 45 for the year. Home run #41 was a monstrous blast of 511 feet into Busch Stadium's upper deck against Brian Bohanon of the Dodgers on July 17. He homered off Antonio Osuna in the same game, a 425-foot shot to left field. At month's end, Big Mac's 45 home runs put him 12 games ahead of Roger Maris and 27 games ahead of Babe Ruth. Sosa trailed with 42 homers and Griffey with 41.

In the pennant races, the Chicago Cubs held down the second spot in the Central Division with a 61–48 record after a torrid 18–9 run in July. They were just 3½ games behind the Astros. McGwire's Cards were rapidly fading from contention in fourth place 13½ games out of first.

The baseball world was buzzing with anticipation as August got underway. McGwire needed just 17 homers in his last 57 games to break Maris' record. His home run frequency was 69 through July. He only needed to average 48 the rest of the way to break the record. Most fans thought it was a lock.

Mark McGwire's life was no longer his own, either on the field or off. He was rapidly becoming a legend in his own time because of his outlandish destruction of official National League baseballs. Batting practice was a spectacle in itself. Fans pushed their way into the ball-park two hours before game time just to see the 6'5" behemoth tee off against batting practice pitcher, Dave McKay, who estimated he had thrown the big redhead about 8,000 B.P. home runs. When the Cardinals arrived in Chicago for a three-game series with the Cubs beginning on August 7, hundreds of fans congregated on Waveland Avenue behind the left field fence in hopes of catching a Mark McGwire blast. And it wasn't just the fans who were mesmerized by the exhibition. Players from both teams stationed themselves around the batting cage to watch in awe as one ball after another sailed out of the park. The batting practice show actually went back to spring training in Jupiter, Florida, where crowds of people stood transfixed behind the batting cage in Roger Dean Stadium, watching one moon-shot after another disappear over the left field fence and explode against the building behind it.

One of the turning points of the season took place on August 18 in Chicago when the Cubs hosted the Cardinals. Mark McGwire had hit only two homers during the first 17 days of the month and was bogged down at 47 homers. Sammy Sosa was on a roll. When he homered off the Astro's Sean Bergman on the 16th, a 360-foot shot to right field, it was his 47th of the year, putting him in a tie with Big Mac.

As the happy-go-lucky Dominican bomber stepped onto the field before the game, he spied McGwire stretching in front of the dugout. He walked over, grabbed Mark's hand, pulled him up, and gave him a giant bear hug. It was his way of letting the Cardinal slugger know that the home run chase and all the media attention was an experience to be enjoyed, not a chore to be dreaded. Whether that meeting changed Mark McGwire's attitude is not known. What is known is that Big Mac seemed to loosen up after the meeting with Sosa and appeared to enjoy the rest of the season. He captivated the fans with his calm demeanor and his class down the stretch.

Chicago took the opener of the series 4–1, with both sluggers taking the collar. The next night, before a wild Wrigley Field gathering of 39,689, Sosa was the first to act. He hit into the left field stands with a man on in the fifth inning to give the Cubs a 6–2 lead. It was his 48th dinger of the season and gave him the home run lead—a lead that lasted less than one hour. Mark McGwire's 48th, a 430-foot shot onto Waveland Avenue in the top of the eighth, tied the game at 6–6, and his 49th in the tenth won it for Tony La Russa's club, 10–8. The rest of the season would be nip and tuck as the two adversaries jockeyed for position. Twice over the final six weeks, Sammy Sosa would grab the lead, only to see McGwire regain it within an hour. Three times they would be tied for the lead in the most exciting home run race in baseball history.

The Chicago management, after watching the media circus in the Cubs locker room with 50 reporters hounding Sosa at his locker while the rest of the team was trying to relax, decided the interviews were a disruption to the team at a time when they were fighting for a playoff spot. They subsequently moved the interviews to an old storage room down the hall. Sosa, seated behind a table, answered questions from the floor for about 20 minutes after every game.

The charismatic Chicago right fielder captivated the fans with his boyish demeanor. When asked whether he expected to finish ahead of McGwire in the home run race, he replied, "Mark's the Man. I'm just a little boy." When he was asked how he was handling the pressure, he said, "What pressure? Pressure is shining shoes when you're seven years old, trying to earn enough money to put food on the table."

On August 22, tabloid journalism reared its ugly head right on schedule, clouding the home run chase. Steve Wilstein, an Associated Press reporter, wrote an article stating that McGwire was taking anrostenedione, a testosterone-producing substance that is banned by the NFL, NCAA, and the Olympics but is legal in the major leagues. Dozens of big league players, in addition to Mark McGwire, take andro and similar supplements as a regular part of their conditioning regimen.

The furor over McGwire's taking a legal substance seemed to be a continuation of the media's "build 'em up, tear 'em down" philosophy of sensationalism, designed to sell more newspapers and magazines. As Mark said, the story resulted from someone "snooping in his locker."

According to McGwire, he started taking androstendione less than two years ago. That being the case, two facts are indisputable. In 1996, "before andro," Mark McGwire averaged 418 feet for each of his 52 home runs. His 1998 average was 423 feet. Also, in 1995 and '96, again "before andro," McGwire averaged 68 home runs for every 550 at bats. His '97-'98 average was 67 home runs.

Obviously, Big Mac didn't need andro to break the record.

Sammy Sosa injected a little humor into the controversy, noting that he took Flinstone chewable vitamins on a routine basis. He said Barney and Fred gave him all the energy he needed.

The home run race went on in spite of the media's attempts to disrupt it. McGwire had hit homers 50 and 51 on August 20 against the Mets in New York before the androstendione expose. He hit another on the 22nd, a 477-foot rocket to right field at Three Rivers Stadium off Francisco Cordova. It was one of only three home runs hit to right field by McGwire during the entire season. The big redhead hit three more homers between August 23 and the end of the month. Number 54 was a 509-foot shot to dead center field while #55 traveled 501 feet in the same direction.

Sammy Sosa kept pace. He homered on the 21st, then took two downtown on the 23rd, his 50th and 51st of the year. Both were hit off Jose Lima of the Houston Astros at Wrigley Field. The first one was a 440 footer onto Waveland Avenue in the fifth inning. The second one landed in the left field bleachers, 380 feet from home plate. Three days later, Sosa homered against the Reds into the upper deck in Cinergy Field. That was followed by #53 against John Thomson of the Colorado Rockies in Coors Field on the 28th.

The slugging spray hitter from the North Side crushed a 482-foot bomb off Darryl Kyle of the Rockies, high up in the left center field stands, on the 30th, and finished out the month with a 364-foot pitching wedge at Wrigley. It was Sosa's 55th home run of the season, once again tying him with Mark McGwire. When Sammy's mother Lucrecia was interviewed by A.P. sports writer, R.B. Fallstrom, about her son's home run achievements, she said, "What I know is that my son will get as many home runs as God wants, not one more or one less."

The month's totals revealed what everyone already knew. The Maris chase was now a two-man race. Ken Griffey, Jr., the remaining challenger, with only six homers in August, was bogged down at 47 with little chance of catching the leaders. The individual stats showed Sammy Sosa at 55 homers, 136 RBIs and a .313 batting average. He had his Cubs three games in front of the New York Mets for the wild card spot in the playoffs. The Cardinals were a distant 21½ games out of first and were just counting the days until they could go fishing. All except McGwire, that is. Big Mac was stinging the ball at a .293 clip with 55 homers and 119 runs batted in.

Sammy Sosa continued to light up the post-game interviews with lines like, "Every day is a holiday for me. What a country." and "I won't lie to you man. I love this country."

Mark McGwire took off like a man trying to catch a train, in September. He ripped two home runs on the first, no's 56 & 57. He tomahawked a fastball by Livan Hernandez of the Marlins in the seventh inning and sent it whistling into the center field stands in Pro Player Stadium, 450 feet from home plate. Two innings later, he hit a longer one, sending a Donn Pall serve in the same direction—only 22 feet farther. The Cards won going away, 7–1.

The next day, in the Friendly Confines of Wrigley Field, Sosa hit his 56th, a 370-foot shot to right center field. The crowds attending the games now, realizing they were on the verge of witnessing history, stood and cheered after each home run until Sosa came out of the dugout for a curtain call. Fans attending the Cardinal games did the same thing to McGwire.

In spite of his heroics, Sammy Sosa lost ground in the home run race. Big Mac crushed no's 58 & 59 in a 14–4 rout of Florida. His first homer was a mammoth 497-foot clout off Brian Edmondson in the seventh inning, giving St. Louis a comfortable 9–0 lead. He finished his day's work in the eighth, smashing a 458-foot blast to left center field off Rob Stanifer.

In spite of all the pressures associated with his pursuit of Roger Maris, Mark McGwire never forgot about his crusade to help abused children. On September 3, Ali Dickson, a good friend of Mark's arrived in St. Louis on business. Ali, who was working for a treatment center for abused children in California, had originally introduced Mark to the traumatic problems faced by some of our young people. Mark immediately took up the baton and formed the Mark McGwire Foundation for Children (MMF), a private, charitable foundation to support organizations that serve children victimized by child abuse. During an off day on the third, Mark spent ten hours with Ali, filming a public service announcement, pleading with children or other knowledgeable people to bring child abuse problems to the attention of the authorities.

When the games resumed on the fourth, the bombardment continued.

Sosa hit his fifth homer in six games, a 387 footer in Three Rivers Stadiumin the first inning, sparking the Cubs to a 5–2 victory. It was the Dominican dandy's 57th, breaking Hack Wilson's Chicago Cubs record of 56 home runs. It also gave the Cubs a three-game bulge over the New York Mets in the wild card race.

September 5th however, belonged to Mark McGwire. In the first inning, with a man on base, the 6'5" pull hitter jumped on a low fast ball from southpaw Dennis Reyes of Cincinnati and drove it into the left field seats, 381 feet from home plate. Busch Stadium exploded in a colorful fireworks display that brightened the evening sky, and an exuberant crowd of 47,994 shook the park to its rafters until the shy Californian came out of the dugout to acknowledge their cheers. Mark joined Babe Ruth and Roger Maris as the only players in the baseball history to hit 60 or more home runs in a single season. And Mark had hit 60 in just 142 games, putting him a stunning 12 games ahead of Ruth and 18 games ahead of Maris.

Mark McGwire drew the collar the next day, then dined with his parents in the evening. His father John was celebrating his 61st birthday the following day, and he said to Mark, "If I can do 61, so can you."

Monday, September 7, was Labor Day, and the festive holiday atmosphere carried over into the 32-year-old stadium along Spruce Street and Stadium Plaza, where Tony La Russa's troops were hosting Jim Riggleman's Chicago Cubs. Mark McGwire's parents were in the stands. So were Roger Maris' children, Mark's former wife Kathy and her husband Tom Williamson, and Baseball Commissioner Bud Selig. Maris' wife Pat was unable to attend the game. She watched from her hotel room after being hospitalized with an irregular heartbeat. Mark's ten-year-old son was the Cardinal batboy, as he had been a number of times since May. Young Matt had seen his father hit several of his tape measure home runs during the season, including no.'s 50, 55, 56, and 57, and he got to keep #50. Now he was about to witness his father's most historic achievement.

McGwire and Sosa held a widely televised, pre-game press conference before 700 media members two hours before the game. It was a light-hearted session with both players thoroughly enjoying themselves. Sammy, as usual, was absolutely giddy, at one point exclaiming in a mock Spanish accent imitating a television comedian, "Baseball has been berry,

berry good to me." When asked about the home run race, he replied smiling, "Mark is The Man in United States. I am The Man in Dominican Republic." He laughed. Mark McGwire applauded, then replied, "God bless America."

The game started on a more serious note, with the Cubs still battling for a playoff berth (they held a slim, one-game lead over the Mets as play started). When McGwire stepped to the plate in the first inning, the clock said 1:21 P.M. With a count of 1–1, the 6'5" slugger drilled a Mike Morgan fast ball 430 feet into the left field stands, for home run #61, tying him with Roger Maris for the most home runs in major league history. A sellout crowd of 50,530 red-shirted Cardinal fans leaped to their feet, screaming and hollering. Big Mac received high fives from Chicago first baseman Mark Grace and third baseman and former teammate Gary Gaetti. Sammy Sosa in right field thrilled for his buddy, pumped his fist in the air, then clapped quietly into his glove. Heading home, the big redhead pointed to the sky in tribute to Roger Maris. After he crossed home plate, he exchanged punches with Ray Lankford, then grabbed his son in a big bear hug and lifted him high in the air, in celebration. He also pointed to his father in the stands, mouthing the words "Happy birthday, Dad," then saluted the Maris family in the stands, tapping his heart, pointing his finger to the sky and blowing the Maris clan a kiss. It was a tender moment at the climax of a most amazing quest. Later in the game, Sammy Sosa, after reaching first base on a single, gave Mark a hug, and said, "Congratulations. But don't get too far ahead. Wait for me."

The Cardinals won the game 3–2, temporarily stalling the Cubs' playoff chase.

If Monday was exciting, Tuesday was absolutely crazy. Busch Stadium welcomed 43,688 Cardinal and Cubs fans to continue the McGwire-Sosa watch. The score stood, Mark 61—Sammy 58, with much more excitement to come. Before the game, McGwire rubbed Roger Maris' 61st home run bat for good luck. When the game started, the Cubs pushed across two runs in the top of the first. Mark grounded out meekly on a 3–0 pitch in the bottom of the inning, as St. Louis put nothing but goose-eggs on the scoreboard through the first three innings. In the fourth, McGwire sat in the dugout caressing his bat, his eyes closed in meditation as he tried to visualize his next at bat. It was the same ritual he had practiced all year, to put himself mentally "in a zone." With two men out and the bases empty, the St. Louis strongman stepped to the plate to face Steve Trachsel, Chicago's 14-game winner. He lashed out at Trachsel's first pitch and hit a low line drive down the left field line. As 44,000 pairs of eyes stared in wonder, the ball barely cleared the left field wall at the 341 foot mark. It was McGwire's shortest home run of the year but his most important. It was #62, setting him apart from every other baseball player who ever played the game. And he accomplished it in 145 games, eliminating the need for an asterisk of any kind. He was now in uncharted territory, and he still had 17 games left to add to his total.

Mark McGwire was in a daze as he began his home run trot. He missed first base and had to be sent back to touch it by first base coach Dave McKay. He got high fives from all the Chicago infielders, plus a big hug from catcher Scott Servais. His teammates mobbed him at home plate as the entire ballpark went ballistic. He gave his favorite batboy another sky high bear hug, then climbed into the stands to hug all the Maris children — Susan Ann, Roger Jr., Kevin, Randy, Richard, and Sandra. Pat Maris missed the historic event, as she was back in the hospital with a case of nerves. After about 11 minutes, Mark McGwire addressed the fans over the PA system, thanking everyone from the Maris family, to the Cubs, his family, and the Cardinals.

Sammy rushed in to give McGwire a big hug. Big Mac picked the 200-pound outfielder off the ground as if he were a little kid and squeezed him tightly. Sosa pounded McGwire on the back and ruffled his hair. After the hug they high-fived each other and exchanged McGwire's famous solar plexus punch.

McGwire's homer cut the Cubs lead to 2–1. The Redbirds put a big five-spot on the board in the sixth, three runs coming on Ray Lankford's 27th homer of the year. They went on to defeat Chicago again, 6–3, dropping the Cubs into a tie with New York and San Francisco for the National League wild card berth.

Once all the furor over the historic event had settled down, the season continued. Mark McGwire relaxed after his unique achievement. Over the next five games, he went 1–14 with six strikeouts. In the meantime, Sammy Sosa was making hay, banging out home run number 59 on the 11th (a 464 footer), and number 60 on the 12th (a 430 footer), against the Milwaukee Brewers. On September 13, the Brewers closed out their season series with the Cubs, in Wrigley Field. The first two games were both slugfests, the Brewers winning 13–11 on Friday and the Cubs taking the Saturday game 15–12. Between them, they had pounded out 68 hits, including 13 home runs. Sunday was no different. Eight more balls left the Friendly Confines before the sun went down. The Brewers drew first blood with single runs in the first and the third for a 2–0 lead. Jim Riggleman's bombers drove Milwaukee starter Brad Woodall to cover under a six-run barrage in the third. A Sammy Sosa home run, a mighty 480-foot blast onto Waveland Avenue, with a man on, brought the score to 8–3, but the Brew Crew was not ready to call it a day. They scored seven runs over the next four innings to take a 10–8 lead into the bottom of the ninth. With one out, Sosa stepped to the plate to face righthander Eric Plunk. The 220-pound fireballer tried to blow a fastball past the Cub slugger, but Sosa was ready for it, and he crushed it, sending it on a high arc toward left field. It landed on Waveland Avenue, 480 feet from home plate, near the spot the first ball landed.

It was #62 and put Sammy Sosa in the history books, alongside Mark McGwire, as the only two players in baseball history to hit as many as 62 home runs in one season. It was a traumatic moment for the former shoe-shine boy from the Dominican Republic as the ecstatic Chicago fans called him out of the dugout for three curtain calls. He said later, according to AP, "I have to say what I did was for the people of Chicago, for America, for my mother, for my wife, my kids, and the people I have around me. My team.... I don't usually cry, but I cry inside. I was blowing kisses to my mother. I was crying a little bit." When Mark McGwire heard the news, he said, "It's awesome, outstanding."

Sammy's fans back home got to see the historic home runs on TV, as Television Dominicana began broadcasting the Cubs games on September 10th. When number 62 left the yard, the entire island nation exploded in celebration. Parties were underway in Santo Domingo. In San Pedro de Macoris, it seemed as if the whole town spilled out into the streets to dance and party. Kids raced through the street screaming sesenta y dos (62). The 30-30 Plaza was sheer bedlam. The crowd watching the game on TV outside the Juancito Sports Shop toasted their hero again and again. When one man was asked how popular Sammy Sosa was in the Dominican Republic, he said, "I think he's leading the Pope right now."

Chicago eventually tied the game in the bottom of the ninth, then won it in the tenth on a Mark Grace home run. The final score was 11–10.

Two days later McGwire recaptured the lead with a 385-foot dinger to left field off Pittsburgh's Jason Christiansen at Three Rivers Stadium. Sosa tied it again in a 6–3 Cubbies victory when he took the Padres' Brian Boehringer down town, in San Diego's Qualcomm Stadium. Mark McGwire answered. He hit number 64 on the 18th and number 65 on the 20th, giving him a two-homer lead over his Chicago adversary, with just five games left in the season.

On the same day in Wrigley Field, 40,117 Chicago fans honored their hero with Sammy Sosa Day. The invited guests included Sammy's family, his business advisor and surrogate father, Bill Chase, Baseball Commissioner Bud Selig, Dominican Republic President Leonel Fernandez, Hall-of-Fame pitcher Juan Marichal, and Chicago General Manager Ed Lynch. Sosa received numerous gifts including a Chrysler Prowler and a painting of himself. After the speeches were completed, Sammy made a tour of the big park, paying special attention to his "bleacher bums" in right field.

Sammy and Sonia Sosa entertained over a dozen guests in their luxury apartment in downtown Chicago overlooking Lake Michigan during the last week of the season. The gathering on the 55th floor above exclusive Lakeshore Drive included Sammy's mother, his four brothers, two sisters, two step-brothers, and an aunt.

While McGwire was putting another ball in orbit, and Sosa was being feted in Chicago, baseball history of another kind was made in Baltimore, Maryland. Cal Ripken, Jr., benched himself, ending a consecutive-games-played streak of 2,632, 502 more than Lou Gehrig. The streak began on May 30, 1982, and lasted more than 16 years. Ryan Minor, who was eight years old when the streak began, when told he would start in place of Ripken at third base, asked, "Does he know?" As soon as the Orioles took the field without Cal Ripken, the New York Yankee players came to the top of the dugout steps to applaud a record that might last forever. Certainly it will last at least another 14 years because Albert Belle has the next longest active streak at 327 games. Ripken came out of the dugout, waved to the crowd, took a bow, then retreated back into the darkness.

Cincinnati swept the three-game weekend series against the Cubs, including the Sunday Sammy Sosa Day game, putting a damper on the day's festivities. The Dominican slugger went 0–13 over the weekend and would see his slump reach 0–21 before he broke out of it. But, like the gentleman he is, he graciously attended every press conference and answered every embarrassing question thrown at him by the aggressive media representatives. All he could say regarding his streak was, "When this happens to me, I know I'm doing something wrong. I just try to relax when I hit. I've got to keep swinging."

On September 23, Sammy Sosa broke out of his slump and closed the gap again, tying Mark McGwire at 65 home runs apiece. Playing in Milwaukee, the 200-pound spray hitter cracked a fifth-inning homer off Rafael Roque, a 344-foot shot down the right field line in County Stadium. In the next inning, he crushed a 410-foot rocket into the center field stands, giving the Cubs a commanding 7–0 lead at that point. Sosa's 65th was his 11th multi-homer game of the season, breaking Hank Greenberg's mark of ten, set in 1938.

On Friday, September 25th, the Chicago Cubs visited the Houston Astros in a night game. In the fourth inning, leading off against countryman Jose Lima, Sammy Sosa hit a titanic blast, 462 feet into the left field seats at the Astrodome. It was his 66th home run of the year, and it gave him the lead over Mark McGwire for just the second time during the season. The first lead, on August 19, lasted 58 minutes. This one disappeared in just 45 minutes as Mark McGwire, playing at home against the Montreal Expos, hit a 375-foot dinger off Shayne Bennett in the fifth inning, sparking the Cardinals to a 6–5 win. The Cubs were beaten 6–2, leaving them in a flat-footed tie with San Francisco and New York for the wild card spot.

In the most memorable home run chase in major league baseball history, the two combatants were deadlocked at an incomprehensible 66 home runs apiece, with just two games remaining in the season.

But, just as suddenly as the race began, it was over. The Chicago Cubs split their two-game set with the Houston Astros to finish the season tied with the San Francisco Giants. Sosa went 4–9 in the series, all singles. The Cubs met the Giants in a one-game playoff for the National League wild card berth in the Windy City on the Monday after the regular season ended. Chicago's finest took the measure of Dusty Baker's troops, 5–3. Sammy Sosa had two hits in four at bats, and scored two big runs. In the Division Series, the Atlanta Braves swept Jim Riggleman's crew three straight, ending Sammy Sosa's season.

In addition to the pressure of the pennant race and the home run chase, the last week of the season was painfully distracting for the man from the Dominican Republic. On Tuesday the 22nd, a devastating hurricane crashed into his country, killing over 500 people and leaving more then 100,000 homeless. It was a tragedy of major proportions, and it left Sosa emotionally drained. He was thankful that his family was with him in Chicago at the time, and not back home, where large sections of San Pedro de Macoris were leveled.

On Saturday, Sosa, along with Chicago outfielder Henry Rodriguez and shortstop Manny Alexander, visited the Dominican Consulate in Houston to help load trucks with emergency medical supplies and food. Sammy's relief efforts continued after the season ended. His Sammy Sosa Foundation collected huge sums of money to be used to help the hurricane victims in his country. He also made large personal contributions to the cause.

Meanwhile, in St. Louis over the final weekend of the season, the redheaded bomber from California absolutely destroyed Montreal manager Felipe Alou's pitching staff. Counting his last two at bats on Friday, Mark McGwire smashed an unbelievable five home runs in his last 11 at bats. On Saturday, September 26, with 48,212 wild-eyed Cardinal fans looking on, he jumped on a first pitch fast ball from Dustin Hermanson and sent it on a line into the left field seats. The 403-foot homer put McGwire in the driver's seat again, 67 to 66. Just two innings later, he crushed a 1–1 serve from Kirk Bullinger and put it into the center field stands, 435 feet from home plate.

On the final Sunday, Mark McGwire was at it again. He took a Mike Thurman fast ball downtown in his second at bat, in the third inning. The 377-foot chip shot into the left field seats, #69 of the year, came with the bases empty and gave St. Louis a 3–2 lead. In the seventh inning, with two men out and two men on base, in a tie game, the home run king hit a 370-foot line drive into the left field seats for home run #70. It was the game winner.

When interviewed after the game, Mark McGwire put it in perspective when he said, "It's unbelievable for anyone to hit 70 home runs. I'm in awe of myself."

Mark McGwire set a new home run record when he smashed an unbelieveable 70 homers in 1998.

Reflecting on the season, Sammy Sosa said, "I'm proud of myself because of where I came from—the guy I used to be—the guy I am now." As reported by Tim Keown in *ESPN Magazine*, Sammy also said, "That boy shining shoes is still who I am. That's why I'm so friendly and nice to people. I believe in God, and God says you have to be a nice person."

The season ended as explosively as it began. Beginning on March 31, Mark McGwire went seven for 16 in his first four games, with a double, four home runs, and 12 runs batted in. In his last 11 at bats of the season, over a 3½ game span, the 6'5" slugger went six for ten, with five home runs and nine RBIs. It was the kind of season that legends are made from.

The game of baseball desperately needed a hero after the 1994 debacle. Thanks to a poor kid from the Dominican Republic and a big redhead from California, it got two.

11. Ruth, Maris, McGwire and Sosa— Side by Side

The preceding chapters have reviewed the lives and careers of Babe Ruth, Roger Maris, Mark McGwire, and Sammy Sosa, the four single-season home run champions, with special emphasis placed on each of their record-breaking seasons.

The four historic seasons covered a period of 72 years, encompassing a world war, a painful depression, several recessions, and a number of small military "land actions" in such places as Korea, Vietnam, Iraq, Panama, and Grenada.

This chapter will study the four combatants side by side comparing the various cultural and social conditions that existed during their careers, as well as the factors in baseball that may have affected each player's home run totals.

Ruth, Maris, McGwire & Sosa— Their backgrounds

Each player's background had a profound effect on his subsequent ability to handle the on- and off-field pressures associated with his pursuit of the home run record. Babe Ruth and Sammy Sosa had similar backgrounds, and those backgrounds may have given them an advantage in their battle for the crown. Psychologists say poverty toughens a person and makes him a survivor. If that's the case, then Ruth and Sosa were survivors.

Ruth, Maris, McGwire and Sosa

George Herman "Babe" Ruth was born into a poor family on the southside of Baltimore, Maryland. He ran in the streets almost from the time he could walk, while his parents tried to carve out a living in a bar. He spent ten of his first 19 years in a home for wayward boys, learning how to fend for himself. Ruth was bigger and stronger than other boys his age, and he used his bulk to exercise control over them. He also learned how to manipulate the people he couldn't intimidate, such as the Xaverian Brothers that ran the Home, the Yankee fans, and the New York newspapermen who followed the team and wrote about his exploits.

Ruth learned to handle pressure as a seven year old. Surviving on the streets of Baltimore, day and night, taught him how to cope with adversity and how to overcome unpleasant situations. Adhering to the strict discipline of "The Home," taught him how to operate within the rules of a system. When he became an adult, he used his survival instincts to become the greatest player in baseball history. He delighted in playing a kid's game for big money. And when he closed in on his own home run record, he was able to do so in a casual and relaxed atmosphere. He controlled his environment.

Sammy Sosa was born into abject poverty in the Dominican Republic. He worked as a shoe-shine boy, after school, from the time he was seven years old. He became street smart at an early age, learning how to charm people with an engaging smile and a keen sense of humor. He struggled to take home $2 a day to help his mother put food on the table.

Young Sosa learned how to handle pressure in his early teens. His struggle to become a professional baseball player to help support his family began when he was just 14. It was a heavy burden to carry. However, it made him into a strong man, who enjoys playing baseball, yet can separate it from the important things in life. In the overall scheme of things, family is important, and being a good person is important. Baseball is just a game.

Roger Maris was born into a blue-collar family in North Dakota. He grew up to be an outstanding high school athlete. He played sports aggressively, both on the football field and the baseball diamond. On the gridiron he was a standout on both offense and defense. On the diamond he could do it all; hit, hit with power, run, field, and throw.

Throughout his amateur and professional career, Maris performed brilliantly on the field of play. But his lack of people skills caused him serious problems off the field when he became the subject of a mini media blitz during his pursuit of Babe Ruth's home run record. His early life had not prepared him for the pressures of celebrity, and the public scrutiny almost destroyed him.

Mark McGwire is the son of a dentist, brought up in an affluent middle-class neighborhood in California. He led a sheltered life, protected from the pressures of the outside world by his mother and father. His day to day life was one of family, study, and athletics. He and his four brothers were all superior athletes, who starred in several sports during their high school and college years.

McGwire traveled through the first 21 years of his life in blissful ignorance of the realities of the world. He never wanted for anything. He had a loving family, a comfortable home, all the luxuries associated with upper middle-class living, a distinguished athletic career, and the advantage of a college education. But, like Maris, he had no experience handling the pressures that were part of his pursuit of the home run record.

Babe Ruth and Sammy Sosa had a significant advantage over both Roger Maris and Mark McGwire, based on their backgrounds. They were survivors of a distressed childhood, who grew up well prepared to handle the off-field pressures associated with their season-long chase of history.

Their Personalities

The personalities of the four home run champions, like their backgrounds, had a significant effect on their ability to handle the off-field pressures associated with their quest.

Babe Ruth was a big, undisciplined kid who never grew up. He played a kid's game, and he played it with enthusiasm. Off the field, he was an extrovert, who lived life to the fullest. He had a good sense of humor and he used it effectively, both for his own well-being and for putting other people at ease. The pressures of early childhood on the streets, combined with the challenges of his teenage years in the "Home," prepared Ruth for any eventuality. Baseball was never a struggle for him. The pursuit of the home run record was not something to be feared. It was just a game. He enjoyed the moment, and whatever happened, happened.

His happy-go-lucky attitude endeared him to both fans and newspapermen. They always supported him in his conflicts with management, and they cheered his every move on the baseball diamond. When he was chasing a new record, they were there, urging him on to new conquests.

Sammy Sosa is an extrovert, an entertainer who enjoys the spotlight and who plays to his audience. The chase for the crown, and the associated media blitz, were sheer pleasure for the former shoe shine boy. Sosa was born into poverty with a smile on his face. He enjoyed life as a child even when the struggle was oppressive. His religion taught him to accept whatever happened with grace and humility. His mother taught him to be a good person. His genes allowed him to face each day with a smile.

His career with the Chicago Cubs has been one long love affair, particularly with the fans in the right field stands. Sosa has endeared himself to the "Bleacher Bums" over a period of seven years, and he never forgets to salute them each time he goes out to his position. They were his secret weapon in his pursuit of the home run record. They kept his adrenaline pumping day after day, with their enthusiastic support. And he, in return, kept their adrenaline pumping with his good-natured friendship and his titanic blasts.

Roger Maris was an introvert who cherished and protected his privacy. His dour personality put him at a decided disadvantage when he became a celebrity and had to face the press. The Yankee right fielder never learned the art of controlling an interview to his own advantage. He answered every question honestly and to the point, without considering the ramifications of seeing his quotes in print. In addition, he lacked the sense of humor needed to charm his interviewers with clever retorts and one-liners.

The North Dakota native was a blue-collar player from a blue-collar background. He expected to do an honest day's work for a day's pay. He couldn't handle the public relations aspect of his job.

Mark McGwire was shy and quiet, but he had a restrained sense of humor which stood him in good stead over the years. He also had a private side, fostered by his father, that did not permit anyone to see his inner feelings. He learned how to get along with people as his baseball career developed, but he was never subjected to strong pressures of any kind until the home run race began.

The big redhead was unprepared for the intense scrutiny of the press during the 1998 season. His claustrophobia increased daily as spring turned into summer, and the size of the media circus grew from a couple of dozen reporters to more than 200 frantic writers and cameramen. He was beginning to wear down when Sammy Sosa came along to support him.

On the field Mark McGwire was better prepared to meet the challenges of the home run race than his three cohorts. He is the ultimate professional hitter, who mentally prepares himself before each at bat, putting himself in a trance-like state and blocking out everything else around him. His ability to visualize the pitch being thrown may be unequaled in baseball history.

Ruth and Sosa had outgoing personalities that disarmed people. They knew how to deal with people, and how to enjoy the media blitz that accompanied the home run chase. On the field, McGwire had a distinct advantage.

Social Climate

When Babe Ruth was entering the peak years of his professional baseball career, the country was just coming out of "The War to End All Wars." Soldiers returning home from the war with the sights and sounds of human slaughter fresh in their memory, had a fatalistic attitude toward life in general. The motto of the "Lost Generation" that populated the United States in the 1920s was "Eat, drink and be merry, for tomorrow we die."

It was also the Golden Age of Sports, when athletes of every type were idolized by the entire country. Heavyweight boxing champion Jack Dempsey and home run king Babe Ruth were the most idolized.

Babe Ruth could do nothing wrong. Every home run was a celebration. Every misdemeanor was forgiven. Babe was not isolated from the hedonistic night life in the big cities around the American League. He was right in the middle of it, often partying until dawn, then making his way back to the hotel. The big, jovial, moon-faced kid was loved by all.

The young slugger broke the home run record four different times— in 1919, 1920, 1921, and 1927. Every time, except the first time, he was chasing his own record, so he was never under any pressure to set a new standard. The New York fans were so blase they didn't even consider it noteworthy when he hit 60 home runs in 1927. They thought he would be setting home run records for years to come.

In Roger Maris' case, it was entirely different. He had the most difficult chore of all, trying to dethrone a god. Ruth was beloved the world over. Baseball fans in general rooted against Maris because they didn't want anyone to unseat the mighty Babe. The Yankee management, fans and players were pulling for Mantle because he was a home-grown player. Maris was considered to be a hired gun, not a genuine New York Yankee. The New York newspapermen were openly hostile toward the new challenger for the same reason. Their questions were often pointed and embarrassing. Even the baseball commissioner plotted against him, declaring that Babe Ruth's record had to be broken in 154 games or it would be identified with an asterisk. It's no wonder Maris' hair began to fall out in clumps before the season ended.

Mark McGwire and Sammy Sosa had an easier task than Maris, although not as easy as Ruth. The quality of baseball declined after 1961, the new-age players were selfish, crude, and greedy, and the strike of 1994 alienated many of the fans. Baseball was in desperate need of a hero—so when McGwire and Sosa came along, they were welcomed with open arms by both the fans and the media alike. Whereas Maris was confronted by 10–20 hostile newspapermen during the last three months of the season, McGwire and Sosa had to face hundreds of reporters, writers, and cameramen daily, but their sessions were generally friendly and light hearted, particularly when Sammy Sosa participated.

Mark McGwire was fortunate that Sosa was a co-challenger, because the happy-go-lucky Dominican taught his American friend that the media attention was something to be enjoyed.

Roger Maris was at a tremendous disadvantage, compared to the other challengers. He was the only one of the four that faced a hostile environment.

Physical Size and Conditioning of the Home Run Champions:

All four challengers were big men, all 6' tall or taller and all weighing 200 pounds or more. Babe Ruth was a big man in his day, standing 6'2" tall and weighing a muscular 215 pounds. Once he became an established star however, he let his finely muscled physique deteriorate. His love of food, drink, and city night life added pounds of fat to his body and affected his play on the field. Periodically, the Bambino would punish himself over the winter to get himself physically fit for the new season. In 1927, he was in top physical condition, having spent the winter in the gym lifting weights, doing aerobics, and running. Back home in the country, he chopped wood, cleared brush, and jogged. He came into the season weighing a trim 220 pounds.

Roger Maris was a solidly built 6', 200-pound slugger, who was always in condition to play. He was a dedicated player who worked out daily during the season and who maintained his weight and physical fitness over the winter.

Sammy Sosa was another rugged 6', 200-pound slugger. Like Maris, he was dedicated to the game, and he worked out religiously during the season lifting weights running and doing various aerobic exercises. He, like many major leaguers, also took a number of legal dietary supplements.

Mark McGwire became a physical fitness fanatic after the 1991 season when his career almost self destructed. His brother J.J., a personal trainer, put Mark on a physical fitness program designed to maximize his strength and stamina. The regimen centered around, but was not limited to, weight training. He added 20 pounds of muscle over the winter of '91-'92, arriving in spring training at a muscular 235 pounds on a big 6'5" frame. He added another 15 pounds over the next six years, bringing his weight up to a full 250 pounds. He also took dietary supplements, including the aforementioned androstendione, but as discussed earlier, the andro did not appear to contribute to his home run surge. He was hitting titanic blasts long before he started taking andro.

As with many things, bigger is better. In boxing, a good big man will always defeat a good small man. In baseball, a good big man will hit more home runs than a good small man. Mark McGwire is a good big man.

The appendix contains a chart showing the physical size of the major league all-star teams from the nineteenth century to the present, as well as the average number of home runs hit by the all-stars. A rough estimate indicates that, all other things being equal, every 3.3 pounds of muscle a player adds will result in one home run a year. The physical size and average number of home runs hit by the four single-season home run champions are shown below.

Name	Height	Weight	Home Runs
Babe Ruth	6'2"	220 lbs.	50
Roger Maris	6'2"	200 lbs.	30
Mark McGwire	6'5"	250 lbs.	49
Sammy Sosa	6'	200 lbs.	32

Using the factor of 3.3 pounds per home run and using Mark McGwire as the base point, if McGwire rapped out 49 home runs, Babe Ruth would be expected to hit 40 home runs (based on his weight), Roger Maris 34, and Sammy Sosa 34. Maris' and Sosa's numbers essentially agree with their actual home run production. The discrepancy in Ruth's numbers indicates that "all other things were not equal"—that Babe Ruth was able to generate more power than the average player his size. The Sultan of Swat belonged in a higher league.

The total number of home runs hit in the major leagues increased from 73 home runs per team per year during the decade from 1920 to 1930, to 140 home runs per team per year during the nine year period from 1990 to 1998 (see appendix). If the estimate of the home run increase on the all-star teams is accurate and can be extended to each major league team roster, then approximately 30 percent of the total increase in home runs over the last seven decades can be attributed to the increased size of the players, as well as the improvement in their physical fitness.

Mark McGwire had a significant advantage in size. All the champions were physically fit during their record year.

Ballparks—Dimensions

The playing field dimensions of baseball stadiums have changed dramatically over the past 70 to 90 years. Until recently, most parks favored left-handed batters, as shown in the tables in the appendix. During Babe Ruth's time, the average distance to right field in American League parks was 329 feet, compared to 386 feet in right center and 446 feet in straight away center. Left field was a healthier 339-foot shot from home plate.

In 1961, when Roger Maris was taking dead aim at Ruth's record, right field was 325 feet from home, the power alley in right center was 380 feet, and center field was 422 feet. Left field was 336 feet.

When McGwire and Sosa were making their run, the average park was symmetrical at 333 feet down the left and right field foul lines, 371 feet to the alleys, and 407 feet to center.

The numbers indicate that the parks have become progressively smaller since Babe Ruth took aim at the fences, particularly in the power alleys and center field. The power alleys are about 15 feet closer to the batter than they were in Ruth's day, and the center field fence is a whopping 39 feet closer. Checking Mark McGwire's home run distances, he hit six home runs to center field that traveled less than the average 446-foot center field distance of Ruth's day, and two home runs less than the 386-foot power alley distance of Ruth's day. However, even if eight home runs were deducted from McGwire's totals, he still would have hit 62 home runs within the 154-game "Ruth benchmark."

Each of the parks associated with the home run champions has a home run factor (HRF) associated with it. The HRF is the number of home runs hit in a particular park compared to the average number of home runs hit in all the league parks. The Yankee Stadium HRF is 1.03 meaning that 1.03 home runs are hit in the stadium for every 1.00 home runs hit in the average league park. The HRF in Wrigley Field is 1.16 while the HRF in Busch Stadium is just 0.79.

Only Sammy Sosa came close to approximating his home park's HRF. Sammy hit 35 of his 66 home runs at home, for a HRF of 1.13. Mark McGwire hit 38 of his 70 home runs at home, indicating the big slugger had more adrenaline pumping when playing before the home folks.

Curiously, both Babe Ruth and Roger Maris hit more home runs on the road than at home. Their detractors have always claimed they set their records by hitting into the friendly right field stands at Yankee Stadium, a 296-foot chip shot from home plate. The facts prove otherwise.

Babe Ruth actually hit 50 percent of his career home runs on the road. Maris hit 54 percent of his Yankee round trippers away from the stadium.

There is one additional factor that affects the home run history of the various major league baseball parks. Teams are now located all across the country, from the Pacific Ocean to the Atlantic and from the Canadian border to Mexico. At the present time, two cities seem to have a decided home run advantage caused by the unique atmospheric conditions surrounding their parks. Home runs fly out of the ballparks in Atlanta at an increase of about 43 percent over the average league park (1.43 HRF). In Denver, balls leave the yard 70 percent more than the average (1.70 HRF).

Mark McGwire and Sammy Sosa had a distinct field advantage (both home and away) over Babe Ruth and Roger Maris.

Equipment—Baseballs and Pitching Mounds

Baseballs have always had a decided effect on the number of home runs hit in the major leagues. When the lively ball was introduced in 1920, the home run became the single most important offensive weapon. In 1930, when the seams of the ball were recessed, home runs jumped up more than 30 percent over 1928. Since 1994, the baseballs have been manufactured in Costa Rica. Coincidentally or not, home runs have increased by 30 percent since that time.

Another modification to the rules that benefitted the batter was lowering the pitcher's mound from a maximum of 15" to 10" in 1969. This change was designed to give parity to the batter, after a decade of pitching dominance in the 1960s.

Mark McGwire and Sammy Sosa have both benefitted from the livelier balls and the lower pitching mounds.

Integration

In 1945, the Brooklyn Dodgers signed Jackie Robinson to play baseball for them, thus ending more than 57 years of segregated major league baseball. Some of the great Negro league players who entered the major leagues at that time, in addition to Robinson, included Willie Mays, Ernie Banks, Monte Irvin, Roy Campanella, and Larry Doby, all Hall-of-Famers.

In Babe Ruth's time, the great black baseball players were not allowed to compete in the major leagues, so they had to play in their own segregated league. As a result, the Bambino did not have to face the likes of Satchel Paige, "Smokey Joe" Williams, "Cannonball" Dick Redding, "Bullet Joe" Rogan, Willie Foster, or dozens of other legendary black pitchers. If he had to bat against the great Negro league pitchers of his day, it is doubtful he could have hit 60 home runs in one season.

Babe Ruth had a big advantage over the other challengers, in not having to bat against the top black pitchers of the 20s and 30s.

Expansion—and a Dilution of Talent

Several major league teams, like the Boston Braves, Brooklyn Dodgers, and New York Giants, moved their franchises to other cities during the 1950s. In 1961, Los Angeles and Washington were added to the American League. The following year New York and Houston were added to the National League.

Over the past 37 years major league baseball has increased from 16 teams to 30 teams. The population of the United States in 1920 was 106 million. However, blacks were not allowed to play organized baseball, so the number of people eligible to play baseball was just 95 million. In 1961, the total population was 175 million, and in 1998 it was 270 million.

It can be assumed from these population numbers that the quality of baseball increased substantially from 1920 to 1961 because the population almost doubled, and integration permitted blacks to play in the major leagues, while the number of teams remained constant. In fact, the period from 1950 to 1965 is frequently referred to as "The Golden Age of Baseball."

Since 1961, several factors have influenced the quality of America's national pastime. First, the population has increased by just 57 percent over that period, while the number of major league teams has increased by a whopping 88 percent. But the true story is even grimmer. Other professional sports have drained away some of the talent that would have previously been channeled into professional baseball.

In 1950, there were 11 professional basketball franchises and 13 professional football franchises. By 1998, these sports had grown to 29 and 30 teams respectively, an increase of 146 percent. Basketball and football are particularly attractive to college athletes because the players can go directly from school into a high-paying professional career, whereas in baseball they usually have to spend four or five years in the minor leagues before they reach the major leagues where the big money is—if they make it at all.

In addition to the above-mentioned sports, baseball has also lost players to tennis, golf, hockey, and a host of minor sports. And now, with college education being more accessible to athletes, some of the finite talent pool is choosing to begin a business career rather than buck the odds to play professional baseball.

Baseball, within its own borders, has seen other areas where talent has been dangerously diluted. It is most noticeable on the mound where pitchers are so protected it is actually causing more physical harm than good. Going back to the Babe Ruth era, major league teams had a four-man pitching rotation, and the starters were expected to finish what they started. During the 1920s, major league teams averaged 80 complete games a year, over a 154-game schedule. During the 40s and 50s, teams averaged 40 to 60 complete games a year. In 1996, the 28 major league teams averaged ten complete games over a 162-game schedule. In 1995, the entire pitching staff of the Colorado Rockies tossed only one complete game!

Today major league teams have five-man pitching rotations, and any pitcher who can throw six innings is considered to be a quality pitcher. Starting pitchers are under a "pitch count" and are removed from the game after reaching a specified limit, usually about 100 pitches. The philosophy is that it is desirable to bring a "fresh arm" into the game after the sixth inning even if it means replacing a Greg Maddux with a Russ Springer. Imagine if Walter Johnson, Lefty Grove, or even Sandy Koufax were under a 100 pitch count. With that scenario, Nolan Ryan never would have made it past the fifth inning. Pitchers today average about two innings per start less than pitchers of 20 to 30 years ago. And yet, the injuries to pitching arms continue to mount. On July 27, 1997, for

Sammy Sosa's relaxed and pleasant persona down the pressure-packed stretch was a highlight of the home run race. (Courtesy James R. Madden, Jr.)

instance, 68 major league pitchers were on the disabled list, an average of more than two per team. Almost a year later, on June 28, 1998, there were a total of 79 pitchers from 30 teams on the D.L. Perhaps today's pitchers need to work more, not less.

Major league pitching quality has deteriorated to the point where it is about on par with the high minor league pitching of the 1950s.

Mark McGwire and Sammy Sosa have a definite advantage facing today's diluted pitching talent. All things considered, taking into account expansion, the drain of other professional sports, and the dilution of pitching talent due to pitch counts and middle relievers, perhaps half the pitchers in the major leagues today are of minor league caliber.

Travel—Night Baseball

Travel and night games affect the performances of the major league players. In the days before expansion, travel was relatively simple. An overnight train ride or a two hour flight was all that was required to reach the most distant city in the major leagues, St. Louis. There were only eight teams in each league, so the 154-game schedule was broken down into 22 games with each opposing team, 11 at home and 11 away.

Travel was much easier for Babe Ruth, somewhat more difficult for Roger Maris, and much more difficult for McGwire and Sosa.

Babe Ruth had another advantage over his three opponents in that he played all his games in the daylight. It was usually more comfortable and easier on the muscles, playing under a warm sun. And the balls carried farther. Night games, with cold, damp weather, create minor health problems and reduce the number of home runs hit in a game.

Sammy Sosa, for example, has hit 32 percent more home runs in the sunlight than he has in the evening. He has played in more than 1,200 major league games during his career, about half of them during the day. In 2,259 daytime at bats, Sosa has averaged 37 home runs for every 550 at bats. Under the moon, he has averaged just 28 home runs in 2,401 at bats.

Babe Ruth had the benefit of having a comfortable travel schedule and of playing all his games in the warm sunlight. Maris, McGwire and Sosa were at a disadvantage in both cases.

Individual Performances

Babe Ruth, Roger Maris, Mark McGwire and Sammy Sosa all dominated their league during their record-breaking season. But no one ever dominated a league like Babe Ruth dominated the American League from 1919 to 1934. In 1919, the last year of the dead ball, the Sultan of Swat hit 29 home runs to break the record for the dead ball era. In the process, he outhomered four of the other seven teams. The next year, the first year of the lively ball, he did even better. He smashed 54 home runs, while the runnerup, George Sisler, had just 19. And Babe outhomered every other team in the American League. In 1921 and 1926 he out-homered five of the seven teams, and in his 60 home run season, he once again outhomered every other team. In fact, the other teams averaged only 40 home runs apiece.

Over a six-year period from 1919 to 1924 Babe Ruth accounted for 10.8 percent of all home runs hit in the American League. From 1926 to 1931 he accounted for 9.5 percent of all home runs hit in the league.

From 1920 through 1933, American League teams averaged 67 home runs a year. Babe Ruth, by himself, averaged 46 home runs a year in just 489 at bats.

In his record year of 1927, the Bambino hit an unbelievable 13.7 percent of all the American League home runs hit that year. To put that in perspective, in 1961 Roger Maris hit 5 percent of all American League home runs (based on an eight-team league). To match Ruth's perfor-mance of hitting 13.6 percent of the league home runs, Maris would have had to hit 167 home runs in 1961. Mark McGwire and Sammy Sosa were in the same boat. McGwire hit 5.5 percent of all the National League home runs (based on an eight-team league) while Sosa hit 5.1 percent. To match Ruth's percentage McGwire would have had to hit 174 homers, and Sosa 177.

Maris, McGwire and Sosa cannot match Babe Ruth's complete domination of a league, statistics-wise. The Babe revolutionized the game.

Summary

McGwire, Sosa, Maris, and Ruth each enjoyed certain advantages over the other three players during their race for the crown. The play-ers, and the areas they enjoyed an advantage in, are shown below.

Ruth, Maris, McGwire and Sosa

Babe Ruth	Roger Maris	Mark McGwire	Sammy Sosa
Background			Background
Personality			Personality
Social climate		Social climate	Social climate
Chasing himself			
		Concentration	
Friendly press		Friendly press	Friendly press
Segregation			
Physical fitness	Physical fitness	Physical fitness	Physical fitness
		Dietary supplements	Dietary supplements
Physical size		Physical size	
Travel	Travel		
Day games			
	Expansion	Expansion	Expansion
		Smaller parks	Smaller Parks
		Atmospheric Conditions	Atmospheric Conditions
		Dilution of Pitching	Dilution of Pitching
		Lively Balls	Lively Balls
		Sosa	McGwire

Certain facts are obvious.

• Babe Ruth set the single-season home run record, not once, but four times. In 1927, when he hit 60 home runs, he outhomered every other team in the league and accounted for 13.7 percent of the league's entire home run production.

The "Sultan of Swat" had a number of advantages in his quest for the home run crown, the most important of which was that he wasn't chasing any record or any record holder. He already held the record. Anything he did over and above that, was a bonus.

• Sammy Sosa was the first man in baseball history to hit 66 home runs in a single season.

• Mark McGwire broke Roger Maris' single-season home run record of 61. He subsequently broke Sammy Sosa's record of 66, then established a new record when he hit his 70th home run on September 26, 1998.

McGwire and Sosa together had advantages in several areas, most notably having a friendly press, enthusiastic fans, smaller parks, livelier baseballs, diluted pitching talent, and each other to feed off.

• Roger Maris, on the other hand, had the worst of all worlds. He was chasing an icon, Babe Ruth, and no one—fans, teammates, or press, wanted him to break the record. His taciturn personality alienated the newspapermen. As noted above, he had almost none of the advantages enjoyed by Ruth, McGwire or Sosa. He was too late to reap the benefits of segregation and of playing his games in the daylight. And he was too early to capitalize on expansion, poor pitching, smaller parks, and livelier baseballs.

Roger Maris had the most difficult task of all the home run challengers. The fact that he was able to break Babe Ruth's home run record under almost unbearable conditions speaks volumes about the heart and courage of this most private baseball player.

It is impossible to compare players from one era with players from another era. Ruth's dominance in the American League occurred during a time when the game was in transition from a Punch and Judy game to a slugging game. He would not have had the same advantage had he played in the 1990s. Modern-day players are bigger and stronger, and most of them are swinging from the heels, going for the long ball. The Babe would still be a great home run hitter, without question, and might still be the major league home run champion. But he would definitely not hit 13.7 percent of the league's home runs. Competition would be stiffer.

All four home run champions were deserving of their achievements and accolades. It is not possible to single out one of the four as the greatest single-season home run champion of all time. They all overcame tremendous obstacles to accomplish a truly amazing feat. Each was a champion in his own time.

PART TWO : THE STATISTICS

1. Playing Statistics

George Herman "Babe" Ruth

Born Baltimore, Md., Feb. 6, 1895; *died* New York, N.Y., Aug. 16, 1948.
Height 6'2"; *weight* 215 pounds
Bats left; *throws* left

Year	Team	League	Pos	G	AB	R	H	D	T	HR	RBI	BA
1914	Boston	AL	P	5	10	1	2	1	0	0	2	.200
1915	Boston	AL	P	42	92	16	29	10	1	4	21	.315
1916	Boston	AL	P	67	136	18	37	5	3	3	15	.272
1917	Boston	AL	P	52	123	14	40	6	3	2	12	.325
1918	Boston	AL	P-OF-1	95	317	50	95	26	11	11	66	.300
1919	Boston	AL	P-OF	130	432	103	139	34	12	29	114	.322
1920	New York	AL	OF-1-P	142	458	158	172	36	9	54	137	.376
1921	New York	AL	OF-1-P	152	540	177	204	44	16	59	171	.378
1922	New York	AL	OF-1B	110	406	94	128	24	8	35	99	.315
1923	New York	AL	OF-1B	152	522	151	205	45	13	41	131	.393
1924	New York	AL	OF	153	529	143	200	39	7	46	121	.378
1925	New York	AL	OF	98	359	61	104	12	2	25	66	.290
1926	New York	AL	OF-1B	152	495	139	184	30	5	47	146	.372
1927	New York	AL	OF	151	540	158	192	29	8	60	164	.356
1928	New York	AL	OF	154	536	163	173	29	8	54	142	.323
1929	New York	AL	OF	135	499	121	172	26	6	46	154	.345
1930	New York	AL	OF-P	145	518	150	186	28	9	49	153	.359
1931	New York	AL	OF-1B	145	534	149	199	31	3	46	163	.373
1932	New York	AL	OF-1B	133	457	120	156	13	5	41	137	.341
1933	New York	AL	OF-P	137	459	97	138	21	3	34	103	.301
1934	New York	AL	OF	125	365	78	105	17	4	22	84	.288
1935	Boston	NL	OF	28	72	13	13	0	0	6	12	.181
Total	22 years			2503	8399	2174	2873	506	136	714	2213	.342

Pitching—career totals

Years	Team	G	IP	W	L	Pct.	SO	BB	ERA
1914–19	Boston Red Sox	158	1190	89	46	.659	483	425	2.20
1920–33	New York Yankees	5	31	5	0	1.000	5	16	5.52

Roger Eugene Maris

Born Hibbing, Minn., Sept. 10, 1934; *died* Houston, Texas, Dec. 14, 1985
Height 6'; *weight* 205 pounds
Bats left; *throws* right

Year	Team	League	Pos	G	AB	R	H	D	T	HR	RBI	BA
1957	Cleve.	AL	OF	116	358	61	84	9	5	14	51	.235
1958	Cleve-KC	AL	OF	150	583	87	140	19	4	28	80	.240
1959	K.City	AL	OF	122	433	69	118	21	7	16	72	.273
1960	New York	AL	OF	136	499	98	141	18	7	39	112	.283
1961	New York	AL	OF	161	590	132	159	16	4	61	141	.269
1962	New York	AL	OF	157	590	92	151	34	1	33	100	.256
1963	New York	AL	OF	90	312	53	84	14	1	23	53	.269
1964	New York	AL	OF	141	513	86	144	12	2	26	71	.281
1965	New York	AL	OF	46	155	22	37	7	0	8	27	.239
1966	New York	AL	OF	119	348	37	81	9	2	13	43	.233
1967	St. Louis	NL	OF	125	410	64	107	18	7	9	55	.261
1968	St. Louis	NL	OF	100	310	25	79	18	2	5	45	.255
Totals	12 years			1463	5101	826	1325	195	42	275	850	.260

The individual playing statistics for Ruth and Maris are from "The Historical Register," compiled by Bob Hoie and Carlos Bauer.

Mark David McGwire

Born Pomona, Calif., Oct. 1, 1963
Height 6'5"; *weight* 250 pounds
Bats right; *throws* right

Year	Team	League	Pos	G	AB	R	H	D	T	HR	RBI	BA
1986	Oakland	AL	3B	18	53	10	10	1	0	3	9	.189
1987	Oakland	AL	1-3-OF	151	557	97	161	28	4	49	118	.289
1988	Oakland	AL	1B-OF	155	550	87	143	22	1	32	99	.260
1989	Oakland	AL	1B	143	490	74	113	17	0	33	95	.231
1990	Oakland	AL	1B	156	523	87	123	16	0	39	108	.235
1991	Oakland	AL	1B	154	483	62	97	22	0	22	75	.201
1992	Oakland	AL	1B	139	467	87	125	22	0	42	104	.268
1993	Oakland	AL	1B	27	84	16	28	6	0	9	24	.333
1994	Oakland	AL	1B	47	135	26	34	3	0	9	25	.252
1995	Oakland	AL	1B	104	317	75	87	13	0	39	90	.274
1996	Oakland	AL	1B	130	423	104	132	21	0	52	113	.312
1997	Oak-St. L.	AL-NL	1B	156	540	86	148	27	0	58	123	.274
1998	St. Louis	NL	1B	155	509	130	152	21	0	70	147	.299
Totals	13 years			1535	5131	941	1353	219	5	457	1130	.264

1. Playing Statistics

Samuel Peralta Sosa

Born San Pedro de Macoris, D.R., Nov. 12, 1968
Height 6'; *weight* 195 pounds
Bats right; *throws* right

Year	Team	League	Pos	G	AB	R	H	D	T	HR	RBI	BA
1989	Tex-Chic	AL	OF	58	183	27	47	8	0	4	13	.257
1990	Chicago	AL	OF	153	532	72	124	26	10	15	70	.233
1991	Chicago	AL	OF	116	316	39	64	10	1	10	33	.203
1992	Chicago	NL	OF	67	262	41	68	7	2	8	25	.260
1993	Chicago	NL	OF	159	598	92	156	25	5	33	93	.261
1994	Chicago	NL	OF	105	426	59	128	17	6	25	70	.300
1995	Chicago	NL	OF	144	564	89	151	17	3	36	119	.268
1996	Chicago	NL	OF	124	498	84	136	21	2	40	100	.273
1997	Chicago	NL	OF	162	642	90	161	31	4	36	119	.251
1998	Chicago	NL	OF	158	639	132	196	20	0	66	158	.307
Totals	10 years			1246	4660	725	1231	182	33	273	800	.264

2. Side by Side Comparisons

	Ruth	Maris	McGwire	Sosa
Date of Birth	2/6/1895	9/10/1934	10/1/1963	11/12/1968
Place of Birth	Baltimore, MD	Hibbing, MN	Pomona, CA	San Pedro de Macoris, D.R.
Residence	Deceased	Deceased	Long Beach, CA	Santo Domingo, D.R.
Religion	Catholic	Catholic	Catholic	Catholic
Height	6'2"	6'	6'5"	6'
Weight, pounds	215	200	250	195
Throws	Left	Right	Right	Right
Bats	Left	Left	Right	Right
Position	1B-P-OF	OF	1B	OF
Primary Team	N.Y. Yankees	N.Y. Yankees	Oakland Athletics	Chicago Cubs
Home Run Record Team	N.Y.	N.Y.	St. Louis Cardinals	Chicago Cubs
Home Run Record, Year	1927	1961	1998	1998
Age, H.R. Record Year	32	27	34	29
Team, League Standing	1	1	3	2
	World Champ	World Champ	—	Playoff
Games, Season	154	163	162	163
Games Played	151	161	155	158
At Bats	540	590	509	639
Base Hits	192	159	152	196
Runs Scored	158	132	130	132
Home Runs	60	61	70	66
HR's per 550 At-Bats	61	57	76	57
Runs Batted In	164	142	147	158
Strikeouts	89	67	155	170
Bases on Balls	138	94	162	73

2. Side by Side Comparisons

	Ruth	Maris	McGwire	Sosa
On Base Percentage	.487	.376	.470	.376
Slugging Average	.772	.620	.752	.648
Batting Average	.356	.269	.299	.307
Awards: Most Valuable Player	No	Yes	No	Yes
Player of the Year	—	—	Yes	Yes

3. Home Run Statistics

	Ruth	Maris	McGwire	Sosa
Year	1927	1961	1998	1998
Home Runs	60	61	70	66
Home Runs by Month				
March	0	0	1	0
April	4	1	10	6
May	12	11	16	7
June	9	15	10	20
July	9	13	8	9
August	9	11	10	13
September	17	9	15	11
October	0	1	0	0
Home Runs by July 4	26	30	37	33
HRs by Labor Day	50	53	60	58
Date, 50th Home Run	Sept. 11	Aug. 22	Aug. 20	Aug. 23
Game	138	125	125	130
Date, #60	Sept. 30	Sept. 26	Sept. 5	Sept. 12
Game	154	159	141	149
Date, #61	—	Oct. 1	Sept. 7	Sept. 13
Game	—	163	143	150
Date, #62	—	—	Sept. 8	Sept. 13
Game	—	—	144	150
Date, #66	—	—	Sept. 25	Sept. 25
Game	—	—	161	160
Date, #67	—	—	Sept. 26	—
Game	—	—	162	—
Date, #70	—	—	Sept. 27	—
Game	—	—	163	—
Home Runs—Home	28	30	38	35
Home Runs—Away	32	31	32	31
HR off RH Pitcher	42	52	55	54
HR off LH Pitcher	18	9	15	12
HR, % of League	13.7	4.0	2.7	2.6

	Ruth	Maris	McGwire	Sosa
HR, % If 8 Team Lge	13.7	5.0	5.5	5.1
Home Runs by Team				
Chicago W.S.	6	13	2	3
Washington	8	9	—	—
Cleveland	9	8	2	0
Phila. A's	9	—	—	—
Detroit Tigers	8	8	0	2
Boston Red Sox	11	7	—	—
St. L. Browns	9	—	—	—
Kansas City A's	—	5	—	—
L.A. CA Angels	—	4	—	—
Minnesota Twins	—	4	1	1
Balt. Orioles	—	3	—	—
K. C. Royals	—	—	1	0
Ariz. D'backs	—	—	4	5
Atlanta	—	—	2	3
Chic. Cubs	—	—	7	—
Cincinnati	—	—	1	4
Colo. Rockies	—	—	2	3
Fla. Marlins	—	—	7	4
Houston Astros	—	—	5	4
L.A. Dodgers	—	—	4	1
Milw. Brewers	—	—	4	12
Montreal Expos	—	—	6	3
N.Y. Mets	—	—	4	2
Phil. Phillies	—	—	5	8
Pitts. Pirates	—	—	3	2
St. L. Cards	—	—	—	3
San Diego	—	—	5	3
San Francisco	—	—	5	3
Totals	60	61	70	66
Home Run Distance				
300-349'	—	—	3	3
350-399'	—	—	20	23
400-449'	—	—	26	34
450-499'	—	—	16	5
500+'	—	—	5	1
Average, ft.	—	—	423	407
Longest, ft.	500+	450 est.	550	500
Total, ft.	—	—	29,610	26,730
Home Run, Direction				
Left Field	—	0	37	13
LCF	—	9	17	15
CF	—		13	18
RCF	—		3	11
Right Field	—		0	9
Home Run, Day	60		21	33

3. Home Run Statistics

	Ruth	Maris	McGwire	Sosa
Home Run, Night	—		49	33
Home Runs, Grass	60	61	60	57
Home Runs, Artificial	—	—	10	9
2-HR games	9	7	8	10
3-HR games	1	0	2	1

4. Day by Day Comparisons

HR No.	Ruth	Maris	McGwire	Sosa
1	04-15	04-26	03-31	04-04
2	04-23	05-03	04-02	04-11
3	04-24	05-06	04-03	04-15
4	04-29	05-17	04-04	04-23
5	05-01	05-19	04-14	04-24
6	05-01	05-20	04-14	04-27
7	05-10	05-21	04-14	05-03
8	05-11	05-23	04-17	05-16
9	05-17	05-28	04-21	05-22
10	05-22	05-30	04-25	05-25
11	05-23	05-30	04-30	05-25
12	05-28	05-31	05-01	05-27
13	05-29	06-02	05-08	05-27
14	05-30	06-03	05-12	06-01
15	05-31	06-04	05-14	06-01
16	05-31	06-06	05-16	06-03
17	06-05	06-07	05-18	06-05
18	06-07	06-07	05-19	06-06
19	06-11	06-11	05-19	06-07
20	06-11	06-11	05-19	06-08
21	06-12	06-13	05-22	06-13
22	06-16	06-14	05-23	06-15
23	06-22	06-17	05-23	06-15
24	06-22	06-18	05-24	06-15
25	06-25	06-19	05-25	06-17
26	07-03	06-20	05-29	06-19
27	07-08	06-22	05-30	06-19
28	07-09	07-01	06-05	06-20
29	07-09	07-02	06-08	06-20
30	07-12	07-02	06-10	06-21
31	07-24	07-04	06-12	06-24
32	07-26	07-05	06-17	06-25

4. Day by Day Comparisons

HR No.	Ruth	Maris	McGwire	Sosa
33	07-26	07-09	06-18	06-30
34	07-28	07-13	06-24	07-09
35	08-05	07-15	06-25	07-10
36	08-10	07-21	06-27	07-17
37	08-16	07-25	06-30	07-22
38	08-17	07-25	07-11	07-26
39	08-20	07-25	07-12	07-27
40	08-22	07-25	07-12	07-27
41	08-27	08-04	07-17	07-28
42	08-28	08-11	07-17	07-31
43	08-31	08-12	07-20	08-05
44	09-02	08-13	07-26	08-08
45	09-06	08-13	07-28	08-10
46	09-06	08-15	08-08	08-10
47	09-06	08-16	08-11	08-16
48	09-07	08-16	08-19	08-19
49	09-07	08-20	08-19	08-21
50	09-11	08-22	08-20	08-23
51	09-13	08-26	08-20	08-23
52	09-13	09-02	08-22	08-26
53	09-16	09-02	08-23	08-28
54	09-18	09-06	08-26	08-30
55	09-21	09-07	08-30	08-31
56	09-22	09-09	09-01	09-02
57	09-27	09-16	09-01	09-04
58	09-29	09-17	09-02	09-05
59	09-29	09-20	09-02	09-11
60	09-30	09-26	09-05	09-12
61		10-01	09-07	09-13
62			09-08	09-13
63			09-15	09-16
64			09-18	09-23
65			09-20	09-23
66			09-25	09-25
67			09-26	
68			09-26	
69			09-27	
70			09-27	

5. Babe Ruth
in 1927

Date	HR No.	Pitcher	Team	Location
04-15	1	H. Ehmke	Phil. A's	New York
04-23	2	R. Walberg	Phil. A's	Philadelphia
04-24	3	S. Thurston	Washington	Washington
04-29	4	S. Harriss	Boston	Boston
05-01	5	J. Quinn	Phil. A's	New York
05-01	6	R. Walberg	Phil. A's	New York
05-10	7	M. Gaston	St. Louis	St. Louis
05-11	8	E. Nevers	St. Louis	St. Louis
05-17	9	R. Collins	Detroit	Detroit
05-22	10	B. Karr	Cleveland	Cleveland
05-23	11	S. Thurston	Washington	Washington
05-28	12	S. Thurston	Washington	New York
05-29	13	D. MacFayden	Boston	New York
05-30	14	R. Walberg	Phil. A's	Philadelphia
05-31	15	J. Quinn	Phil. A's	Philadelphia
05-31	16	H. Ehmke	Phil. A's	Philadelphia
06-05	17	E. Whitehill	Detroit	New York
06-07	18	T. Thomas	Chicago	New York
06-11	19	G. Buckeye	Cleveland	New York
06-11	20	G. Buckeye	Cleveland	New York
06-12	21	G. Uhle	Cleveland	New York
06-16	22	T. Zachary	St. Louis	New York
06-22	23	H. Wiltse	Boston	Boston
06-22	24	H. Wiltse	Boston	Boston
06-30	25	S. Harriss	Boston	Boston
07-03	26	H. Lisenbee	Washington	Washington
07-08	27	D. Hankins	Detroit	Detroit
07-09	28	K. Holloway	Detroit	Detroit
07-09	29	K. Holloway	Detroit	Detroit
07-12	30	J. Shaute	Cleveland	Cleveland
07-24	31	T. Thomas	Chicago	Chicago
07-26	32	M. Gaston	St. Louis	New York

5. Babe Ruth in 1927

Date	HR No.	Pitcher	Team	Location
07-26	33	M. Gaston	St. Louis	New York
07-28	34	L. Stewart	St. Louis	New York
08-05	35	G. Smith	Detroit	New York
08-10	36	T. Zachary	Washington	Washington
08-16	37	T. Thomas	Chicago	Chicago
08-17	38	S. Connally	Chicago	Chicago
08-20	39	J. Miller	Cleveland	Cleveland
08-22	40	J. Shaute	Cleveland	Cleveland
08-27	41	E. Nevers	St. Louis	St. Louis
08-28	42	E. Wingard	St. Louis	St. Louis
08-31	43	T. Welzer	Boston	New York
09-02	44	R. Walberg	Phil. A's	Philadelphia
09-06	45	T. Welzer	Boston	Boston
09-06	46	T. Welzer	Boston	Boston
09-06	47	J. Russell	Boston	Boston
09-07	48	D. MacFayden	Boston	Boston
09-07	49	S. Harriss	Boston	Boston
09-11	50	M. Gaston	St. Louis	New York
09-13	51	W. Hudlin	Cleveland	New York
09-13	52	J. Shaute	Cleveland	New York
09-16	53	T. Blankenship	Chicago	New York
09-18	54	T. Lyons	Chicago	New York
09-21	55	S. Gibson	Detroit	New York
09-22	56	K. Holloway	Detroit	New York
09-27	57	L. Grove	Phil. A's	New York
09-29	58	H. Lisenbee	Washington	New York
09-29	59	P. Hopkins	Washington	New York
09-30	60	T. Zachary	Washington	New York

6. Roger Maris in 1961

Date	HR No.	Pitcher	Team	Location
04-26	1	P. Foytack	Detroit	Detroit
05-03	2	P. Ramos	Minnesota	Minnesota
05-06	3	E. Grba	Los Angeles	Los Angeles
05-17	4	P. Burnside	Washington	New York
05-19	5	J. Perry	Cleveland	Cleveland
05-20	6	G. Bell	Cleveland	Cleveland
05-21	7	C. Estrada	Baltimore	New York
05-24	8	G. Conley	Boston	New York
05-28	9	C. McLish	Chicago	New York
05-30	10	G. Conley	Boston	Boston
05-30	11	M. Fornieles	Boston	Boston
05-31	12	B. Muffett	Boston	Boston
06-02	13	C. McLish	Chicago	Chicago
06-03	14	B. Shaw	Chicago	Chicago
06-04	15	R. Kemmerer	Chicago	Chicago
06-06	16	E. Palmquist	Minnesota	New York
06-07	17	P. Ramos	Minnesota	New York
06-09	18	R. Herbert	Kansas City	New York
06-11	19	E. Grba	Los Angeles	New York
06-11	20	J. James	Los Angeles	New York
06-13	21	J. Perry	Cleveland	Cleveland
06-14	22	G. Bell	Cleveland	Cleveland
06-17	23	D. Mossi	Detroit	Detroit
06-18	24	J. Casale	Detroit	Detroit
06-19	25	J. Archer	Kansas City	Kansas City
06-20	26	J. Nuxhall	Kansas City	Kansas City
06-22	27	N. Bass	Kansas City	Kansas City
07-01	28	D. Sisler	Washington	New York
07-02	29	P. Burnside	Washington	New York
07-02	30	J. Klippstein	Washington	New York
07-04	31	F. Lary	Detroit	New York
07-05	32	F. Funk	Cleveland	New York

6. Roger Maris in 1961

Date	HR No.	Pitcher	Team	Location
07-09	33	B. Monbouquette	Boston	New York
07-13	34	E. Wynn	Chicago	Chicago
07-15	35	R. Herbert	Chicago	Chicago
07-21	36	B. Monbouquette	Boston	Boston
07-25	37	F. Baumann	Chicago	New York
07-25	38	D. Larsen	Chicago	New York
07-25	39	R. Kemmerer	Chicago	New York
07-25	40	W. Hacker	Chicago	New York
08-04	41	C. Pascual	Minnesota	New York
08-11	42	P. Burnside	Washington	Washington
08-12	43	D. Donovan	Washington	Washington
08-13	44	B. Daniels	Washington	Washington
08-13	45	M. Kutyna	Washington	Washington
08-15	46	J. Pizarro	Chicago	New York
08-16	47	B. Pierce	Chicago	New York
08-16	48	B. Pierce	Chicago	New York
08-20	49	J. Perry	Cleveland	Cleveland
08-22	50	K. McBride	Los Angeles	Los Angeles
08-26	51	J. Walker	Kansas City	Kansas City
09-02	52	F. Lary	Detroit	New York
09-02	53	H. Aguirre	Detroit	New York
09-06	54	T. Cheney	Washington	New York
09-07	55	D. Stigman	Cleveland	New York
09-09	56	M. Grant	Cleveland	New York
09-16	57	F. Lary	Detroit	Detroit
09-17	58	T. Fox	Detroit	Detroit
09-20	59	M. Pappas	Baltimore	Baltimore
09-26	60	J. Fischer	Baltimore	New York
10-01	61	T. Stallard	Boston	New York

7. Mark McGwire
in 1998

Date	HR No.	Pitcher	Location	Distance	Direction
03-31	1	R. Martinez	L.A. @ St. Louis	364	LF
04-02	2	F. Lankford	L.A. @ St. Louis	368	LF
04-03	3	M. Langston	S.D. @ St. Louis	367	LF
04-04	4	D. Wengert	S.D. @ St. Louis	430	CF
04-14	5	J. Suppan	Ariz. @ St. Louis	424	LF
04-14	6	J. Suppan	Ariz. @ St. Louis	347	LF
04-14	7	B. Manuel	Ariz. @ St. Louis	462	CF
04-17	8	M. Whiteside	Phil. @ St. Louis	410	LF
04-21	9	T. Moore	Montreal	440	LCF
04-25	10	J. Spradlin	Philadelphia	410	CF
04-30	11	M. Pisciotta	Chicago	380	LCF
05-01	12	R. Beck	Chicago	362	LCF
05-08	13	R. Reed	New York	358	LF
05-12	14	P. Wagner	Milw. @ St. Louis	527	LCF
05-14	15	K. Millwood	Atlanta @ St. Louis	381	RCF
05-16	16	L. Hernandez	Florida @ St. Louis	550	CF
05-18	17	J. Sanchez	Florida @ St. Louis	478	LF
05-19	18	T. Green	Philadelphia	440	CF
05-19	19	T. Green	Philadelphia	471	LCF
05-19	20	W. Gomes	Philadelphia	451	LF
05-22	21	M. Gardner	San Fran. @ St. Louis	425	LF
05-23	22	R. Rodriguez	San Fran. @ St. Louis	366	LF
05-23	23	J. Johnstone	San Fran. @ St. Louis	477	LCF
05-24	24	R. Nenn	San Fran. @ St. Louis	394	LF
05-25	25	J. Thomson	Colo. @ St. Louis	432	LF
05-29	26	D. Miceli	San Diego	388	LCF
05-30	27	A. Ashby	San Diego	423	LCF
06-05	28	O. Hershiser	San Francisco	410	CF
06-08	29	J. Bere	Chic. White Sox	358	LF
06-10	30	J. Parque	Chic. White Sox	410	CF
06-12	31	A. Benes	Arizona	451	LF
06-17	32	J. Lima	Houston	349	LF

7. Mark McGwire in 1998

Date	HR No.	Pitcher	Location	Distance	Direction
06-18	33	S. Reynolds	Houston	450	LF
06-24	34	J. Wright	Cleveland	433	LF
06-25	35	D. Burba	Cleveland	461	LF
06-27	36	M. Trombley	Minnesota	431	LCF
06-30	37	G. Rusch	K. C. @ St. Louis	471	LF
07-11	38	B. Wagner	Houston @ St. Louis	463	LF
07-12	39	S. Bergman	Houston @ St. Louis	403	LCF
07-12	40	S. Elarton	Houston @ St. Louis	403	LF
07-17	41	B. Bohanon	L.A. @ St. Louis	511	LF
07-17	42	A. Osuna	L.A. @ St. Louis	425	LF
07-20	43	B. Boehringer	San Diego	454	LCF
07-26	44	J. Thomson	Colorado	452	LF
07-28	45	M. Myers	Milw. @ St. Louis	414	RCF
08-08	46	M. Clark	Chic. @ St. Louis	377	LF
08-11	47	B. Jones	Mets @ St. Louis	467	LCF
08-19	48	M. Karchner	Chicago Cubs	430	LF
08-19	49	T. Mulholland	Chicago Cubs	406	CF
08-20	50	W. Blair	New York	369	LF
08-20	51	R. Reed	New York	385	LF
08-22	52	F. Cordova	Pittsburgh	477	RCF
08-23	53	R. Rincon	Pittsburgh	392	LCF
08-26	54	J. Speier	Florida @ St. Louis	509	CF
08-30	55	D. Martinez	Atlanta @ St. Louis	501	CF
09-01	56	L. Hernandez	Florida	450	CF
09-01	57	D. Pall	Florida	472	CF
09-02	58	B. Edmondson	Florida	497	LF
09-02	59	R. Stanifer	Florida	458	LF
09-05	60	D. Reyes	Cinci. @ St. Louis	381	LF
09-07	61	M. Morgan	Cubs @ St. Louis	430	LF
09-08	62	S. Traschel	Cubs @ St. Louis	341	LF
09-15	63	J. Christiansen	Pitt. @ St. Louis	385	LCF
09-18	64	R. Roque	Milwaukee	414	LCF
09-20	65	S. Karl	Milwaukee	422	LF
09-25	66	S. Bennett	Mont. @ St. Louis	375	LF
09-26	67	D. Hermanson	Mont. @ St. Louis	403	LF
09-26	68	K. Bullinger	Mont. @ St. Louis	435	CF
09-27	69	M. Thurman	Mont. @ St. Louis	377	LF
09-27	70	C. Pavano	Mont. @ St. Louis	370	LF

8. Sammy Sosa
in 1998

Date	HR No.	Pitcher	Location	Distance	Direction
04-04	1	M. Valdes	Mont. @ Cubs	371	RF
04-11	2	A. Telford	Montreal	350	RCF
04-15	3	D. Cook	New York	430	LF
04-23	4	D. Miceli	S.D. @ Cubs	420	CF
04-24	5	I. Valdes	Los Angeles	430	CF
04-27	6	J. Hamilton	San Diego	434	CF
05-03	7	C. Politte	St. L. @ Cubs	370	LCF
05-16	8	S. Sullivan	Cincinnati	420	CF
05-22	9	G. Maddux	Atlanta	440	CF
05-25	10	K. Millwood	Atlanta	410	RCF
05-25	11	M. Cather	Atlanta	420	CF
05-27	12	D. Winston	Phil. @ Cubs	460	LF
05-27	13	W. Gomes	Phil. @ Cubs	400	RF
06-01	14	R. Dempster	Florida @ Cubs	430	LCF
06-01	15	O. Henriquez	Florida @ Cubs	410	LCF
06-03	16	L. Hernandez	Florida @ Cubs	370	LCF
06-05	17	J. Parque	Chic. W.S. @ Cubs	370	RCF
06-06	18	C. Castillo	Chic. W.S. @ Cubs	410	CF
06-07	19	J. Baldwin	Chic. W.S. @ Cubs	380	CF
06-08	20	L. Hawkins	Minnesota	340	RF
06-13	21	M. Portugal	Philadelphia	410	RF
06-15	22	C. Eldred	Milw. @ Cubs	420	RCF
06-15	23	C. Eldred	Milw. @ Cubs	410	LF
06-15	24	C. Elderd	Milw. @ Cubs	415	LCF
06-17	25	B. Patrick	Milw. @ Cubs	430	LF
06-19	26	C. Loewer	Phil. @ Cubs	380	LCF
06-19	27	C. Loewer	Phil. @ Cubs	378	LF
06-20	28	M. Beech	Phil. @ Cubs	366	LCF
06-20	29	T. Borland	Phil. @ Cubs	500	LF
06-21	30	T. Green	Phil. @ Cubs	380	RF
06-24	31	S. Greisinger	Detroit	390	CF
06-25	32	B. Moehler	Detroit	400	CF

8. Sammy Sosa in 1998

Date	HR No.	Pitcher	Location	Distance	Direction
06-30	33	A. Embree	Ariz. @ Cubs	364	LF
07-09	34	J. Juden	Milwaukee	432	RCF
07-10	35	S. Karl	Milwaukee	450	CF
07-17	36	K. Ojala	Florida	440	CF
07-22	37	M. Batista	Mont. @ Cubs	365	RCF
07-26	38	R. Reed	Mets @ Cubs	420	CF
07-27	39	W. Blair	Arizona	349	RF
07-27	40	A. Embree	Arizona	430	RCF
07-28	41	B. Wolcott	Arizona	395	LCF
07-31	42	J. Wright	Colo. @ Cubs	378	RCF
08-05	43	A. Benes	Ariz. @ Cubs	377	LCF
08-08	44	R. Croushore	St. Louis	400	CF
08-10	45	R. Ortiz	San Francisco	366	CF
08-10	46	C. Brock	San Francisco	420	LCF
08-16	47	S. Bergman	Houston	360	RCF
08-19	48	K. Bottenfield	St. L. @ Cubs	368	LF
08-21	49	O. Hershiser	San Fran. @ Cubs	430	CF
08-23	50	J. Lima	Houston @ Cubs	440	LCF
08-23	51	J. Lima	Houston @ Cubs	380	LCF
08-26	52	B. Tomko	Cincinnati	439	LCF
08-28	53	J. Thomson	Colorado	414	RCF
08-30	54	D. Kile	Colorado	482	LCF
08-31	55	B. Tomko	Cinci. @ Cubs	364	LF
09-02	56	J. Bere	Cinci. @ Cubs	370	RF
09-04	57	J. Schmidt	Pittsburgh	387	CF
09-05	58	S. Lawrence	Pittsburgh	411	RCF
09-11	59	B. Pulsipher	Milw. @ Cubs	464	RF
09-12	60	V. de Los Santos	Milw. @ Cubs	430	LF
09-13	61	B. Patrick	Milw. @ Cubs	480	LF
09-13	62	E. Plunk	Milw. @ Cubs	480	LF
09-16	63	B. Boehringer	San Diego	434	LF
09-23	64	R. Roque	Milwaukee	344	RF
09-23	65	R. Henderson	Milwaukee	410	CF
09-25	66	J. Lima	Houston	462	LF

9. Major League Park Field Dimensions

American League—1927

Location	Distance, Feet				
	LF	LCF	CF	RCF	RF
Yankee Stadium	281	395	490	429	295
Shibe Park	312	405	468	393	307
Comiskey Park I	365	375	455	375	365
Fenway Park	321	379	488	405	359
Tiger Stadium	345	365	467	370	370
Griffith Stadium	358	391	421	378	328
Sportsmans Park III	355	379	430	354	320
League Park II, Cleveland	376	415	420	400	290
Average	339	388	446	386	329

American League—1961

Location	Distance, Feet				
	LF	LCF	CF	RCF	RF
Yankee Stadium	301	402	461	407	296
Fenway Park	315	379	420	380	302
Tiger Stadium	340	365	440	370	325
Memorial Stadium, Baltimore	309	380	410	380	309
Comiskey Park I	352	375	415	375	352
Cleveland Stadium	320	380	410	380	320
Metropolitan Stadium, Minneapolis	329	402	412	402	329

9. Major League Field Dimension

Location	Distance, Feet				
	LF	LCF	CF	RCF	RF
Griffith Stadium	388	372	421	373	320
Wrigley Field,					
Los Angeles	340	345	412	345	339
Municipal Stadium,					
Kansas City	370	390	421	387	353
Average	336	379	422	380	325

National League—1998

Location	Distance, Feet				
	LF	LCF	CF	RCF	RF
Joe Robbie Stadium	330	380	434	380	345
Shea Stadium	338	371	410	371	338
Veterans Stadium	330	371	408	371	330
Olympic Stadium	325	375	404	375	325
Turner Field	335	380	401	390	330
Three Rivers Stadium	335	375	400	375	335
Busch Stadium	330	375	402	375	330
Wrigley Field	355	368	400	368	353
County Stadium,					
Milwaukee	315	392	402	392	315
Riverfront Stadium	330	375	404	375	330
Astrodome	330	375	400	375	330
Dodger Stadium	330	375	400	375	330
Qualcomm Stadium	327	370	405	370	327
3Com Park	335	365	400	365	335
Bank One Ballpark	330	369	407	371	334
Coors Field	347	390	424	375	350
Average	333	375	407	375	334

Major League Stadiums— Home Run Factors (HRF)

Location	HRF
Yankee Stadium	1.03
Busch Stadium	0.79
Wrigley Field	1.16
Kingdome Seattle	1.41

HRF-The no. of home runs hit in that park compared to the average no. of HRs hit in the league.

10. Home Run Factors

Major League Home Runs

Factors Affecting Major League Home Runs—From 1920 to 1998

Average major league team home runs per year:

1920	39 home runs per team per year
1998	140 home runs per team per year
	An increase of 121 home runs

Factors

	% home run increase (decrease)/ team/year	No. of HR increase (decrease)/ team/year
Player size, physical fitness, weight training, personal trainers, dietary supplements	9	11
New livelier basenball, 1994	18	21
Homer friendly parks, dimensions	3	4
Atmospheric conditions, Colorado, Atlanta	3	4
Babe Ruth syndrome	49	59
Ralph Kiner syndrome	27	33
Integration	8	10
Designated hitter	5	6
Night Baseball	(-8%)	(-10)
Expansion, travel, free agency	(-14%)	(-17)
Total	100%	121

Babe Ruth Syndrome

Babe Ruth's home run heroics affected the batting philosophy of a generation of home run hitters, but the full effect of his influence on home run production wasn't felt until the next generation of hitters arrived on the scene in the 1930s. Ruth's contemporaries, except in a few cases, could not, or did not want to, change their batting strokes.

Ralph Kiner Syndrome

This was similar to the Babe Ruth syndrome. Kiner's effect on home run output was noticeable during the 1950s and 60s. His famous comment, "Home run hitters drive Cadillacs. Singles hitters drive Chevys," influenced a whole generation of young hitters.

Integration

The Negro League players were, in general, more productive home run hitters than the average major league player. The effect of the movement of these players into the major leagues was noticeable during the 1950s and 60s.

Major League Home Run Production

Average Home Runs per Year per Team
Based on a 154-Game Schedule

Years	Home Runs/Team/Year	Comments
1921–30	73	16 major league teams
1931–40	84	16 major league teams
1941–50	84	16 major league teams
1951–60	133	16 major league teams Integration
1961–70	136	18 to 24 major league teams
1971–80	115	24 to 26 major league teams Changed baseball manufacturer from Spalding to Rawlings in 1976
1981–90	125	26 major league teams Baseballs manufactured in Haiti
1991–98	147	26 to 30 major league teams
1991	124	26 teams
1992	111	26 teams
1993	137	28 teams
1994	154	28 teams—Baseballs manufactured in Costa Rica
1995	156	28 teams

Years	Home Runs/Team/Year	Comments
1996	168	28 teams
1997	165	28 teams
1998	160	30 teams

Number of Home Runs Hit per Team per Year

```
            170
            165
            160
            155
            150
            145                                                    X
            140
Home Runs   135                          X     X
            130
Per Team    125                                            X
            120                                      X
Per Year    115
            110
            105
            100
             95
             90
             85              X     X
             80
             75        X
             70
                   1921-30 31-40 41-50 51-60 61-70 71-80 81-90 91-98
                                        Year
```

The Effect of Player Size on Home Runs

Period	Major League All-Star Team Average Size of 18 Players		Avg HRs/Man adjusted for Lively ball	Comments No. of players weighing 200 pounds or more
19th Century	5'10"	175 pounds	15	Brouthers, Connor, Thompson
1901–25	5'10"	181 pounds	15	Bresnahan, Wagner, J. Jackson
1926–50	6'	188 pounds	20	Gehrig, Ruth, Williams, Greenberg, Terry

Period	Major League All-Star Team Average Size of 18 Players		Avg HR's/Man adjusted for Lively ball	Comments No. of players weighing 200 pounds or more
1951–75	6'	194 pounds	25	Campanella, Bench, Hodges, J. Robinson, McCovey, Killebrew
1976–99	6'1"	195 pounds	19	Fisk, Murray, Ripken Winfield, Puckett
1990–99	6'2"	208 pounds	26	I. Rodriguez, Thomas, M.Vaughn, McGwire, Baerga, Ripken M. Williams, Caminiti, Griffey J. Gonzalez, Belle, Bichette, Buhner, J. Carter

All other things being equal, the bigger the batter, the more home runs he will hit. From 1926 to 1999, the average number of home runs increased by six, and the average weight of the players increased by 20 pounds.

Added muscle = more home runs

Example: Mark McGwire at 250 pounds weighs 50 pounds more than Sammy Sosa, which would give him a formidable 15 home run edge.

Through 1998, McGwire has averaged 49 home runs for every 550 at bats during his career. Sosa has averaged 32 home runs for every 550 at bats during his career.

Effect of Player Size on Home Runs

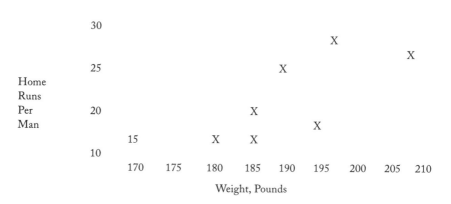

11. Top Home Run Seasons, per At-Bat

Player	Team	Year	AB	HR	HR per 550 AB
Mark McGwire	St. Louis Cardinals	1998	509	70	76
Mark McGwire	Oakland Athletics	1995	317	39	68
Mark McGwire	Oakland Athletics	1996	423	52	68
Babe Ruth	New York Yankees	1920	458	54	65
Babe Ruth	New York Yankees	1927	540	60	61
Babe Ruth	New York Yankees	1921	540	59	60
Mark McGwire	Oakland-St. Louis	1997	540	58	59
Mickey Mantle	New York Yankees	1961	514	54	58
Hank Greenberg	Detroit Tigers	1938	556	58	57
Roger Maris	New York Yankees	1961	590	61	57
Sammy Sosa	Chicago Cubs	1998	639	66	57
Hank Aaron	Atlanta Braves	1973	392	40	56

Note: Seasons with less than 10.00 at bats per home run

12. Top Home Run Careers, per At-Bat

Player	AB	HR	HR/550 AB	Weight, lbs.
Babe Ruth	7,289	665	50 (1920-1935)	220
Mark McGwire	5,131	457	49 (through 1998)	250
Ralph Kiner	5,205	369	39	195
Harmon Killebrew	8,147	573	39	210
Albert Belle	4,684	321	39 (through 1998)	200
Ted Williams	7,706	521	37	205
Ken Griffey, Jr.	5,226	350	37 (through 1998)	205
Mickey Mantle	8,102	536	36	201
Dave Kingman	6,677	442	36	215
Jimmie Foxx	8,134	534	36	195
Mike Schmidt	8,352	548	36	195
Hank Greenberg	5,193	331	35	210
Hank Aaron	12,364	755	34	190
Willie Mays	10,881	660	33	187
Eddie Mathews	8,537	512	33	195
Sammy Sosa	4,660	273	32 (through 1998)	205
Reggie Jackson	9,864	563	31	195
Roger Maris	5,101	273	30	195

Bibliography

Bamberger, Michael. "Sammy: You're the Man." *Sports Illustrated*, September 28, 1998, 44–50.

Baseball Weekly. Arlington, Va: Gannett, 1998.

Beard, Charles A., and Mary R. Beard. *The Rise of American Civilization*. New York: Macmillan, 1937.

Benson, Michael. *Ballparks of North America*. Jefferson, N.C.: McFarland, 1989.

Brown, Gene, Arleen Keylin and Daniel Lundy, eds. *Sports of the Times*. New York: Arno, 1982.

Carter, Craig, ed. *Daguerreotypes*. 8th ed. St. Louis: Sporting News, 1990.

Castle, George. *Sammy Sosa: Clearing the Vines*. Champaign, Ill.: Sports Publishing, 1998.

Cohen, Richard M. and David S. Neft. *The World Series*. New York: Collier, 1986.

Creamer, Robert W. *Babe, the Legend Comes to Life*. New York: Fireside, 1992.

Davenport, John Warner. *Baseball's Pennant Races*. Madison, Wis.: First Impressions, 1981.

Friend, Tom. "Crush Hour." *ESPN*, September 1998, 122–126.

Gallagher, Mark. *The Yankee Encyclopedia*. Champaign, Ill.: Sagamore, 1996.

"The Great Home Run Race," *Sports Illustrated*. Time Inc. 1998.

Hoffman, Robert M., ed. *News of the Nation*. Englewood Cliffs, N.J.: Prentice-Hall, 1975.

Honig, Donald. *A Donald Honig Reader*. New York: Fireside, 1988.

Houk, Ralph, and Robert W. Creamer. *Season of Glory*. New York: G.P. Putnam's Sons, 1988.

Johnson, Lloyd, and Miles Wolff, eds. *Encyclopedia of Minor League Baseball*. Durham, N.C.: Baseball America, 1993.

Kaplan, David A., and Brad Stone. "Going...Going...." *Newsweek*, September 14, 1998, 54–56.

Kermisch, Al. "The Babe Ruth Beginning." *Baseball Research Journal*, 4 (1975):45–51.

Koenig, Bill. "The Babe." *Baseball Weekly*. no. 21 (1998): 28–31.

Krich, John. *El Beisbol*. New York: Prentice Hall, 1989.

Lowry, Philip. J. *Green Cathedrals*. Reading, Mass.: Addison-Wesley, 1992.

The Mac Attack: The Road to 62 and Beyond. Tulsa, Okla.: Paragon Communications Group, 1998.

Bibliography

McConnell, Bob, and David Vincent, eds. *SABR Presents the Home Run Encyclopedia*. New York: Macmillan, 1996.

McGwire, Mark, with Tom Verducci. "Where Do I Go from Here?" *Sports Illustrated*, September 21, 1998, 52–55.

McKinney, Susan M., ed. *Home Run: The Year the Records Fell*. Champaign, Ill.: Sports Publishing, 1998.

McNeil, William F. *The Dodgers Encyclopedia*. Champaign Ill.: Sports Publishing, 1997.

_____. *The King Of Swat*. Jefferson, N. C.: McFarland, 1997.

Menke, Frank G. *The New Encyclopedia of Sports*. New York: A.S. Barnes and Company, 1947.

Morse, Joseph Laffan, ed. *The Universal Standard Encyclopedia*. New York: Unicorn, 1954.

Muskat, Carrie. "Sammy Sosa." *Cubs Quarterly*, 16, no. 1 (1997): 34–41.

Nemec, David. *Great Baseball Feats, Facts, & Firsts*. New York: New American Library, 1987.

Oh, Sadaharu, and David Falkner. *Sadaharu Oh*. New York: Vintage Books, 1985.

Okrent, Daniel, and Steve Wulf. *Baseball Aanecdotes*. New York: Harper & Row, 1990.

Oleksak, Michael M., and Mary Adams Oleksak. *Beisbol*. Indianapolis: Masters Press, 1986.

Peary, Danny, ed. *Cult Baseball Players*. New York: Fireside, 1990.

Pirone, Dorothy Ruth. *My Dad, the Babe*. Boston, Mass.: Quinlan Press, 1988.

Rains, Rob. *Mark McGwire, Home Run Hero*. New York: St. Martins, 1998.

Reichler, Joseph L. ed. *The Baseball Encyclopedia*. New York: Macmillan, 1979.

Reichler, Joseph, and Jack Clary. *Baseball's Great Moments*. New York: Gallahad Books, 1990.

Reidenbaugh, Lowell. *Baseball's Hall of Fame, Cooperstown*. New York: Arlington House, 1988.

Reilly, Rick. "The Good Father." *Sports Illustrated*, September 7, 1998, 32–45.

Rice, Grantland. *The Tumult and the Shouting*. New York: A.S. Barnes, 1954.

Ritter, Lawrence, and Mark Rucker. *The Babe, a Life in Pictures*. New York: Ticknor & Fields, 1988.

Rodriguez Suncar, Osvaldo, ed. *La Pelota Nuestra*. Santo Domingo, Dominican Republic: Productores Asociados, n.d.

Ruiz, Yuyo. *The Bambino Visits Cuba*. San Juan, Puerto Rico: La Esquina Del Left Field, n.d.

Rushin, Steve. "Sam the Ham." *Sports Illustrated*, September 14, 1998, 34–35.

Shatzkin, Mike, ed. *The Ballplayers*. New York: Arbor House, 1990.

Smelser, Marshall. *The Life that Ruth Built*. Lincoln, Nebr.: University of Nebraska Press, 1975.

Smith, Gary. "Heaven and Hell." *Sports Illustrated*, December 21, 1998, 54–72.

_____. "The Mother of All Pearls." *Sports Illustrated*, September 14, 1998, 56–59.

_____. "The Race Is On." *Sports Illustrated*, September 14, 1998, 48–51.

Smith, Ron, ed. *Celebrating 70*. St. Louis, Mo.: Sporting News, 1998.

Sports Illustrated, October 7, 1998.

Thorn, John, et al., eds. *Total Baseball*. 5th ed. New York: Viking, 1997.

Torres, Angel. *The Baseball Bible*. Glendale, Cali.: GWP, 1983.

Veducci, Tom. "Larger Than Life." *Sports Illustrated*, October 7, 1998, 24–31.

_____. "The Greatest Season Ever." *Sports Illustrated*, October 5, 1998, 38–52.

_____. "Goin' Yard." *Sports Illustrated*, October 7, 1998, 36–41.

_____. "Stroke Of Genius." *Sports Illustrated*, December 21, 1998, 44–63.

_____. "Making His Mark." *Sports Illustrated*, September 14, 1998, 30–33.

Wendel, Tim. "Roger Maris." *Baseball Weekly*, 8, No. 22, August 19–25, 1998.

Index

Index

Index

Index

Index